Inhalt

Allgemeiner Teil 2

Topicbegleitender Teil

Topic 1: Shakespeare and his time
Didaktisches Inhaltsverzeichnis 6
Unterrichtsverlauf 7

Topic 2: Shakespeare's language
Didaktisches Inhaltsverzeichnis 20
Unterrichtsverlauf 21

Topic 3: Shakespeare's theatre
Didaktisches Inhaltsverzeichnis 35
Unterrichtsverlauf 36

Topic 4: Shakespeare the dramatist
Didaktisches Inhaltsverzeichnis 50
Unterrichtsverlauf 52

Topic 5: Not for an age, but for all time
Didaktisches Inhaltsverzeichnis 87
Unterrichtsverlauf 88

Anhang

1 Sequenzplaner – Differenzierungshinweise GK/LK 99

2 Kopiervorlagen 102

3 Lösungen zu den Kopiervorlagen 123

4 Klausurvorschläge 124

5 Erwartungshorizont zu den Klausurvorschlägen 134

6 Erwartungshorizont zu den *Revision files* 141

AT | Allgemeiner Teil

Allgemeiner Teil

Reihenkonzept
Das Heft *Shakespeare* ist ein Themenheft aus der Reihe „Abi Workshop Englisch". Diese Reihe bietet eine Sammlung von Themen- und Methodenheften, die speziell auf die Erfordernisse der G8-Oberstufe und der zentralen Abiturprüfung ausgerichtet sind und ohne den Einsatz eines Oberstufen-Lehrwerks eine gründliche Vorbereitung des Abiturs gewährleisten.

Methodenhefte
Während die Methodenhefte konsequent methoden- und kompetenzorientiert sind, bieten die Themenhefte einen landeskundlich-interkulturell ausgerichteten Überblick über ein relevantes

Themenhefte
Abiturthema. Im Themenheft *Shakespeare* sind die konzeptionellen Neuerungen der Reihe „Abi Workshop Englisch" auf folgende Weise realisiert:

Dokumenten CD-ROM

CD-ROM
Auf der Dokumenten CD-ROM sind die Hörtexte, die Filmsequenzen und die *Vocabulary sheets* enthalten. Dadurch, dass die CD-ROM den Schülern und Schülerinnen (künftig: S) und Lehrern und Lehrerinnen (künftig: L) gleichermaßen zur Verfügung steht, können wichtige Lernbereiche deutlich intensiver behandelt werden als bisher. Für die S besteht die Möglichkeit zur Nachbereitung der Lernbereiche Hörverstehen bzw. Hör-/Sehverstehen sowie zu einer systematischen selbstständigen Wortschatzarbeit in der Oberstufe. Für die L bietet sich die Gelegenheit, diese Lernbereiche in die Unterrichtsvorbereitung durch die S einzubeziehen und sie zusätzlich auch für Hausaufgaben zu nutzen. Das Themenheft *Shakespeare* enthält dementsprechend ausführliche Aufgabenstellungen.

Hör-/ Sehverstehen
Für die weitere Schulung des Hör-/Sehverstehens stehen vier Videoclips zur Verfügung, die mit einem ausführlichen Aufgabenapparat im Schülerheft versehen sind. Die Benutzung der Filmausschnitte im Klassenzimmer ist ausdrücklich gestattet. Darüber hinaus enthält das Themenheft *Shakespeare* zahlreiche Aufgaben und Online-Links, sodass Hör-/Sehverstehen ohne die üblichen Probleme bei der Materialbeschaffung möglich ist. Insgesamt wird die Behandlung dieses Lernbereichs erheblich ausgeweitet und intensiviert.

Vokabelkonzept
Das Themenheft *Shakespeare* ermöglicht den S eine systematische und erfolgsorientierte Wortschatzarbeit in der Oberstufe, die eine optimale Vorbereitung auf das Abitur gewährleistet. Dazu wurde die Vokabelarbeit folgendermaßen organisiert:

Wortschatz im Themenheft

Topics
Der in den *Topics* angegebene Wortschatz dient ausschließlich dem Verständnis der Texte bzw. als Hilfe für die Bewältigung von Aufgaben. Der im Textteil angegebene Wortschatz ist **nicht identisch** mit dem Lernvokabular auf der CD-ROM. Die Wörter sind in unterschiedlicher Weise aufbereitet:

Annotations
Die *Annotations* dienen zur Erklärung nicht erschließbarer, für das Textverständnis zentraler Wörter und Begriffe. Sie stehen in der Randspalte und enthalten bei Bedarf auch die phonetische Umschrift.

Word bank
Unter dem Titel *Word bank* erhalten die S eine Zusammenstellung von auf das Thema bezogenen Wörtern – bekannten und neuen – zur sprachlichen Bewältigung der Diskussions- oder Kommentierungsaufgaben. Die roten Kästchen stehen unmittelbar bei den Aufgaben.

Vocabulary sheets auf der CD-ROM

CD-ROM
Die Organisation des Wortschatzes geschieht mit Hilfe der *Vocabulary sheets* auf der CD-ROM. Das Schülerheft bzw. Themenheft enthält lediglich zwei Seiten als Muster mit Erläuterungen

Allgemeiner Teil | AT

(Seite 57/58). Das Themenheft bietet eine dreispaltige Vorlage zur Gestaltung der *Vocabulary sheets* an:

Gestaltung Die linke Spalte ist für die zu erlernende Vokabel bestimmt (Einzelwort oder Wendung). Die mittlere Spalte kann Antonyme, Synonyme, Bezüge zur Wortfamilie usw. enthalten. Bei Einzelwörtern in der linken Spalte bietet sie vor allem wichtige Kollokationen. Die rechte Spalte ist für die deutsche Übersetzung der Lernvokabel und wichtiger Kollokationen vorgesehen.

Editierbar Die *Vocabulary sheets* werden für die S in einer Version mit Lücken angeboten. In der Regel ist nur die linke Spalte gefüllt und damit der zu lernende Wortschatz definiert. Es ist die Aufgabe der S, die leeren Spalten im Rahmen der Textarbeit zu füllen. Auf diese Weise erarbeiten sie sich den chronologischen Wortschatz weitgehend selbstständig. Der Inhalt der mittleren und rechten Spalte wird nur punktuell vorgegeben, um Variationsmöglichkeiten zu eröffnen und den S immer wieder Hinweise auf Vernetzungstechniken für die Wortschatzarbeit zu geben. Durch die Editierbarkeit der Word-Dokumente haben die S die Gelegenheit, jederzeit nach Wunsch weiteres Vokabular hinzuzufügen.

Online-Link 601015-0001 Für L steht das komplett ausgefüllte Vokabular zusätzlich online bei www.klett.de zur Verfügung. Der Online-Link des Lehrerheftes lautet: 601015-0001. Auf diese Weise besteht die Möglichkeit, jederzeit Vokabeltests schreiben zu lassen und diese auf komfortable Weise korrigieren zu können.

Organisation der Wortschatzarbeit

Chronologisch Aus der Reihenfolge der Vokabeln in den Texten ergibt sich ein chronologischer textbezogener Aufbau des Lernwortschatzes. Insgesamt können die S auf diese Weise einen Lernwortschatz von ca. 400–500 Wörtern pro Themenheft aufbauen. Die CD-ROM bietet zusätzlich *Vocabulary sheets* zu bestimmten Themengebieten an. In diesen Listen sind die wichtigsten Vokabeln pro Themengebiet enthalten. Ein Großteil dieser Vokabeln ergibt sich aus den Texten und ist bereits im chronologischen Wortschatz zu finden. Wichtiger, noch fehlender Wortschatz wird

Thematisch ergänzt, sodass die S am Ende thematisch gruppierte Lernwortlisten vorliegen haben, die es ihnen ermöglichen, sich optimal auf die mündliche oder schriftliche Textproduktion zu einem bestimmten Thema vorzubereiten. Der Inhalt der Wortlisten zu bestimmten Texten oder Themen kann von L als verbindlich erklärt und ggf. in Vokabeltests überprüft werden. L und S können somit unabhängig voneinander entscheiden, ob sie nur mit den chronologischen oder auch mit den thematischen Wortlisten arbeiten möchten.

Topics im Themenheft

Topics Das Themenheft *Shakespeare* enthält fünf *Topics:*
Topic 1: Shakespeare and his time
Topic 2: Shakespeare's language
Topic 3: Shakespeare's theatre
Topic 4: Shakespeare the dramatist
Topic 5: Not for an age, but for all time

Tasks Die *Topics* bieten ein vielseitiges und abwechslungsreiches Übungsangebot mit dem Ziel, die S zu einer textsortengerechten Produktion von gesprochener und geschriebener Sprache zu befähigen. Dabei stehen die Anforderungen der Abiturprüfung selbst und die Bewältigung der verschiedenen Lern- und Arbeitsbereiche der Oberstufe im Mittelpunkt. Grundsätzlich orientiert sich das Übungsangebot an den Anforderungsbereichen *Comprehension, Analysis*

Operatoren und *Evaluation* sowie an der Erarbeitung der jeweiligen Operatoren. Darüber hinaus ermöglicht die Übungsfolge in dem Themenheft *Shakespeare* einen lebendigen und motivierenden Unterricht. Neben den textanalytischen Fragestellungen spielen auch Aufgaben zu den

Kompetenzen Kompetenzen eine wichtige Rolle. Dies sind u. a. *Discussing, Debating,* Recherche (auch über Online-Links), Präsentation, Projekte, *Creative writing,* Wortschatzaufbau, *Mediation,* Hörver-

3

AT | Allgemeiner Teil

Sozialformen stehen, Hör-/Sehverstehen, Ergebnissicherung. Die Übungen sind für die unterschiedlichsten Sozialformen konzipiert. Häufig wird Gruppen- oder Partnerarbeit empfohlen. Durch die sinnvolle Kombination der verschiedenen Aufgaben entsteht so ein anregendes Übungsangebot, das die zielgerichtete Vorbereitung auf die Abiturprüfung gewährleistet, gleichzeitig aber die immer wiederkehrende Umwälzung durch nur wenige gleichförmige Übungsformate verhindert. Das Übungsangebot im Themenheft *Shakespeare* orientiert sich damit auch an der Verwendung der englischen Sprache über das Abitur hinaus.

Servicematerial im Anhang

Projects Das Themenheft *Shakespeare* enthält im Anhang (Seite 53–56) drei Projektvorschläge:
Project 1: Adaptations of Shakespeare
Project 2: Shakespeare and you – a photo story
Project 3: A Shakespeare museum
Die *Projects* sind in mehrere *Steps* untergliedert. Die S erhalten Hinweise zur Umsetzung (*Hints for audiences while watching a Shakespearean play*) sowie nützliche Hinweise zur Durchführung der *Projects*.

Worksheets Nach den *Projects* bietet das Themenheft Informationen zur Konzeption der Wortschatzarbeit (Seite 57/58). Hier wird die Organisation der *Vocabulary sheets* erläutert und die S finden Muster einer textbezogenen chronologischen und einer thematischen Wortschatzseite mit Hinweisen zur Verwendung:
*   *How to work with the text-based vocabulary files*
*   *How to work with the thematic vocabulary files*

Revision files Zu den fünf *Topics* werden fünf methodisch jeweils modifizierte *Revision files* angeboten (Seite 59–63), in die die S die wichtigsten Daten und Informationen eintragen können. Die *Revision files* sind ein Instrument zur Ergebnissicherung und zur Wiederholung. Sie können gezielt zur Klausur- oder Prüfungsvorbereitung eingesetzt werden. Ein Erwartungshorizont befindet sich hier im Lehrerheft im Anhang (Seite 141–145/Umschlagseite 3).

Methodenhefte

Methodenhefte Das Themenheft *Shakespeare* kann ideal ergänzt werden durch eine Auswahl aus den ebenfalls im „Abi Workshop Englisch" zur Verfügung stehenden Methodenheften. Je nach den Notwendigkeiten der Lerngruppe können gezielt Defizite aufgearbeitet oder besondere Schwerpunkte gesetzt werden. Auch die individuelle Förderung von S ist möglich. Alle Methodenhefte sind konsequent auf die Anforderungen der Oberstufe und des Abiturs ausgerichtet. Sie sind sowohl für den Klassenunterricht als auch für das Selbststudium geeignet. Die jeweils beiliegende CD-ROM enthält alle Lösungen und Erwartungshorizonte.

Lehrerheft

Lehrerheft Das Lehrerheft setzt sich zum Ziel, einen wirksamen Beitrag zu einer effektiven und zeitsparenden Unterrichtsvorbereitung und -durchführung zu leisten. Die folgenden Elemente dienen in besonderer Weise zur Arbeitserleichterung:

Didaktisches Inhaltsverzeichnis Eine Erstinformation über die Inhalte der *Topics* bietet ein didaktisches Inhaltsverzeichnis, das in knapper und übersichtlicher Form über Textsorte/Thema, Unterrichtsmethoden, *Input boxes*, Kompetenzen und Textproduktion informiert. Hier sind außerdem die Textlängen (Wortanzahl) und Erscheinungsjahre der Originaltexte verzeichnet.

Unterrichtsverlauf Es folgen Hinweise zum Unterrichtsverlauf, einschließlich der Hintergrundinformationen, methodischen Schritte, dem Lernvokabular, aller Unterrichtsergebnisse, Querverweise, Alternativen, Hausaufgaben, Zusatzmaterialien usw. Die methodisch-didaktischen Erläuterungen werden zugunsten einer knappen, übersichtlichen Benutzerführung z.T.

Allgemeiner Teil | **AT**

Ergebnis-sicherung stichwortartig angeboten. Besonderer Wert wurde auf die Sicherung der Unterrichtsergebnisse in Form von Lösungsvorschlägen gelegt. Bei zahlreichen Texten und Übungen gibt es ausführlichere Vorschläge, insbesondere dann, wenn die Unterrichtsergebnisse für die Klausur- und Prüfungsvorbereitung relevant sind und sich auf elementare oder für die S schwierige Lernbereiche erstrecken (z. B. bei den Form-Inhalt-Beziehungen). Die S erhalten so die Chance, ihr Wissen und ihre Methodenkompetenz systematisch aufzubauen, das Gelernte zu vernetzen und – vor allem – noch einmal nachzuschauen, wenn sie etwas vergessen haben.

Servicematerial im Anhang

Sequenzplaner Im Anhang des Lehrerhefts befinden sich weitere nützliche Materialien für die Unterrichts-planung. Den Auftakt bildet ein Sequenzplaner (Seite 99–101), der in knapper und übersicht-licher Form Aufschluss über die Kernsequenzen und die Vertiefungsmaterialien gibt. Damit wird die Zuordnung der Texte für Grund- und Leistungskurse auf einen Blick deutlich.

Kopiervorlagen Es folgen zu jedem der fünf *Topics* weiterführende Arbeitsblätter als Kopiervorlagen (Seite 102–122). Die Kopiervorlagen (KVs) vertiefen die behandelten Themen und dienen entweder zur Festigung des Lernwortschatzes oder zur inhaltlichen Erweiterung der Themenbereiche.

Lösungen Die Lösungen (Seite 123) stehen ebenfalls als Kopiervorlage zur Verfügung. Sie können den S zur Selbstkontrolle ausgehändigt werden.

Klausur-vorschläge Neben den Kopiervorlagen befindet sich im Anhang zu jedem *Topic* ein Klausurvorschlag (Seite 124–133). Die sechs Klausurvorschläge (zu *Topic* 4 stehen zwei Klausurvorschläge zur Auswahl zur Verfügung) decken unterschiedliche Textsorten ab, z. B. Prolog, Sonett, Drama und Sachtexte. Der notwendige Wortschatz wird unter dem Text als *Annotations* angeboten, darauf folgt eine Auswahl an abwechslungsreichen *Tasks*.

Erwartungs-horizont Zu den sechs Klausurvorschlägen gibt es für die Hand der L einen Erwartungshorizont (Seite 134–140). Neben den Lösungsvorschlägen zu den *Tasks* befinden sich hier die nötigen Textinformationen und Quellenangaben.

Revision files Den Abschluss des Serviceteils im Lehrerbuch bildet der Erwartungshorizont zu den *Revision files* (Seite 141–145/Umschlagseite 3).

Topic 1: Shakespeare and his time

pp. 4–11

Didaktisches Inhaltsverzeichnis

Bearbeitungszeitraum: 6–8 Unterrichtsstunden

Textsorte/ Thema	Unterrichts- methoden	*Input boxes*	Kompetenzen	Textproduktion
Lead-in: Shapespeare and his time				SB, Seite 4/5, LB, Seite 7–12
Combination of visuals, quotes, timeline/Eliza- bethan theatre	Kursgespräch Online-Link: 601005-0001 Zusatzmaterial: Kopiervorlage 1	*Fact files: Elizabethan England – Theatre in London*	Orientierungswissen Bildbeschreibung/ -analyse Leseverstehen Gespräche führen Recherchieren Mediation	*Describing and assessing pictures Writing a report Evaluating information Giving an explanation*
The Shakespeare portrait, 2009 (684 words)				SB, Seite 6/7, LB, Seite 12–14
Factual informa- tion, visuals/ Likenesses	Kursgespräch Online-Link: 601005-0002	*Word bank: Talking about possibilities VIP file: William Shakespeare*	Orientierungswissen Leseverstehen Gespräche führen	*Writing a summary Assessing pictures Giving a presentation*
Book burning, 2006 (661 words)				SB, Seite 8/9, LB, Seite 15–17
Novel excerpt, factual information/ Censorship in Elizabethan England	Kursgespräch Online-Link: 601005-0003	*Word bank: Censorship Fact files: Censorship – Henry VIII*	Leseverstehen Gespräche führen Argumentieren	*Describing pictures Analysing facts*
Life in the suburbs, 2004 (467 words)				SB, Seite 10/11, LB, Seite 17–19
Novel excerpt, quotations/ Punishment in Shakespeare's time	Kursgespräch Gruppenarbeit Zusatzmaterial: Klausurvorschlag 1	*Word bank: Crime and punishment*	Leseverstehen Hör-/Sehverstehen Gespräche führen Recherchieren	*Summing up facts Discussing effects*

Shakespeare and his time   Lead-in: Shakespeare and his time

1

Unterrichtsverlauf

Photos/Quota-
tion/Timeline

| Lead-in: Shakespeare and his time | pp. 4–5 |

HINTERGRUNDINFO

William Shakespeare was baptised in Stratford-upon-Avon on St George's Day, April 23, 1564, the son of John Shakespeare, glover, and Mary Arden, from a prestigious Warwickshire family. John Shakespeare was a very well respected Stratford citizen. He was an alderman and bailiff in Stratford. However, he stopped attending council meetings in 1578, because taking the Oath of Supremacy, an oath of allegiance to the Queen in religious matters, was expected of anyone who wanted to hold public office. His name appears on the list of Stratford Catholics who refused to accept the new faith (list of recusants), just like his granddaughter Susanna's name some years later. Shakespeare must have been a pupil at Stratford grammar school, where he would have received an excellent education in Latin and rhetoric. Usually the sons of well-to-do citizens were sent to university for further training, and one would have expected the same of William Shakespeare. But he left school when he was 14, the same year that his father began to mortgage or sell property on a large scale.

He married Anne Hathaway when he was only 18 years old. His wife was six years older and already pregnant with their first child, Susanna. They married in Temple Grafton, which was unusual since neither bride nor groom lived there. Records show that the vicar at Temple Grafton at the time was a priest of the old faith, and since Anne and William chose neighbours from Henley Street who were also known for their Catholic beliefs as godparents for their children (Judith and Hamnet Sadler both figure on the list of recusants), one may assume that the religion of the priest who was to marry them was important enough to William and his wife to apply for the special licence which was required if one wanted to marry in a place different from one's hometown. The Shakespeares lived with William's parents in their house in Henley Street, where the twins Judith and Hamnet were born in 1585.

*Shakespeare was first mentioned as a **playwright** in London in 1592 in Robert Greene's pamphlet "A groatsworth of writ", in which he calls Shakespeare "an upstart crow, beautified with our feathers, that with his Tygers heart wrapt in a Players hide supposes he is as well able to bombast out a blank verse as the best of you; and, being an absolute Johannes Factotum, is in his own conceit the only Shake-scene in a country". It seems that by this time Shakespeare had made it in London, so he*

must have been there long enough to have Robert, and probably others too, turn green with envy. He probably left Stratford in 1585 after his twins were baptised, but there are no records as to where he was in the meantime. It seems likely, though, that he toured the country with the famous acting company, The Queen's Men. Stratford council records reveal that they performed in Stratford that year, and also that they had fallen a man short when one actor was killed in a tavern brawl. They had been set up by Francis Walsingham as the government's propaganda troupe. Their task was both to boost morale for the impending war with Spain and to spy on the people; the fear of rebellion, treason and conspiracy was the driving force of most government activities in Elizabeth's reign. Shakespeare later borrowed freely from their plays, as a look at The Queen's Men's repertoire of the time suggests: Shakespeare's early plays "Two Gentlemen of Verona" and "Titus Andronicus" rely on plays previously performed by The Queen's Men, and both "The Famous Victories of Henry V" and "The True Tragedy of Richard III" were performed by them before Shakespeare wrote plays with similar titles.

The last years of the 16th century and the first of the 17th were highly successful for Shakespeare. During the years of the plague he had published his long poems, dedicated to his close friend Lord Wriothesley, Earl of Southampton, earning him a reputation as a poet. When he joined the Burbages' company of players, The Lord Chamberlain's Men, his financial situation greatly improved, too. The Burbages built the Globe Theatre, and sold shares to finance it. Shakespeare was one of the shareholders in both the theatre and the company, so he now had a vested interest in writing good plays. Those he sold to other companies would only pay him four or five pounds, but if his plays were a box office hit in the Globe, his profits soared. William must have travelled home at least once or twice each year, as documents show. He bought and sold, let and rented land and estates in his home town, went to court to be paid his debts, and acquired Stratford's second largest house, New Place, for his family. However, he himself remained a tenant in London. The only property he ever bought there was the eastern gatehouse of Blackfriars, doing so only after he had sold his shares in the Globe and returned to Stratford. The eastern gatehouse had various back entrances, alleys, secret vaults and hiding places "in which

7

Papists had been sought" without success, and secret passageways that led directly to the Thames. The gunpowder plotters escaped through this house, and the neighbouring northern gatehouse was used for secret Catholic services. It seems that Blackfriars was the epicentre of London's underground Catholicism at the time. Shakespeare bought the house with two trustees whose task it was to look after matters while he was in Stratford. Shakespeare died in Stratford on April 23, 1616, shortly after having written his will, in which he left the bulk of his property to his daughter Susanna, some money to his daughter Judith – safe from access by her husband, who seems to have been a troublemaker – and makes sure that all his friends are awarded a souvenir. Ben Jonson, who knew him well, wrote about him: "He was, indeed, honest, and of an open and free nature; had an excellent fancy, brave notions, and gentle expressions, wherein he flowed with that facility that sometime it was necessary he should be stopped. [...] Many times he fell into those things, could not escape laughter, as when he said in the person of Caesar, one speaking to him: 'Caesar, thou dost me wrong.' He replied: 'Caesar did never wrong but with just cause;' and such like, which were ridiculous. But he redeemed his vices with his virtues. There was ever more in him to be praised than to be pardoned."

For more information, see: http://www. englishhistory.info/Shakespeare/shakespeares-catholicism.html, http://205.153.158.30/life.htm.

James Burbage was originally trained as a joiner, but became London's most important theatre builder, actor and impresario. His son Cuthbert followed in his father's footsteps as a theatre manager, whereas Richard, the younger son, became an actor.

The Theatre was London's first permanent theatre building. It opened in 1576 and served as a playhouse to London's most renowned theatre companies. William Shakespeare played here with his company, The Lord Chamberlain's Men. James Burbage built the Theatre on leased land in Shoreditch, where he and his family lived. When the lease ended in 1599, problems arose with the proprietor, Giles Allen, who claimed that with the expiry of the lease the building became his property, and Burbage's sons Richard and Cuthbert decided to move the Theatre. They got carpenter Peter Street to dismantle the entire building. The timbers were transported across the Thames and used to construct the Globe on Bankside. Remainders of the Theatre were found by archaeologists in August 2008.

The Queen's Men were an Elizabethan theatre company which had Elizabeth I as its patron. It is assumed that Elizabeth's spymaster Lord Francis

Walsingham was behind the foundation of The Queen's Men. Walsingham saw this company as a means to regulate the London theatre scene, but it may have been that the court wanted to protect the most important and famous actors from the regulations of the city authorities, who considered actors as little more than vagabonds and thieves. Their most celebrated actor was the clown Richard Tarlton.

The Lord Chamberlain's Men were Shakespeare's theatre company. It was founded in 1594 by James Burbage, who functioned as the company's impresario until his death in 1597. Both his sons Richard and Cuthbert were members of the company, although Cuthbert did not act. The company itself consisted of eight shareholders, who shared profits and debts: The Burbages, William Kempe (the company's famous clown), who played Bottom in "A Midsummer Night's Dream", and Dogberry in "Much Ado About Nothing"), Thomas Pope, Augustine Philips, George Bryan, Henry Condell and John Heminges. The latter too are best remembered today for publishing the First Folio edition of Shakespeare's plays. William Shakespeare himself was also a shareholder, an actor and the company's playwright. Some hired men played smaller parts, and a couple of boys, some of them apprenticed to an adult actor, were employed to play the female parts. The Lord Chamberlain's Men operated under the patronage of Henry Carey, 1st Baron Hunsdon, then the Lord Chamberlain. After Queen Elizabeth's death and James's ascension to the throne in 1603, they became The King's Men.

The Globe Theatre, built in 1599, was Shakespeare's "Wooden O". Constructed on marshy land outside the city boundaries, and thus out of reach of London's authorities, it was of polygonal shape – twenty-sided, as it seems – and could house up to 3,000 spectators. There are only very few and not very detailed contemporary illustrations of the Globe, but it must have been an amphitheatre with three storeys, an apron stage with a trap door and a roof to protect the actors from rain. Another trap door in the roof allowed for the sudden entrance of ghosts or spectres, and two or three doors in the back wall of the main level led into the tiring house, where actors awaited their entrance and costumes were kept. The balcony was reserved for the musicians, but frequently also integrated into the plays, as in the famous balcony scene in "Romeo and Juliet".

Queen Elizabeth I, the daughter of Henry VIII and his second wife Anne Boleyn, was considered illegitimate by those who refused to accept Henry's separation from the Church of Rome – hence her trouble with Mary Stuart, Queen of Scots, who was

Shakespeare and his time — Lead-in: Shakespeare and his time — 1

seen as the legitimate successor to the throne and thus focus of a number of conspiracies against Elizabeth. Henry VIII was first succeeded by his son Edward, who died aged 15, and then by Mary, daughter of Henry's Catholic first wife Catherine of Aragon, and an ardent Catholic herself. Mary was bent on reintroducing Catholicism in England, but had to face stubborn refusal from the English lords who had been rewarded for their loyalty with former church possessions by her father. Elizabeth was a Protestant. She succeeded Mary in 1558 at the age of 25, and one of her first acts as Queen was the establishment of an English Protestant Church with herself as its supreme governor. Elizabeth relied on a small number of trusted advisors like William Cecil or Francis Walsingham for her reign, and often preferred observing and ignoring what she saw to rash actions. Some of her counsellors were vexed by this attitude, regarding it as indecisiveness, especially when military campaigns or the question of her marriage were concerned. Elizabeth disliked wars and spending money on them, so neither the expeditions to France, nor those to the Netherlands or Ireland were much of a success. However, the defeat of the Spanish Armada in 1588 – to a large extent due to unfavourable winds for the Spanish – contributed greatly to her popularity: she was "Gloriana, the Virgin Queen" or "Good Queen Bess" to her people. Towards the end of her 44-year reign, however, a number of military and economic crises weakened her popularity. She was succeeded by James, son of Mary Stuart, who had been beheaded on Elizabeth's orders.

Shakespeare's plays and money: For almost a quarter of a century, Shakespeare wrote as many as two, sometimes even three plays per year. With attending rehearsals, learning new roles and taking care of his family back in Stratford, he must have been a very busy man. The plays earned him about four pounds: once the play was finished, it was sold to a playing company who then owned all the rights. Elizabethans had a rather lax attitude towards copyright or plagiarism, so making money out of a play was a difficult job. Shakespeare, however, was a clever businessman who held shares not only in The Lord Chamberlain's Men and the Globe, but also in the Blackfriars Theatre. So selling his plays to these consortia to a certain degree meant selling them to himself, and being highly interested in their financial success: the money the plays earned would at least in parts go into his pockets, too.

First Folio edition: In Shakespeare's times, plays were written to be played, not to be printed. Most of the plays that were staged in Elizabethan times are lost today, and we only know they existed because they are referred to in other sources. Like most other playwrights, Shakespeare himself did not seem to be interested in preserving his plays for posterity by having them printed. However, seven years after his death, two of his former colleagues from The Lord Chamberlain's Men compiled "Mr. William Shakespeare's Comedies, Histories, & Tragedies" and had them printed in folio format. Other folio editions followed. The book contains 36 Shakespeare plays, half of which had never been printed before. Two plays which did not find their way into the folio edition have survived ("Pericles, Prince of Tyre", and "Two Noble Kinsmen"), and two other Shakespeare plays ("Cardenio", "Love's Labours Won") have been lost. The First Folio edition, of which 1000 copies were printed, was originally sold for one pound (about 160 euros today). In 2008, the value of a copy was estimated at about 24 million euros by the Folger Shakespeare Library in Washington DC.

Lernwortschatz	playwright, theatre company, south bank, accession, folio edition, to be bent on doing sth, to persecute, conspiracy, outbreak of the plague, to stage a play, audience, to overcome difficulties, a public art form, migration, to direct a film, to star in a film, in the countryside, to reign, public execution, venue, juggler, to tour the countryside, temporary stage, affordable, reputation, to seek, nobility, social acceptance
Materialien	→ Online-Link: 601005-0001

Comprehension

1 [💻] *Look at the timeline and discuss the importance ...*

Die S können die Bedeutung der Daten aus unterschiedlichen Perspektiven betrachten: Welches Datum war für Shakespeare das wichtigste, welches Datum für uns? Aufgabe **b)** kann in Gruppenarbeit gelöst werden: Personen, Politik, Kunst und Erfindungen werden auf jeweils eine Gruppe aufgeteilt, die Ergebnisse in Form von Postern der Lerngruppe präsentiert. Hinweis auf die *Fact file* zu *Elizabethan England*.

Alternative Die S erhalten Kopien mit Abbildungen bedeutender Persönlichkeiten oder mit Bildern von Gegenständen, die für die Zeit von Bedeutung waren (z. B. Leonardo da Vincis „Vitruvmann", die „Santa Maria" von Christopher Columbus, Galileos Teleskop, eine Seite aus einer Gutenberg

9

1 Shakespeare and his time   Lead-in: Shakespeare and his time

Bibel). Von jeder Abbildung sollten mindestens zwei Kopien vorliegen. Die S haben nun die Möglichkeit, sich die Abbildung auszuwählen, zu der sie glauben, am meisten sagen zu können. Danch suchen sie den Partner/die Partnerin, die die gleiche Abbildung gewählt hat. Gemeinsam werden Informationen zusammengetragen und anschließend der Gruppe vorgestellt.

Lösungsvorschlag   a) *Students might argue that the first date is the most important one; without it we wouldn't even be talking about Shakespeare. Another very important date was the building of the first permanent theatre, as it changed the entertainment scene drastically. As a shareholder of The Lord Chamberlain's Men and the Globe Theatre, Shakespeare might have considered 1592 and 1599 as particularly important dates. For us, one might argue that 1623 is particularly important: without the First Folio edition we would have lost a large part of Shakespeare's work.*

b) ***Famous artists:*** *Tintoretto (Jacopo Comin, 1518–1594), Caravaggio (1571–1610), Paul Rubens (1577–1640), etc.*
Famous discoverers and scientists: *Galileo Galilei (1564–1642; invented a telescope through which stars could be seen that were unknown till then), René Descartes (1569–1659; French philosopher, mathematician, scientist, "cogito ergo sum"), etc.*

Brief report: *The Middle Ages were over; Italy was the centre of a new interest in art and ideas. Some of the most talented men in all of history lived at this time. The printing press had just been invented: more people had access to books; it was a time of great learning. Travelling became easier, and more people left their native villages and towns to visit foreign countries than ever before. The role of the Roman Catholic Church as spiritual authority for all of Europe declined, strong national governments developed. The era is called the Renaissance.*

Analysis   ## 2 Look at the quotes from Shakespeare's dramas.

Diese Aufgabe kann auch als **Hausaufgabe** erledigt werden.

Lösungsvorschlag   *"**The game is up.**" – Someone who has been playing tricks can no longer deceive others, they see through his tricks. It might be an impostor, someone who for instance tries to trick a girl into marrying him. German:* Das Spiel ist aus.
*"**A horse! A horse! My kingdom for a horse.**" – A king must have said these words in a moment in which his horse has either run away from him, or been stolen, and he badly needs it. German:* Ein Pferd! Ein Pferd! Mein Königreich für ein Pferd.
*"**Though this be madness, yet there is method in it.**" – This might have been said by someone who comments on a person who only pretends to be mad, probably in order to hide his proper intentions. German:* In dem Wahnsinn steckt Methode.
*"**To be or not to be – that is the question.**" – A very sad and indecisive person who does not know whether he wants to live or die could have said this. German:* Sein oder nicht sein, das ist hier die Frage.
*"**Love is blind.**" – This might have been said by a friend or relative of someone who has fallen in love with a person with obvious flaws. Everyone else sees the imperfections of that person, except for the one who is in love with him. German:* Liebe macht blind.

Analysis   ## 3 Look at the pictures of the Globe Theatre and its modern ...

Hinweis auf die *Fact file* zu *Theatre in London.*

Lösungsvorschlag   ***Elizabethan Theatre***
- *amphitheatre without roof for most of the audience*
- *there was no curtain*
- *many people stood on the ground in front of the stage*
- *stage had a roof, so actors were protected from bad weather*
- *there is no backdrop*
- *theatre had to compete with very cruel forms of entertainment*
- *theatre going was a very new form of entertainment and highly popular*

Shakespeare and his time Lead-in: Shakespeare and his time

- groups of actors and jugglers tour the country and perform on makeshift stages
- actors have a very low reputation

Theatre in our times
- usually large buildings with a roof so that nobody gets wet
- a curtain hides the stage; when the curtain opens the play begins
- cinema, TV, Internet as competitors
- very few companies tour the country; if they come, they use the buildings which are there
- actors are admired, often well paid; if they are good, they can become millionaires

Erweiterung Weitere Informationen zum elisabethanischen Theater sind im Internet zu finden. Hier eine Auswahl an geeigneten Links:
www.globe-theatre.org.uk/elizabethan-theatre.htm
www.william-shakespeare.info/elizabethan-theaters.htm
www.elizabethan-era.org.uk/elizabethan-theatre.htm

Evaluation **4 Imagine you were Shakespeare and wanted to stage a new play.**

Lösungsvorschlag Shakespeare had to work without electricity, in broad daylight, without a curtain. In modern theatres, lights go out to announce the beginning of a play; when the curtain opens the lights go on and illuminate only the stage. The darkness in which the audience sits contributes to its silence; attention focuses on what is happening on the stage. So as Shakespeare, you have to deal with the following difficulties:
- Making sure everyone realises when the play begins. (Music? An actor or someone else who loudly announces the beginning of the play?)
- The light is always the same, cannot be dimmed to indicate night time. (Props, like a candle? The actors actually say things like "Look at the stars!", or "What a dark night it is!")
- Special effects are limited, there is no music on tape. (Musicians are placed somewhere in the theatre and play on cue? Wet wood is burned to produce smoke that looks like fog? Trapdoors and pulleys help people appear or disappear?)
- The audience is used to loud and cruel forms of entertainment. (Some of the cruelty is part of the plays, in fighting scenes, or in the description of events, acrobatics catch the audience's attention?)
- People need to be told where the play is set. (Costumes? Actors talk about it? Someone gives an explanation to the audience before the play starts?)
- etc.

Today, difficulties can easily be overcome by using modern devices. A loud bell sounds to invite the audience to their seats before the play begins; turning off the lights usually is enough to provide for silence. Dry ice can be used to produce fog, backdrops tell the audience something about the setting of the play.

Erweiterung Mehr Informationen zu Shakespeares Leben im Internet (kleine Auswahl):
http://www.shakespeare-online.com/biography/ Webportal zu Shakespeares Biographie.
http://www.bardweb.net/works.html Webportal zu Shakespeares Werken.
http://search.eb.com/shakespeare Webportal der Encyclopaedia Britannica zu Shakespeare.

Evaluation **5 In Shakespeare's days, theatre was the major public art form.**

Zusatzmaterial → Kopiervorlage 1a–c (Who stole the manuscript of *Richard II*?)

HINTERGRUNDINFO

Shakespeare was not interested in having any of his plays printed; in fact, the only work he ever saw through the printing press himself was "Venus and Adonis", one of his lengthy poems. But others soon realised that they could make money with his plays. Andrew Wise, for instance, published not only "Richard II", but also "Richard III", "Henry IV Parts 1 and 2" and "Much Ado about Nothing". Of course Shakespeare himself had no share in the profit that was made with the printed versions of his plays; he had sold the manuscript to his company, and that was that. Elizabethans had

1 Shakespeare and his time   The Shakespeare portrait

no laws against the violation of copyrights or plagiarism, so there was nothing Shakespeare could have done about it. The persons in this role play are for the most part real Londoners who lived there in Shakespeare's time, and the information about their lives is taken from historical sources. The only invented characters are Jenny and Sally, servants at the Mermaid Tavern. The Mermaid itself was well known to Shakespeare. His landlord is one of Shakespeare's trustees in the purchase of the eastern gatehouse of Blackfriars in 1613, and it can safely be assumed that Shakespeare was a regular customer. Nat and Dick are also invented characters, but most of the company's permanent actors really took on boy apprentices. Another invented character is Nicholas Sandon. However, Elizabeth's police state would hardly have worked without people like him. Marie Mountjoy was Shakespeare's landlady; his name appears as that of a witness in the court records of the Bellot-Mountjoy court case. Elizabeth Vernon may have been the dark lady of Shakespeare's sonnets. Her husband was Shakespeare's good friend and patron Henry Wriothesley, Earl of Southampton, but he only married her when she was already eight months pregnant. Their daughter Penelope looks suspiciously like Shakespeare and very little like Henry.

Lösungsvorschlag   *Theatre was fascinating for a number of reasons. It was a very new form of entertainment: when Shakespeare established himself in London, the first permanent theatre building was only ten years old. People had very few alternatives, and probably not everybody liked them because of their cruelty (public executions and bear baiting are gory and gruesome). Only very few people could read; books were expensive; there was neither TV, nor Internet, nor radio, not even newspapers; and travelling to the next town or even abroad was an adventure that only very few dared to embark on, or had the money for. People learned about strange places and famous persons at the theatre.*

Erweiterung   Am Ende dieses Abschnitts bietet sich der Einsatz von **Kopiervorlage 1a–c** (Seite 102–104) an. Die Arbeitsblätter enthalten ein Rollenspiel, bei dem die S Personen spielen, die tatsächlich gelebt haben bzw. so hätten existieren können. Das bietet die Möglichkeit, das Leben in Shakespeares London im Klassenraum erfahrbar zu machen. Die Rollenkarten und Handlungsanweisungen werden ausgeschnitten und an die S verteilt. Thema des Rollenspiels ist der Diebstahl eines Shakespeare Manuskripts. Es bietet sich an, für dieses Rollenspiel den Klassenraum zu verlassen. Das Rollenspiel versetzt die S als Zeitreisende zurück in die Zeit Shakespeares. Sie nehmen die Identität eines Londoner Bürgers an. Die Titelkarte mit der Einführung wird an alle S ausgeteilt, dann erhält jeder S seine eigene Rolle zugewiesen, die er den anderen nicht zeigt. Nachdem alle S sich mit ihrer Rolle vertraut gemacht haben, geht es nun darum, durch gegenseitiges Befragen ausgehend von einer zufälligen Gesprächssituation (z. B. *Excuse me, can you tell me the way to the Globe theatre?*) herauszufinden, ob der Gesprächspartner möglicherweise der Dieb des Manuskripts sein könnte. Die S unterhalten sich mit möglichst vielen Mitschülern, befragen sich gegenseitig und geben Informationen über sich selbst weiter. Diese Informationen können anschließend in einem Tafelbild festgehalten werden.

Factual information/Photos   ## The Shakespeare portrait   pp. 6–7

HINTERGRUNDINFO

*According to a German Shakespeare scholar, Hildegard Hammerschmidt-Hummel, there are four **likenesses** (pictures that really show Shakesepare) today. The first of them is the Flower portrait, which was probably done in 1609 on a canvas that had previously been used for a painting of a Madonna and the Christ-child in the late 15th or early 16th century. X-Rays show the old painting. At present a debate is going on on whether the portrait that is still held by the Royal Shakespeare Company, and which was dated as a 19th century painting in 2005, is the original Flower portrait or a fake. The Chandos portrait from 1610 is another portrait for which Shakespeare in all probability sat himself. Both portraits show symptoms of a disease which is known as Mikulicz Syndrome, a chronic condition characterized by the abnormal enlargement of glands in the head and neck, including those near the ears, the eyes and the mouth. The swelling is distinctly visible over Shakespeare's left eye both in the Flower and in the Chandos portrait. The painters could only have known about these swellings from seeing them for themselves. In the course of time, the condition grew worse, the swellings larger,*

Shakespeare and his time   The Shakespeare portrait

1

as can be seen in the Darmstadt death mask of Shakespeare. Scientists in Germany scanned the Davenant bust and the death mask using computerised imaging techniques to show that they match up with the Chandos and the Flower portrait of the Bard. Based on these findings Hammerschmidt-Hummel concludes that these four – the Chandos portrait, the Flower portrait, the Davenant bust and the death mask – are true likenesses of Shakespeare.

When in 2009 a supposedly new portrait was discovered, it did not find acceptance to this short list of thought to be true likenesses, despite it was claimed to be the only painting produced during Shakespeare's lifetime. Although the international reception of this portrait has shown quite controversial voices as to this being a true depiction of Shakespeare, the finding of this picture alone has stirred up the discussion again between the various

factions supporting different interests as to any historical reference to Shakespeare. (The question that remains for many Shakespeareans though, is whether such a discussion is really worthwhile with regard to the preoccupation with Shakespeare's works in general.)

For more information see: http://news.bbc.co.uk/2/hi/entertainment/4742716.stm, http://www.sciencedaily.com/releases/2009/04/090421142316.htm, http://www.hammerschmidt-hummel.de/das-cobbe-portraet/The%20Cobbe%20portrait%20-%20Press%20Release%20-%2021.04.%2009%20-%20Univ.%20of%20Mainz.pdf, http://www.telegraph.co.uk/news/uknews/1511251/Lump-above-eye-that-killed-Shakespeare.html, http://www.independent.co.uk/arts-entertainment/art/news/how-restorers-ruined-the-last-portrait-of-shakespeare-1656028.html.

Lernwortschatz   *the Bard, mansion, to sell at auction, to be at the disposal of sb, balding, serene, likeness, to venerate, disposition, the latter, prosperous, to dye, glover, to fall short of sth, shareholder, lawsuit, to purchase, scholar*

Materialien   → Online-Link: 601005-0002

Brainteaser   **1 *Before you read: Look at the preceding two pages and the fact files.***

Lösungsvorschlag   *Shakespeare lived in a very interesting time. England saw many changes: Queen Elizabeth established Protestantism as the state religion, Catholics were persecuted; more and more people moved to London, a teeming city; the theatre in its modern form had just been invented and drew large numbers of spectators. Shakespeare himself left his native Stratford and went to London, too, to earn a living as an actor, playwright and shareholder of London's best theatre company, The Lord Chamberlain's Men, which later gained the protection of King James. This company of actors had its own theatre on Bankside, the Globe.   (98 words)*

Erweiterung   Die S können im Internet weitere (vermeintliche) Porträts Shakespeares ausfindig machen oder als Farbfolie vorgestellt bekommen, diese miteinander vergleichen und diskutieren, warum so großes Interesse daran besteht zu wissen, wie Shakespeare aussah.

Analysis   **2 *Summarise the information the text gives us about ...***

Die S können zusätzlich die *VIP file* zu *William Shakespeare* heranziehen.

Alternative   Statt einer *summary* bietet sich auch ein Interview an, das ein Reporter mit einem Zeitgenossen Shakespeares führt, z. B. seiner Frau oder einem seiner Kollegen.

Lösungsvorschlag   **a)** *Shakespeare must have been rather successful and wealthy in the time between 1590 and 1610. He was unconventional, like other artists of the time. Maybe he was also discreet because he did not wear much jewellery, or he was not rich enough to buy much jewellery and show off his wealth as was the custom at the time. He must have been self-confident, and he also looks a bit bold. The information on Shakespeare that the portrait reveals corresponds to the facts presented on the lead-in pages: Shakespeare was an artist – actor and playwright – and he probably earned a handsome amount of money because his company was London's most respected one and quite successful, protected by the King himself, and because many people went to see plays in those days.*

13

1 Shakespeare and his time   The Shakespeare portrait

b) *The portrait is from the time in which Shakespeare was successful in London. It shows someone who is unconventional, self-confident and not too poor – all of which were true of Shakespeare. It has been said for a very long time that it does show Shakespeare, and it resembles all other portraits of Shakespeare that are known. What speaks against the assumption is that some people say the person in the portrait is too dark-skinned, too foreign-looking to be a great English poet, and they dislike the look on his face: apparently they believe that the greatest poet of all times should look more sophisticated. Besides, the history of the portrait can only be traced back to 1747, so nothing can be said of its origin or owners before that time.*

Analysis

3 Compare the two portraits of Shakespeare shown here.

Hinweis auf die *Word bank* zu *Talking about possibilities.*

Lösungsvorschlag **a)–c)** *The Chandos portrait shows a person who might have been a member of the not too poor middle class in Elizabethan times: his entirely black clothing and the fact that he could afford a portrait, though not a very good one, reveal that much. The facial expression shown in the Chandos portrait seems quite true to life, the portrayed person looks attentively, maybe even a bit mockingly at the beholder. The second portrait resembles the Chandos portrait: the same receding hairline, moustache, and somewhat prominent nose. However, the golden earring is missing, the clothes are much more refined, and the curve of the eyebrow and half-smile give the portrayed person an air of wealth, sophistication and arrogance. Apparently the painter of this portrait used already existing likenesses of Shakespeare for his painting, but decided to portray Shakespeare as the person he thought him to be.*

Evaluation

4 As with the portrait, the life of Shakespeare ...

Lösungsvorschlag *At the root of the authorship debate lies the assumption that a simple man from a village in Warwickshire with no university training could never have written such refined poetry, let alone plays filled with so many stories from foreign countries and history. Various contemporaries of Shakespeare have been suspected of being the true author of the plays, among them Christopher Marlowe, a young and highly talented poet and Cambridge graduate; Edward de Vere, Earl of Oxford, a man of great learning and wealth; and even Queen Elizabeth herself. Those who believe that Shakespeare did not really write the plays argue that Marlowe, a troublesome youth, spy, and atheist, had to flee to Italy and continued to write his plays fromthere (hence the frequent choice of Italian settings in Shakespeare's plays), using Shakespeare's name as a cover for his own work. However, it is rather certain that he was killed in a tavern brawl in 1593, well before Shakespeare wrote some of his greatest masterpieces.*

The case for the Earl of Oxford is based on the idea that a nobleman at the time could not very well be associated with the theatre, seeing as actors had such a low reputation. Therefore, wishing to remain anonymous, he used Shakespeare as a frontman. The Earl, however, died in 1604, when Shakespeare was yet to write "Macbeth", "King Lear", "Cymbeline", "The Tempest" and six other plays. The Oxfordians still defend their position by arguing that the Earl wrote these plays before he died, kept them in stock and ordered that they should be staged after his death. As far as Queen Elizabeth is concerned, she certainly had a very good education, was fluent in a number of foreign languages, and was greatly interested in the theatre. The point that is made for her is the way in which women are shown in Shakespeare's plays: often they are self-confident, sometimes even headstrong, and outwit their male counterparts. The Queen herself was like that – but did she really have the time to write 39 plays? And besides, she, too died in 1603, well before Shakespeare ended his literary career.

Erweiterung Anhand der zahlreichen Informationen hierzu im Internet können die S in Gruppenarbeit ihren persönlichen Favoriten auswählen und die Argumente, die für ihn als Autor der Dramen Shakespeares sprechen, auf Postern zusammenstellen. Eine Debatte zwischen *Stratfordians* und *Oxfordians*, in der die Argumente ausgetauscht werden, bietet sich ebenfalls an.

Shakespeare and his time   Book burning   **1**

| Novel excerpt/ Photos | **Book burning** | pp. 8–9 |

HINTERGRUNDINFO

James Shapiro's "1599: A Year in the Life of William Shakespeare" focuses on just this one year in Shakespeare's life, beginning with a description of the dismantling of James Burbage's old Theatre in Shoreditch in a cloak-and-dagger operation (the parts were used to build the Globe) in the last winter days of 1598 and ending with the political crisis caused by the Earl of Essex's untimely return from his unsuccessful campaign in Ireland. Essex was a close friend of Shakespeare's; and the Earl's political downfall presumably caused the Bard some distress. James Shapiro is a professor of English at Columbia University in New York. "1599" won him the Samuel Johnson Prize in 2006.

Censorship: Throughout Elizabeth's reign, there was a constant fear of conspiracies. Most suspect of conspiracy were Catholics, who since Henry VIII's Act of Supremacy, which was renewed by Elizabeth, suffered from discrimination. Extremely strict penal laws directed against them concerned all religious writings, too, not only Catholic, but also Puritan, so the most commonly burned books at the time were prayer books, missals and writings such as the Borromeo testament. In these testaments, which were brought to England by Jesuit missionaries, Catholics solemnly professed their faith and belief in the Virgin Mary and the saints. One such testament, signed by John Shakespeare, William's father, was found in the Shakespeares' house in Henley Street.

Christopher Marlowe was one of the most colourful persons of the time: a blasphemous, iconoclastic, university graduate and the star of the theatre scene. His patron was Thomas Walsingham, the brother of Elizabeth's spymaster Francis Walsingham, and he was on Francis's payroll – as a secret service agent. Careless remarks about the flaws of Protestantism and virtues of Catholicism were overheard by another spy and brought about his downfall. He was murdered in a government safe house run by the widowed Mrs Bull, a distant relative of the Walsinghams. Whether he was killed by Nicholas Skeres, spy, Ingram Frazer, spy, or Robin Poley, a major player in Elizabeth's secret service, can not be said for sure. Robin Poley, who later also caught Antony Babington (of the Babington plot), was a next door neighbour of Shakespeare's in Silver Street.

Political drama in the publishing world: In the spring of 1599, two books on the ruler who had disposed Richard II were on sale in London, one by Shakespeare ("The History of Henry the Fourth"), and one by John Hayward ("The First Part of the Life and Reign of King Henry IV"). Hayward presented the book to an official for approval without a dedication or preface. The official was Samuel Harnsett, known for his rather lax attitude, who later admitted he had only really looked at the first page of the book. Hayward then dedicated the book to the Earl of Essex, thus capitalising on contemporary events. The Earl's demand to have the dedication page cut out of the book after 500 copies had already been sold only served to further enhance sales, of course, and when a second edition was printed Hayward added a preface in which he aggressively rejected all imputations attributed to his book. This, of course, prompted the readers all the more to look for evidence of criticism of the authorities, which was not very hard to find: similarities between Richard II and Elizabeth I were obvious, especially when it came to the dangers of a childless ruler. The Earl of Essex, when he tried to stage his rebellion in the following year, paid Shakespeare's company a handsome amount of money for a performance of "Henry IV" on the eve of his rebellion – demanding that the deposition scene, which had not been printed, be played at all events. The players had to report to the authorities in the course of the ensuing Essex trial.

Lernwortschatz	*censorship, approval, abdication, coincide, dissident, crackdown, livelihood, imminent, arbitrary, impoverished, to conspire, accost, to humour, rioter, to sway sb, haze, to seep, maw, annulment, to proclaim, to appeal, treasury, to succeed, to surrender, gentry, to impose, penalty*
Materialien	→ Online-Link: 601005-0003
Evaluation	**1 *Describe the picture to the left. What effect was ...?***
Lösungsvorschlag	*The public burning of books aimed at setting an example to the people watching and at demonstrating power. The burning of religious writings was meant to instill fear, since burning at the stake was still a common punishment for heresy, and the message probably was that what happened to the book could just as well happen to its reader or author.*

1   Shakespeare and his time   Book burning

Analysis   **2   Explain why the text is entitled "Book burning".**

Hinweis auf die *Word bank* zu *Censorship*.

Lösungsvorschlag   *As the fact file explains, all books that were to be printed needed official approval by a "censor". If a book was not officially approved, or a play had not been stamped by the Master of the Revels, the book could not be printed, the play not performed. So Shakespeare, like all other writers at the time, had to make sure that his writings would pass muster with the officials. This is what the text is about, and as the most extreme form of censorship is the public burning of books, the title "Book Burning" quite fittingly describes the atmosphere created by such censorship.*

Comprehension   **3   The text starts by telling you that Shakespeare was facing ...**

L verweist auf die *Fact file* mit den Hintergrundinformationen zur politischen Situation.

Lösungsvorschlag   *In the spring of 1599, Shakespeare was writing a play for the opening of the Globe Theatre that same year, and since he was a shareholder in this new building, he had a vested interest in making it a success. What troubled Londoners at the time was an aging, childless ruler, a hero (the Earl of Essex) sent off on a suicide mission to Ireland, and the grim repression of all criticism through the authorities. Many of the former stars of the theatre scene had either been killed, like Christopher Marlowe, or imprisoned, or tortured to death. So Shakespeare had to make up his mind and decide if he wanted to join in the chorus of criticism, which might draw the people to the performances of his forthcoming new play and guarantee a full house for a couple of nights, or play it safe and avoid any critical or even ambiguous remarks about the present ruler and her government. This might put off the audience, but keep him out of trouble. Shakespeare decided not to criticise the ruler, but to criticise censorship instead by describing the violent deaths of two poets onstage, thus echoing the fates of his fellow writers Thomas Kyd and Marlowe.*

Analysis   **4   Analyse the way in which Shapiro links ...**

Lösungsvorschlag   *Shapiro mentions the fate of some of Shakespeare's fellow writers, who had either been imprisoned for their writings, or died from torture, or had been murdered. Being a writer at the time must have been a fairly dangerous job. It was easy to come into conflict with political authorities, and difficult to come out unharmed. Shapiro quotes from the play Shakespeare was writing that year, "Julius Caesar", and which was performed on the opening night of the Globe. In the scenes he quotes the murder of two innocent poets by an angry mob who is not interested in the truth. His argument is that Shakespeare did not introduce this scene, which is nowhere to be found in the historical sources, by accident, but on purpose, and by doing so found his own way of criticising censorship. He seems to warn his fellow poets not to invite trouble, but to steer clear of it. The lynching of the poet onstage not only mirrors the murder of Julius Caesar in an earlier scene of the play, but also the deaths of many innocent people who were killed for their beliefs or political attitudes. Thus, current events left their mark on Shakespeare's writings.*

Shakespeare and his time — Life in the suburbs

Novel excerpt/Quotes/Photos — **Life in the suburbs** — pp. 10–11

HINTERGRUNDINFO

Literary critic and theorist **Stephen Greenblatt** is a professor of literature at Harvard University and one of the founders of New Historicism, an academic movement with a set of critical principles he himself refers to as cultural poetics. His Shakespeare biography "Will in the World: How Shakespeare Became Shakespeare" was on the New York Times bestseller list for nine weeks. In it he investigates how social events and circumstances influenced the works of Shakespeare and to what extent he chronicled them in his plays.

Punishment in Elizabethan England was cruel and often unjust. Elizabeth's state was a police state with spies everywhere. Her government was obsessed by the fear of conspiracies and rebellions and saw to it that any person suspected of treason ended on the rack or the scaffold, usually both. As the spy who reported on a suspect was rewarded with one third of the convict's belongings, being an informant was a well-paid job. Once accused of a capital crime such as high treason, blasphemy, spying, witchcraft, alchemy or rebellion, the defendant was often tortured to "find out the truth" and had no right to legal counsel. Chances of receiving an acquittal during the trial were extremely slim, so an accusation of having committed one of these crimes often led to the defendant's execution.

Shakespeare's family more than once felt the hand of the state: his father was fined for illegal wool trading, and also had to pay a handsome sum for not appearing before court; his daughter Susanna was fined for not attending Protestant mass; and the recusant Edward Arden, a relative from his mother's side, was accused of conspiring against the Queen in the Somerville plot because of his staunch Catholic beliefs. He was hanged, drawn and quartered – the usual penalty for traitors – despite lack of evidence. It is hard to imagine that such events left no mark on Shakespeare's writings.

In **Elizabethan England**, you got hanged for treason, murder, stealing goods worth more than five pence or repeated minor offences such as tramping. This is why the playing companies who toured the country and who were often seen as vagabonds by the town authorities were bent on finding a nobleman as a patron to protect them. During Elizabeth's reign, an average of 1800 executions took place per year, several hundred of them in London, so that the statistical likelihood for Elizabethans to be executed was just as high as for today's citizen to be killed in a road accident. In a world where bear baiting, by today's standards an extremely cruel sport, was officially approved of and by royal order encouraged by the Church, watching an execution was just another form of entertainment. However, even Elizabethans had their limits: when the Babington plotters were executed, eleven in a row, the audience shouted and screamed at the executioner to stop the bloody spectacle after the eighth execution.

For more information, see: http://www.william-shakespeare.info/elizabethan-crime-punishment.htm, http://www.eyewitnesstohistory.com/punishment.htm, http://www.ewtn.com/library/CHISTORY/PENALAWS.HTM, http://www.springfield.k12.il.us/schools/springfield/eliz/Torturepun.html, http://www.springfield.k12.il.us/schools/springfield/eliz/crimeandpunishment.html.

Lernwortschatz — to execute, traitor, pillory, ferocity, to mete out, gory, ghastly, to lop off, to vanquish, to reconcile, rape, mutilation, scaffold, to deem, offender, rack, gallows, inept, villain, to chop off

Comprehension — **1 Describe the way in which Elizabethan authorities …**

Hinweis auf die Word bank zu Crime and punishment.

Lösungsvorschlag — Elizabethan authorities dealt with offenders in an extremely harsh manner. Many of the offences that were severely punished at the time are not punishable offences at all today, like tramping or begging, and the punishments themselves often involved physical pain or mutilation, such as whipping, cutting parts of the body off, or executions. The offenders were punished in public, probably to scare others off, and the punishments were so pitiless and cruel that it is hard to imagine that they did not work as a deterrent.

1   Shakespeare and his time   Life in the suburbs

Comprehension

2 Summarise the extent to which Shakespeare incorporated …

Lösungsvorschlag

Shakespeare was no stranger to the cruel scenes of torture and punishment that took place in London every day and incorporated such scenes to a fair extent into his plays. In one of his earliest plays, "Titus Andronicus", Lavinia is mutilated and raped; in "Richard III" and "Macbeth" traitors are executed by decapitation, and their heads are displayed to the audience. Even in his comedies such as in "Much Ado About Nothing" there is a reference to the cruel punishment that awaits the villain.

Research

3 [🖥] Browse the Internet to find out the following: What was the worst …?

Lösungsvorschlag

The worst punishment
This was reserved for those who had committed a crime against the state, such as treason or rebellion, and were also not of noble origin. They were drawn from the prison to the place of execution on a sled or a hurdle, and then hanged until they were half dead. Next, they were taken down and quartered alive. If they survived this, they could witness how their limbs and bowels were cut from their bodies and burned in a nearby fire. Noblemen were simply decapitated, and their heads exposed on stakes – a row of such heads greeted everyone who entered London from the South through the entrance gate of London Bridge.

Offences for hanging
You could be hanged for stealing goods worth more than five pence, for begging repeatedly, for poaching at night, for tramping, but also for religious beliefs. An Act of Parliament from 1581 made reconciliation with the Catholic Church treason, and another Act in 1585 "against Jesuits and seminary priests" declared as treason the mere presence of a Catholic priest in England. Sheltering or assisting him was a felony and equally punishable by hanging.

Other punishments
- *the pillory and the stocks (part of the body was locked between two slabs of wood, usually for drunkards or criminals whose more severe punishment had not yet been decided upon)*
- *whipping (for adultery)*
- *branding (this was deemed necessary to expose repeated offenders)*
- *ducking stools (for talkative, or free-speaking women; the procedure consisted of strapping the women to a stool and ducking them under water, but often resulted in the woman's drowning)*
- *cutting off various parts of the anatomy – hands, ears etc. (for cutpurses and thieves)*
- *the gossip's bridle or the brank (an iron framework placed on the head of the offenders, usually women, with a metal strip that fit into the mouth and due to its shape caused severe pain or injury with any movement of the tongue; the offenders were led through the streets by a chain, then tied to a whipping post or pillory and thus exposed to the verbally abusive public)*
- *the drunkard's cloak (a public punishment for drunkenness, the cloak being a weighty barrel)*

Discussion

4 [👥] Discuss: What effect did these real-life spectacles have …?

Lösungsvorschlag

The effects on the Elizabethans might have been that they got used to violence, blood, torture, and cruelty at a very early age. Apparently, they were taught not to feel or show any pity or sympathy for the offender, but on the contrary to take delight in others' misery. If public punishment was a form of entertainment, then gloating over the others' misfortune must have been a widespread social emotion revealing little or no respect for human life. After all, with high rates of infant mortality and devastating plague years, death was more or less omnipresent. Today we probably react differently to the violence in Shakespeare's plays. Such violence as displayed in "Titus Andronicus" or in "Richard III" seems draconian to us, and we might feel put off by such shows of cruelty on stage. But then we are very used to realistic

Shakespeare and his time   Life in the suburbs   1

shows of violence on TV and in film in our everyday lives, and the media fill us with stories of abominable crimes every day. In a time where the executions of criminals and tyrants such as Saddam Hussein are watched by millions on YouTube, it is doubtful that we are so much different from the Elizabethans.

Evaluation

5 Look at the quotations below. Which of them do you find particularly …?

Zusatzmaterial   → Klausurvorschlag 1 • Revision file 1

Lösungsvorschlag   *Individual solutions. The ones that might have impressed Elizabethans were probably the quote from "Macbeth". Cruelty against infants, in this case a baby, was even by Elizabethan standards more than extreme. The quote from "Henry V" may also have impressed them, but probably rather for the fact that the dead French soldiers had been killed by an otherwise outnumbered English army, which left the field victoriously.*

Erweiterung
- Als Zusatzaufgabe bietet es sich an, dass sich die S noch näher mit den Lebensgewohnheiten der Elisabethaner beschäftigen: *Find out more about everyday life in Elizabethan times. What did Elizabethans eat and drink? What did they wear? Were there any rules for clothes? What was travelling like in those times? etc.*

- Zum Abschluss des *Topics* füllen die S *Revision file* 1 (Themenheft, Seite 59) aus. Ein Lösungsvorschlag befindet sich hier im Lehrerheft auf Seite 141.

2 | Shakespeare's language Didaktisches Inhaltsverzeichnis

Topic 2: Shakespeare's language

pp. 12–19

Didaktisches Inhaltsverzeichnis
Bearbeitungszeitraum: 10–12 Unterrichtsstunden

Textsorte/Thema	Unterrichts-methoden	*Input boxes*	Kompetenzen	Textproduktion
Elizabethan English (209 words)				SB, Seite 12, LB, Seite 21–23
Factual information, quotes/Elizabethan English	Kursgespräch		Orientierungswissen Leseverstehen Gespräche führen	*Matching expressions to modern counterparts Analysing stylistic devices*
Working with Shakespeare's language (188 words)				SB, Seite 13, LB, Seite 23/24
Factual information, quotes/Shakespeare's language	Kursgespräch Online-Link: 601005-0004		Orientierungswissen Leseverstehen Gespräche führen	*Matching expressions to definitions Translating expressions into German*
Shakespeare's use of prose and verse (542 words)				SB, Seite 14/15, LB, Seite 25–27
Factual information/ Prose and verse	Kursgespräch Zusatzmaterial: Kopiervorlage 2	*Fact file: Understanding the language*	Orientierungswissen Leseverstehen Gespräche führen Argumentieren	*Discussing the change in meaning due to stress Splitting verse lines into stressed and unstressed syllables Dramatic reading*
Prose and verse in *Romeo and Juliet* (333 words)				SB, Seite 16, LB, Seite 27
Drama excerpt/Act II, scene iv	Kursgespräch		Leseverstehen Gespräche führen	*Analysing language conventions Rewriting a scene Acting out a scene*
[1🖰] Shakespeare's poetry/[1◉] Sonnet 73 (213/121 words)				SB, Seite 17, LB, Seite 28–30
Factual information, poem, video clip/Love poetry, history of London	Kursgespräch Online-Link: 601005-0005	*VIP file: Henry Wriothesley Fact file: Sonnets*	Leseverstehen Hör-/Sehverstehen Gespräche führen Argumentieren	*Analysing poetic devices and tone Comparing sonnets Commenting on history*
[2◉] Sonnet 116 (109 words)				SB, Seite 18, LB, Seite 30–32
Poem, quote/Marriage	Kursgespräch Partnerarbeit		Orientierungswissen Leseverstehen Hörverstehen Gespräche führen Argumentieren	*Evaluating a poem Making a comment Finding metaphors Giving a presentation*
[3◉] Sonnet 94 (107 words)				SB, Seite 19, LB, Seite 32–34
Poem/Hurt feelings	Kursgespräch Zusatzmaterial: Klausurvorschlag 2		Leseverstehen Hörverstehen Gespräche führen Argumentieren	*Summing up a message Pointing out key words Analysing structure Comparing sonnets Writing a statement*

| Shakespeare's language | Elizabethan English | **2** |

Unterrichtsverlauf

| *Factual informa- tion/Quotations* | **Elizabethan English** | p. 12 |

HINTERGRUNDINFO

History of the development and origins of English:
The history of the English language really started during the 5th century, when the Angles, Saxons and Jutes, coming from what is today Denmark and northern Germany, invaded Britain during the 5th century AD. The words for English and England come from one of these tribes, the Angles, who came from 'Englaland' and spoke a language called 'Englisc'. In the 5th century, the inhabitants of Britain were Celts and spoke a Celtic language, but they were driven to Wales, Ireland and Scotland by the invaders, where Celtic languages are still spoken by a minority today. As the languages spoken by the invaders were similar, they quickly developed into a common language we now call Old English, and which was spoken in England from around 450 to 1100 AD. Very few texts in Old English survive, the most famous of which is "Beowulf", a narrative poem. Although these texts are very difficult to understand even for native English speakers today, many of the most commonly used words in modern English have Old English roots, like "water", "be", or "strong".

Things changed drastically with the arrival of the Normans in **1066**. The new conquerors spoke a variety of French, which became the language of the ruling classes while the lower classes continued to speak English. During the course of the 14th century, English once again became the dominant language in Britain, but now with many French words added. This language, called Middle English, was spoken from around 1100 to 1500 and used by the great poet Chaucer, but is still very different from the language spoken by today's native speakers. From around 1500 to 1800 people spoke early modern English, which is the language that Shakespeare spoke. Towards the end of the 15th century, people started to pronounce words differently. Vowels became shorter – a change in pronunciation which is called the Great Vowel Shift. In addition, the world itself changed: British people started to travel abroad and had contact with other people from around the world. The renewed interests in classical literature lead to the introduction of many Greek and Latin words into the English language. More people were taught to read and write, books could now be printed, grammar and spelling were standardised, and the dialect of southern England – especially London, where most publishing houses were – became the standard.

When asked what is so difficult about Shakespeare, even many native English pupils will answer "the language". However, the main difference between their language – (Late) Modern English – and Shakespeare's English is vocabulary. The Industrial Revolution and technology made it necessary to create new words, and so did the political situation. Toward the end of the 19th century, Britain had become a huge empire, and foreign words from many countries were adopted.

David Crystal proves in **"Think On My Words"** (Cambridge, 2008) with the help of almost endless textual examples that Shakespeare's language is a challenge that can be taken up. "What we have are the plays and poems as dramatic and literary wholes, expressed in a language which is sometimes different from what we know today, and sometimes difficult." (p. 41). He presents and explains some of the real differences and also demystifies some of the seeming problems. Some of his major claims include:

- Shakespeare invented about ten percent of his words, but only five percent of the words in his plays have changed their meaning from Early Modern to Modern English.
- Ninety percent of the language he used does not need to be explained. To understand the remaining part there are a number of methods, like reading in context or building analogies, which make this part even smaller.
- It is almost impossible to analyse Shakespeare's oeuvre in worthwhile categories, yet it is quite possible to come to conclusions about differences in usage when analysing the language of characters, genres, or periods.
- The spelling in the "First Folio" is roughly 70 percent identical with Modern English. The relatively small number of different forms that happen to have a high frequency today leads us to believe otherwise.
- The same result is true for the differences in punctuation. Differences in punctuation usually serve a dramatic purpose.
- The use of rhyme and verse show Shakespeare's development in his skill and his urge to use rhythmical variation within the limits of strict forms. The form of the iambic pentameter, which became popular when rhyming went out of fashion, suits the normal lengths of units in everyday conversation today.

2 Shakespeare's language Elizabethan English

- Too much emphasis is often put on looking at the vocabulary that remains difficult rather than using the skill of learning this vocabulary with the help of the context or antonyms.
- As opposed to popular belief, Shakespeare showed his inventiveness much stronger by giving existing words new meanings in a different context than by actually inventing most of these new terms.
- Looking at the development of the language of Shakespeare's plays, we see that there is a great difference in usage before and after 1600.
- "Poets especially love to break normal collocation rules, and Shakespeare is one of the greatest rule-breakers the language has seen." (p. 173)
- When students study Shakespeare's grammar, too much work is done on morphology and far too little on sentence structure; e.g. there are only a few pronouns used in the old language variety yet they are very common. The different use of these pronouns must be studied to understand the various and varying relationships between characters. The expression of tenses increasingly took over the form we are used to today. Many more differences to Modern English occur in the sentence structure due to metrical requirements.

- Apart from looking at individual features of language ("bottom up"), it is just as necessary to look at the perspective of discourse ("top down"). This study of the language of communication reveals the differences of the usage of verse and prose as well as that of "high" or "low style".

David Crystal's systematic look at **Shakespeare's language**, which he supports with a large amount of relevant data, shows where some of the difficulties in the study of Shakespeare's plays might come up. With his findings he clearly supports the didactic approach of facilitating the study of Shakespeare by trying to become actively involved rather than speculating on some singular features. As Crystal puts it:
"There is an intimate relationship between Early Modern English and Shakespeare. [...] We should not try to study Early Modern English and then study Shakespeare. Rather, we should study Early Modern English alongside and through the medium of Shakespeare. Examining the way an author manipulates linguistic rules give us insights into the nature of the rules themselves." (p. 231.)

Lernwortschatz to invert, to suit a purpose, to estimate, elaborate, wordy, imagery, metaphor, insult

Comprehension **1 Many Shakespearean expressions seem strange at first, …**

Lösung 1 – D, 2 – F, 3 – E, 4 – H, 5 – I, 6 – J, 7 – C, 8 – G, 9 – K, 10 – A, 11 – B

Modern English	Elizabethan English
A no painted backdrop	10 How now?
B a recess	11 I pray you
C a small gallery	7 God grant you mercy
D Excuse me	1 Pray pardon
E Wow!	3 In sooth!
F Really? No kidding?	2 Is it even so?
G I swear it!	8 Now, by my faith!
H Oh no! Too bad!	4 God a-mercy!
I Hello!	5 What ho!
J Goodbye	6 Fare thee well
K See you soon.	9 I shall see thee anon.

Analysis **2 In the quotations above say what stylistic device is used …**

Lösungsvorschlag The stylistic device used in all three quotations is **metaphor**.

Shakespeare's language — Working with Shakespeare's language — 2

- *"Sir, in my heart there was a kind of fighting that would not let me sleep."*
  With this metaphor, Shakespeare illustrates to what extent Hamlet's thoughts are controversial and occupy him so much that he cannot sleep. The effect is that the audience visualises a fight, and realise that Hamlet's troubles are becoming worrisome.

- *"Life's but a walking shadow, a poor player …"*
  In this quote, Shakespeare compares life to an unimportant actor (walking shadow), who worries and brags about his or her chance on stage, yet the day never comes. The actor is gone and the audience never even knew they were there. The effect achieved is that the meaninglessness Macbeth sees in life seems to suddenly play a part on the stage itself.

- *"Blow, winds, and crack your cheeks!"*
  As in picture books for children, the wind is depicted as having a mouth and cheeks to blow with, and is thus someone Lear can address directly. Directors are tempted to invent visual and sound effects for the storm, but Shakespeare's words are, if correctly pronounced, so powerful that the audience can easily imagine the wind without any special effects.

Factual information

Working with Shakespeare's language — p. 13

HINTERGRUNDINFO

In the epilogue to **"Think On My Words"**, David Crystal suggests a three-stage process is required to understand Shakespeare's language better. After first finding a difficult passage, the students should describe the construction as precisely as possible before trying to explain why that feature is there. It is not enough to stop at "feature spotting", though. This way we try to put ourselves into the position of the playwright who had a choice in using this particular feature. The question is why he used it. After answering this question, the work begins on trying to understand the language "within a wider literary, dramatic, historical, psychological and social frame of reference". This is where the active work in the classroom sets in. The justification for being experimental in the attempt to get closer to an understanding of Shakespeare is the attitude the playwright himself had.

Shakespeare shows us how to achieve effects with language, how to try new things out. Linguistic inventiveness can lead to new words like "unshout", "unspeak" or "unsex" that were formerly unknown. New verbs can be made from nouns, as with "to lethargy" or "to dialogue". Finally, Shakespeare was also able to challenge standard word order to make it fit his poetic purposes as in 'Musicke do I heare / Ha, ha? Keepe time'. For David Crystal, Shakespeare is a role model for bending and breaking linguistic rules most effectively (p. 233).

Lernwortschatz — to coin, to integrate, assassin, to make sth up from scratch, gossip(er), to make one's hair stand on end, to accomplish, to expose, resentful, gender

Materialien — → Online-Link: 601005-0004

Comprehension

1 Match the expressions from the list above to …

Lösung

You use this expression …
… to describe an attempt to accomplish something nearly impossible.   **E**
… to describe a person who makes his feelings obvious to everyone.   **G**
… about someone who is too friendly to another person.   **H**
… if something lasts indefinitely.   **I**
… if you do not understand something at all.   **A**
… if something nice becomes unpleasant because you have more than you need.   **F**
… to express how you may react when something makes you feel afraid.   **C**
… when a deception is exposed.   **B**
… if you feel that something is not right.   **D**

2 Shakespeare's language   Working with Shakespeare's language

Comprehension

2 How can you translate these expressions into German?

Lösungsvorschlag

A Ich verstehe nur Bahnhof.
B Das Spiel ist aus.
C Das lässt einem die Haare zu Berge stehen.
D Ich traue dem Frieden nicht./Es liegt etwas in der Luft.
E Das ist ein sinnloses Unterfangen.
F Das ist zu viel des Guten.
G Er trägt sein Herz auf der Zunge.
H Sie erschlägt ihn mit ihrer Zuneigung.
I Für immer und ewig.

Analysis

3 Which of the expressions from the list above could be used ...

Teilaufgabe b) kann in Partnerarbeit oder als schriftliche **Hausaufgabe** gelöst werden.

Lösungsvorschlag

a)

- *I don't really trust the committee's decision. I think **there's something in the wind**.*
- *John is extremely resentful. He'll remember that **forever and a day**.*
- *Do you realise that everyone knows what Sally thinks about this? She **wears her heart on her sleeve**.*
- *I was looking forward to snow, but **this is too much of a good thing** – it's April and I want sunshine.*

b)

John: *Oh, hi there, Paul, what are you doing here?*
Paul: *I'm waiting for Sally. We wanted to have a drink here first and then go to the cinema.*
John: *What film are you going to see?*
Paul: *Baz Luhrman's "Romeo and Juliet". I'll take her out to dinner afterwards at a nice little restaurant and ask her to marry me.*
John: *Wow, how romantic! She'll remember that **forever and a day**, I'll bet.*
Paul: *That's the idea. But I wonder where she is – she should have been here half an hour ago.*
John: *Why don't you call her?*
Paul: *I've tried, but she just texted back that she couldn't speak right now. I guess she is still in that meeting.*
John: *What's that meeting all about?*
Paul: *The new boss is presenting his ideas on how to deal with the economic crisis. I think **there's something in the wind**. He'll try to get rid of some of the employees, I guess. The company lost a fair amount of money last year, and the management will want to cut costs.*
John: *As long as it is not you or Sally.*
Paul: *Who knows? Sally **wears her heart on her sleeve**. She often says things that do not go down very well with the other members of the management. These men like to be surrounded by good-looking women – but one of them as a member of the board of executives, **that's maybe too much of a good thing** for them.*
John: *Let's hope for the best. Look, here she comes now! And she doesn't look as if she had been fired. Have a nice evening then, the two of you! Bye!*
Paul: *Thanks, John, bye!*

Erweiterung

Oft werden Ausdrücke von Shakespeare als Überschriften in Zeitungsartikeln verwendet (z. B. *All's well that ends well, Much ado about nothing, What's in a name?*, etc.). Die S können aufgefordert werden, von einer Liste mit Ausdrücken oder Zitaten aus einem bestimmten Stück eine Auftaktseite für eine Zeitung zu gestalten. Die Texte können entweder selbst verfasst oder aus dem Internet übernommen werden. Wird der Auftrag in Gruppenarbeit erledigt, kümmert sich ein Teil der S um die Materialbeschaffung und der Rest der Gruppe um die Gestaltung der Fotos und Texte.

Shakespeare's language Shakespeare's use of prose and verse | **2**

| Factual information | **Shakespeare's use of prose and verse** | pp. 14–15 |

HINTERGRUNDINFO

A quite comprehensive, yet very palatable study on the use of verse and prose in Shakespeare is offered by **Ben Crystal** in "Shakespeare on Toast, Act 4, Catch the Rhythm", (Cambridge, 2008, pp. 113–138). The linguistic areas covered by the Fact file are discussed in great detail by **David Crystal** in "Think On My Words" (Cambridge, 2008). Some of his findings with regard to the individual categories are in brief:

Pronouns: Although the total number of old forms is quite high, there are only a few different old forms to be learnt. It is important to notice, however, that English took over much of the French usage of 'tu' and 'vous', using 'you' as a form of address from inferior to superior people. A very important consequence would be to look out for changes in the forms of the pronouns by the same characters in a passage (pp. 178–183).

Word order: Most of the deviations from Modern English can be seen where verse was used to meet the demands of the metre. Ideally the end of the line coincides with the end of the sentence. Yet sometimes the rhythm or speed of the language required the thought to occupy more than a line or the line to be shared by a number of speakers. The more the metre forces deviations from grammatical rules within one line, the more difficult a passage becomes. So metre is not just a question of sound; metrical choices result in a number of grammatical consequences (pp. 199–206).

Vocabulary: The number of words than cannot be explained through context or forms of analogy is below ten percent. It usually is the experimental use or introduction of new word combinations, e.g. as new phrasal verbs or collocations that causes most of the necessary work. Difficult words that have an important bearing on the meaning have to be learnt like modern vocabulary, whereby learning them in context or as linguistic chunks is an advisable method (pp. 152–177).

Lernwortschatz prose, verse, low status character, to follow rules slavishly, to switch to, overwhelming, iambic pentameter, syllable, to resemble, irregularity, mood, to tell apart, discernible, pattern, capitalisation, couplet, punch, climax

Hinweis auf die *Fact file* zu *Understanding the language.*

Erweiterung Folgende Aufgaben eignen sich, um das Verständnis der Sachtexte auf dieser Doppelseite zu überprüfen:
1. *Explain in your own words what "verse" in a Shakespeare play means.*
2. *Point out the differences between Shakespeare's use of prose and verse which are mentioned in the text.*
3. *Find categories for the examples of the elements of Elizabethan English mentioned in the Fact File, then find examples for these categories in the quotes from Shakespeare's plays in the first five pages of chapter 2 (pp. 12–16).*

Mögliche Lösung:
1.
- *Shakespeare's verse I called "blank verse".*
- *A line consists of five unstressed and five stressed syllables.*
- *The syllables alternate, beginning with an unstressed syllable → iambic pentameter.*
- *The lines usually do not rhyme.*
- *Sometimes a line ends with a rhyme to give special emphasis to it.*

2. **Prose is used for/by**
- *written texts that were read out loud, such as letters,*
- *low status characters,*
- *funny lines, comedy,*
- *express madness.*

Verse is used by/for
- *high status characters,*
- *situations of dramatic dimensions,*
- *matters of great importance such as state affairs, issues of life and death.*

2 | Shakespeare's language   Shakespeare's use of prose and verse

3. *Categories and examples of Elizabethan English*
- *Pronouns: Fare thee well, I shall see thee anon (p. 12), That summons thee to hell (p. 15)*
- *Verbs: What wilt thou tell her? Thou dost not mark me. (p. 16, l. 15)*
- *Syntax: Hear it not, Duncan (p. 15), And there she shall at Friar Laurence' cell be shriv'd and married (p. 16, l. 20 ff.).*
- *Words: afore (p. 16, l. 1); in sooth (p. 12), scurvy knave (p. 16, l. 2).*

Brainteaser

1 Stress changes the meaning of a line. Change the stress in the following ...

Die Diskussion erfolgt als Einstieg direkt im Plenum.

Comprehension

2 Choose one of the verse lines from the text above, or from any other excerpt ...

Zusatzmaterial

→ Kopiervorlage 2 (Shakespeare's quotes)

Erweiterung

- Ergänzend kann **Kopiervorlage 2** (Seite 105) eingesetzt werden. Die Zitate auf der Kopiervorlage werden entweder auseinandergeschnitten, sodass jeder S ein Zitat erhält, oder die S bekommen alle Zitate und suchen sich eines davon aus. L gibt den S einige Minuten Zeit, um das Zitat zu lesen, das Verständnis zu klären und ggf. geeignete Gestik und Mimik zu überlegen, mit der das Zitat begleitet werden kann. Anschließend gehen die S durch den Raum und begrüßen einander mit ihrem jeweiligen Zitat. Es bietet sich bei dieser Übung an, nach Möglichkeit den Raum zu verlassen und z. B. auf den Flur oder in einen größeren, möglichst leeren Raum zu wechseln, da zum einen dann kein Mobiliar stört und zum anderen der Wechsel des Raums bereits zu einer für diese Übung notwendigen Lockerung der Unterrichtsatmosphäre führt.

- Als Erweiterung können die S versuchen, einen oder mehrere geeignete Dialogpartner zu finden und die sich ergebenden Kurzdialoge anschließend der ganzen Gruppe vorsprechen. Eine weitere Möglichkeit besteht darin, bekannte Dialoge aus Shakespeare-Dramen zu kürzen, Namen wegzulassen, sie auseinanderzuschneiden und zu verteilen. Die S suchen nun den Partner, der die passenden Dialogteile hat und üben gemeinsam. Die Dialoge werden anschließend der gesamten Lerngruppe vorgetragen. Für diese Vorgehensweise geeignete Dialoge sind:

  "Wilt thou be gone? it is not yet near day:
  It was the nightingale, and not the lark,
  That pierced the fearful hollow of thine ear;
  Believe me, love, it was the nightingale."
  – It was the lark, the herald of the morn,
  I must be gone and live, or stay and die."
  ("Romeo and Juliet", Act III, scene v)

  "Revenge his foul and most unnatural murder."
  – "Haste me to know't, that I, with wings as swift
  As meditation or the thoughts of love,
  May sweep to my revenge."
  ("Hamlet", Act I, scene v)

  "I have done the deed. Didst thou not hear a noise?"
  – "I heard the owl scream and the crickets cry. Did not you speak?"
  ("Macbeth", Act II, scene ii)

Analysis

3 Read a line from a Shakespeare text and experiment with different ways ...

Alternative

L wählt einen Monolog (entweder von einem Stück, das noch mit den S bearbeitet wird oder von einem beliebigen anderen Schauspiel) aus und lässt ihn abwechselnd zeilenweise von einem S-Paar lesen. Geeignete Monologe für diese Übung sind:

	Shakespeare's language Prose and verse in Romeo and Juliet	**2**

"Macbeth", Act I, scene vii: "If it were done when 'tis done, …"
"Hamlet", Act III, scene i: "To be, or not to be."
"Romeo and Juliet", Act II, scene ii: "Romeo, oh Romeo." (leave out Romeo's line)
"The Merchant of Venice", Act III, scene i: "Hath not a Jew eyes?"
"Julius Caesar", Act III, scene ii: "Friends, Romans, countrymen."

Erweiterung ***Tudor talk – role play activity***

Die S verwenden ihre neu erworbenen Kenntnisse zu Shakespeares Englisch und schreiben in Partnerarbeit einen Dialog in *Tudor English*. Es bietet sich an, dass L eine Situation vorgibt, z. B. ein Streitgespräch darüber, wer was in der Familie erledigt; eine Diskussion zwischen einem Elternteil und der Tochter über deren Freund; eine Auseinandersetzung zwischen Nachbarn, bei denen sich einer über den Lärm des anderen in der Nacht beklagt. All diese Situationen sind typische Szenarien aus Shakespeares Stücken. L kann natürlich auch eine Situation aus einem Schauspiel wählen, das mit dem Kurs noch gelesen werden soll. Die ausgearbeiteten kurzen Gespräche werden zunächst einem anderen S-Paar vorgestellt und anschließend der gesamten Lerngruppe präsentiert. Ein Hinweis auf Websites mit weiterführenden Informationen zu *Elizabethan English* oder zu *Shakespeare insult generators* kann hilfreich sein.

Drama excerpt

Prose and verse in *Romeo and Juliet*	**p. 16**

Die S lesen die Szene in Stillarbeit.

Analysis

1 *Use the information from the previous text to find out …*

Diese Aufgabe kann in Verbindung mit Aufgabe 2 als **Hausaufgabe** gegeben werden.

Lösungsvorschlag *Prose lines are the nurse's lines, Romeo's lines in ll. 11–12 and l. 15. From l. 19 onwards Romeo switches to verse, while the nurse continues to speak in prose.*

Analysis

2 *Analyse the way in which Shakespeare handles language …*

Lösungsvorschlag *Romeo mostly uses verse, and the nurse uses prose. Prose is the appropriate language for low-status characters, such as the nurse, whereas Romeo as a member of the upper class mostly uses verse. However, at the beginning of the excerpt Romeo uses prose, too, and so does the nurse throughout the play, so this is what the audience watching the play would be used to. But at the beginning of this part the nurse is very angry and upset, and Romeo tries to distract her from the source of anger, which is one explanation for their both switching to prose.*

Evaluation

3 *Verse and prose are no longer used today to show differences …*

Lösungsvorschlag *Differences could be marked by the way in which Romeo addresses the nurse, and by his choice of words. He might use formal or polite expressions such as "Nurse, I would be very grateful if you could give my regards to your lady, and please believe me that …", whereas the nurse might use a dialect or slang, so that her line might read "Sure, I'll tell her you fancy her, and I reckon that'll turn her on." Another possibility to express the difference in status is by actually playing the roles accordingly. Romeo, for instance, would barely be looking at the nurse, while the nurse would humbly look up at him and show with gestures that she knows how much she is below him in status.*

Erweiterung Im Internet finden sich Versionen von Shakespeares Dramen in modernem Englisch, z. B. unter http://nfs.sparknotes.com/. Sie können den S die Arbeit am Textauszug erleichtern.

27

2 Shakespeare's language   Shakespeare's poetry

Factual information   **Shakespeare's poetry**   p. 17

HINTERGRUNDINFO

The first edition of Shakespeare's sonnets was not published until 1609, but evidence of the fact that Shakespeare circulated his sonnets among close friends dates to 1598. Their language suggests that Shakespeare started writing them in the early 1590s, when sonnets had come into fashion with Elizabethans – so much so, that some 1200 sonnets from the 1590s alone survive. Most poets chose to name their beloved, so we know that Philip Sidney's muse in "Astrophil and Stella" was Elizabeth Devereux; but Shakespeare never did. He neither names his muse in the title nor does he mention a name in the sonnets themselves.

Another tradition was to publish the sonnets in a grouping called "sequence" and to finish this sequence with an elegiac poem known as a "complaint". Shakespeare follows this tradition in that the first edition of his sonnets ends with "A Lover's Complaint". The sequence itself can be divided into three basic groups. The first of these includes sonnets 1–126, in which a young man is addressed: in the first 17 sonnets, he is encouraged to marry and have children in order to guarantee the survival of his virtues. However, Shakespeare is also convinced that poetry itself may preserve these virtues for posterity: the final couplet of sonnet 17 claims "but were some child of yours alive that time, / You should live twice, in it and in my rhyme." Defying death and decay by poetry is a central topic in the sonnets, as Sonnet 18 strongly suggests: "So long as men can breathe or eyes can see, / So long lives this, and this gives life to thee." Some believe that since the addressee of these sonnets is a young man, Shakespeare must have been a homosexual. But the sonnets do not express any consistent experience – neither of sexuality nor of anything else. Shakespeare's youth, it seems, was his muse for about three years, and in the course of that time his view of the young man changed. Sometimes he worships him or is enchanted by him, and at other times he is confused or disenchanted. The famous 'dark lady' enters the sequence with Sonnet 127, and as with the young man, his feelings for the lady are anything but static: there is passionate love, disgust at himself for their adulterous love affair, and deep disappointment, as Sonnet 147 suggests: "For I have sworn thee fair, and thought thee bright / Who are as black as hell, as dark as night." Some lines in the first group of sonnets hint that the young man is having an affair, and others in the second group of sonnets suggest that the dark lady is having an affair with him. In

sonnets 76–86, a rival poet makes his appearance; and in Sonnet 86 Shakespeare suspects that because of the verses this rival poet writes about the young man, he himself is incapable of continuing to praise his virtues in elaborate verses. This is paradoxical, of course, as he expresses these feelings in a refined poem, as he does in all his other sonnets. No matter how vexed, jealous, hurt or in love he claims to be, and how much these feelings supposedly prevent him from adequately expressing himself: he is an unparalleled master at capturing these intricate, mixed and volatile feelings in the formal language of the sonnets.

Henry Wriothesley, Earl of Southampton, was educated at the University of Cambridge and at Gray's Inn, London. When he was 17 years old, he was presented at court, where he was favoured by Queen Elizabeth I and befriended by Robert Devereux, 2nd Earl of Essex. In 1598, he married Elizabeth Vernon, lady-in-waiting to Queen Elizabeth and seven months pregnant at the time. Their marriage brought down the Queen's anger on both of them, so that they spent some time in Fleet Prison. Some scholars believe Elizabeth Vernon to be the dark lady of Shakespeare's sonnets: in her book "Das Geheimnis um Shakespeare's Dark Lady", Shakespeare scholar Hildegard Hammerschmidt-Hummel from Mainz argues that Elizabeth Vernon was pregnant with Shakespeare's child when she married Southampton. Portraits of their daughter Penelope indeed reveal a far greater resemblance to Shakespeare then to Henry Wriothesley. Since Penelope married the Earl of Spencer, an ancestor of Lady Di's, this would mean that Shakespeare's blood flows in the veins of Prince William, the heir apparent to the English throne.

Another interesting link between Southampton and Shakespeare is triangular and has to do with a mutual friend, the **Earl of Essex**. The group of Shakespeare patrons included the Walsingham-Sidney-Pembroke-Essex literary circle, also referred to as either the Wilton or Essex circle, the names deriving from the principal places (Essex/Wilton house) that they met. Essex fell from grace after his disastrous Ireland expedition in 1599, and started to act treasonably afterwards, making plans with the Earl of Southampton to capture the Queen and take over the Court. Essex was executed, and Southampton's sentence commuted to imprisonment for life.

Lernwortschatz   outbreak, plague, to tour the country, narrative, quarto, to scorn, refined

Shakespeare's language Sonnet 73 | **2**

| Materialien | → Online-Link: 601005-0005 |

Hinweis auf die *VIP file* zu Henry Wriothesley.

[₁◉] Sonnet 73 — p. 17

Lernwortschatz *to behold (fml), bough (fml), to fade, to seal (up), to expire (fml), to consume*

Materialien → CD, Track 1

[₁◉] L präsentiert den Textauszug von der CD. Hinweis auf die *Fact file* zu *Sonnets*. Da die Diktion des Sonetts einfach ist, bietet sich eine Hörverständnisübung an. Eine Vokabelvorentlastung ist nicht notwendig, allerdings kann mit passenden Bildern als Farbfolie (z. B. Kirchenruine, herbstlicher Baum, Dämmerung, verlöschendes Feuer), die jeweils passend zu den drei *quatrains* aufgelegt werden, das Verständnis erleichtert werden.

Comprehension

1 What is the main topic of this sonnet? What does …?

Sonette haben einen eigenen Rhythmus und eine besondere Sprache. Eine Möglichkeit, dies den S nahe zu bringen, besteht darin, Sonette in einzelne Zeilen aufzuteilen, den S jeweils eine Zeile zum Auswendiglernen zu geben und ihnen Zeit einzuräumen, sich Gedanken darüber zu machen, wie diese Zeile gesprochen werden sollte. Wenn möglich sollte man dafür den Klassenraum verlassen. Anschließend werden die Zeilen zusammengesetzt und das Sonett von der S-Gruppe in der richtigen Reihenfolge vorgetragen.

Lösungsvorschlag *The main topic of the sonnet is the transience of everything that lives. Death and decay govern life, and the sonneteer, like everything and everyone else, is subject to this. The poet himself is aging, here displaying and metaphorically commenting on his physical condition to the addressee of the sonnet, a younger man. The lesson provided to the listener is that there is a counter-force to the tyranny of death: the couplet concludes that although the young man sees all the signs of old age in the poet, his love is strong and youthful, thus defying death itself.*

Erweiterung Weitere Vertonungen des Sonetts finden sich im Internet, z. B. auf *YouTube*.

Analysis

2 The poet uses a number of metaphors to express …

Lösungsvorschlag **List of metaphors and their meaning**
Each of the three quatrains of the sonnet evolves around a major metaphor. The first metaphor compares old age to a time of year, autumn, the second to the end of day, and the third to a dying fire. It is notable that there is a progression in the metaphors themselves: whereas it takes some time for spring to turn into autumn, twilight is only a few hours away from dawn, and a fire can expire within a couple of minutes.

"that time of year"
The speaker's age is like a time of year, autumn, when almost all "yellow leaves" have fallen from the trees and the boughs "shake against the cold." Those metaphors indicate that winter, which often stands for loneliness and melancholy, is close at hand. The leafless boughs are compared to "bare ruin'd choirs, where late the sweet birds sang". This metaphor compares the bare trees to the remains of a dilapidated church. The choir is the part of the church at the eastern end, in the chancel, where the choristers ("sweet birds") stood and sang. There are four relevant meanings to the word "bare" here: it refers to the speaker's middle age, the leaves gone from the boughs, the birds from the trees, and the singers from the choir. Only this fourth meaning is directly stated.

"the twilight of such day"
Again, an image from nature and time is used to describe the speaker's age, this time anticipating the end of his life by continuing the metaphors in the following lines: as night takes away all daylight and puts all beings to sleep, so does death "seal up all in rest". Death is often compared to sleep, or portrayed as Death's brother.

2 Shakespeare's language   Sonnet 116

"In me thou see'st the glowing of such fire"
In this metaphor Shakespeare is comparing himself to the fire. The fire is still glowing, as he himself is still alive, but as the fire dies on its ashes, the remains of that which nourished it first, so must the poet himself die.

In the first metaphor, the speaker looks up at the church choirs and trees, then raises his vision to the sky in the second metaphor, but down to earth in the last quatrain, which with its imagery of destruction is the deepest and darkest of all three metaphors.

The overall tone of the poem is not so much one of despair or anguish, but rather one of melancholy and sad resignation at the inevitability of death and decay.

Analysis

3 Comment on the poet's choice of words.

Lösungsvorschlag

Most words Shakespeare uses in this sonnet are simple, monosyllabic words of Anglo-Saxon origin, except for "expire", "consumed" and "perceivest". Some of the key words in the sonnet like "bare" have multiple meanings (see answer to task 2), or evoke certain colours – grey ashes and ruins, brown and yellow leaves, black boughs, which contribute to the melancholy tone of the sonnet. The power of the sonnet obviously does not lie in difficult or unusual words, but in their function as effective similes and metaphors.

Evaluation

4 Compare this sonnet to Sonnet 116 on the following page.

Lösungsvorschlag

Both sonnets deal with the effects of time and circumstance on love. Sonnet 73 asks the addressee to love a person who is no longer as desirable as he was in younger years, and Sonnet 116 talks about the difficulties and changes love faces. This might be seen as unusual for a love poem, in which one rather expects the poet to romanticise a relationship, or to praise the virtues of the beloved one than to bemoan his own weaknesses. In Sonnet 116 the poet raises the concept of love to the level of an absolute value, superior to death and decay. If the poet is right about this, then the addressee in Sonnet 73 will not mind the poet's growing old. Love "bears it out even to the edge of doom", so someone who has reached the twilight phase of his life can still be sure to be loved despite the signs of old age.

Comment

5 [1🖰] Watch the video and comment on the history of London ...

Materialien

→ Film 1 (Great Britons)

[1🖰]

Diese Aufgabe eignet sich gut als **Hausaufgabe**. Mit einigen zusätzlichen Fragen kann das Verständnis des gesamten Videoclips überprüft werden:
- *Which of the pictures that were shown do you remember?*
- *What information did you get with these pictures?*
- *What information do we get about the political situation in England?*
- *What does the speaker say about the link between Shakespeare the person and his sonnets?*
- *How much did you understand about the sonnet that was recited?*

Lösungsvorschlag

When the plague struck London, Shakespeare took to writing poetry. All public buildings, among them, of course, the theatres, were shut down, and the theatre companies left town. London became a place of death and disease, with hundreds of people dying every day. Most actors and playwrights left the city, but not Shakespeare. He stayed and wrote sonnets.

[2◎] Sonnet 116 p. 18

Lernwortschatz

banns of marriage, impediment, matrimony (fml), to alter, mark, obstacle, doom, tempest, couple, rhyme scheme, procedure, legal

Materialien

→ CD, Track 2

30

Shakespeare's language   Sonnet 116   2

Brainteaser

1 [👥] *The 'banns of marriage' are the public announcement …*

Lösungsvorschlag

The law in most countries states that people who are already married are not allowed to marry again until the first marriage is dissolved. Some people may believe that if one or both people are unable to have children, then they should not get married. Yet others may think that if one of the two is in love with someone else besides the betrothed, then the marriage should be called off. This situation can be seen in many romantic comedies today. Serious illnesses or the inability to sustain oneself financially may also be hindrances.

Comprehension

2 Say in your own words what the sonnet is about.

[2 ◎]

L präsentiert den Textauszug von der CD. Eine Vokabelvorentlastung ist hier sinnvoll. In schwächeren Arbeitsgruppen sollten die S die Möglichkeit haben, das Sonett mitzulesen.

Lösungsvorschlag

The sonnet talks about the characteristics of true love. The poet claims that true love changes neither when circumstances change, nor when the lovers themselves change. It is permanent and unshakeable and serves as a guiding light to the lovers, although they probably do not realise this. Love does not change when the lovers grow old or die. The poet is so convinced that this idea of love is right that he does not believe that he can ever be proved wrong.

Analysis

3 What obstacles to love does the speaker in this sonnet name?

Hinweis

Vor der weiteren Bearbeitung der Fragen sollte das Detailverständnis geklärt werden. Ausführliche Erläuterungen zu Shakespeares Sonetten befinden sich unter http://www.shakespeares-sonnets.com/116comm.htm.

Lösungsvorschlag

The poet names a number of obstacles to love. The first one is in line 3, in which he talks of the changes that may occur in a loving relationship and which can cause the end of it. In the next line he mentions a "remover", which might either be an unfaithful person who leaves a loving relationship, or death which takes one of the two lovers away. Death is referred to again in line 12, in which the poet says that true love continues till the very end. Time itself is another obstacle: as lovers grow older, their appearances change, and often their character, too, which may lead to the end of love. Impediments in our times could be financial problems, alcoholism or serious illnesses, unemployment, problems with children, etc.

Analysis

4 The speaker does not say directly what love is, but …

Hinweis

Die Aufgabe sollte zunächst in Stillarbeit oder als **Hausaufgabe** vorbereitet werden.

Lösungsvorschlag

"marriage of true minds" (l. 1)
The poet does not have a real marriage in mind, but a relationship in which all physical considerations are of secondary importance. It is the mental equivalence that matters. "True" here probably does not just mean faithful, but rather complementary: the poet has two people in mind who understand each other and complement one another.

"an ever-fixèd mark" (l. 5)
In former times, sailors used well-known and prominent features on land – such as a lighthouse – to determine their position at sea. Such features could neither be moved by storms nor be easily taken down by mankind. The point of the metaphor is that such features were unchangeable, not even in times of trouble, and always there to guide the person who needed it.

"the star to every wandering bark" (l. 7)
In the northern hemisphere, the North Star appears to stay exactly where it is, with all other stars circling around it in the northern sky. That is why it was important for sailors: like the prominent features on land, they used it to determine their position at sea by calculating the distance between the horizon and the star ("although his height be taken") with a quadrant when land was not in sight. Such a constant guiding light at sea was of great value to the sailors.

2 Shakespeare's language   Sonnet 94

Love's not Time's fool (l. 9)
Either the poet is referring to the fool at court who lived at the whim of his master, or in more general terms to someone who can easily be outsmarted. Love is not like that; time can neither change nor influence it.

Analysis

5 Look at the sonnet and describe its rhyme scheme (abab, etc.).

Lösungsvorschlag

The rhyme scheme of the sonnet is abab cdcd efef for the quatrains, and looks as if it was gg for the couplet. However, when read aloud the rhyme scheme does not always seem to work: in modern English, "come" does not rhyme with "doom", and "proved" does not seem to rhyme with "loved". These words were pronounced differently in Shakespeare's day, so that the words rhymed when he wrote the sonnet. Sometimes, pairs of words are used that work as "eye rhymes", words which, when written, look as if they rhyme.

Erweiterung

Die S können weitere sprachliche Auffälligkeiten heraussuchen, Gründe für die Unterschiede überlegen und die Textstellen in modernes Englisch setzen.

Analysis

6 Analyse the structure of the sonnet and explain...

Diese Aufgabe eignet sich als **Hausaufgabe**.

Lösungsvorschlag

True to the form of the Shakespearean sonnet, this one too consists of three quatrains and a couplet. The first quatrain says what love is not, the second explains what love is, and the third quatrain again explains more specifically what love is not. There is no twist – or 'volta' – in the sonnet, and the rhyming couplet simply serves as a closing statement to express the poet's certainty that his conception of love is true. The sonnet's main topic is a declaration of what love should be, and the simplicity of the structure with its definition of love in both negative and positive terms supports this declaration.

Comment

7 [👥] What is love to you? And what is important for a good relationship?

Lösungsvorschlag

Individuelle S-Beiträge.

Erweiterung

In beiden Sonetten bedient sich Shakespeare einer sehr bildhaften Sprache. Eine Aufgabe für kreative S wäre es, passend zu einem Sonett ihrer Wahl Bilder auszuwählen und diese in eine PowerPointPräsentation einzubauen, in der der Text der Sonette zu den Bildern eingeblendet wird. Die Präsentation kann mit einem geeigneten Musikstück untermalt werden, von Liedern mit Text ist aber abzuraten. Die musikalische Untermalung dient dazu, die Stimmung des Sonetts einzufangen. Weitere Sonette bzw. Gedichte von Shakesepare, die auf Grund ihrer Bildhaftigkeit dafür sehr geeignet sind, sind z.B. *Sonnet 128 (How oft when thou, my music, music play'st)* oder *"Fear no more"* aus *Cymbeline*.

Sonnet

[3◎] Sonnet 94   p. 19

Lernwortschatz

to inherit, to husband, steward, base, weed, dignity, to fester

Materialien

→ CD, Track 3

[3◎]

L präsentiert das Sonett von der CD.

Comprehension

1 Summarise the message of this sonnet in two sentences.

Lösungsvorschlag

a) *This sonnet is considered by a number of critics to be very difficult, particularly as there are a number of different possibilities of interpretation, mainly due to ambiguous expressions and the uncertainty of the addressee, which could lead to an ironic reading.*

Shakespeare's language   Sonnet 94

One basic reading without a double meaning could be: Powerful people who do not harm others and don't show their emotions are to be praised. Like a flower that does not consider its own beauty, their self-control may protect their virtues, but if they become corrupt, they are far more terrible than the lowest of people.

b) *The speaker could be referring either to people who have a superior position (e.g. rulers), who could use political or even physical power to reign over others either fairly or tyrannically, or to lovers and friends who could hurt others by not showing their true emotions, respect, etc.*

2 Point out the key words for the message of the sonnet.

Lösungsvorschlag   **a)** *"They" vs. "others'" the power to hurt; to temptation slow; inherit heaven's graces; husband riches; owners of their faces; the flower to itself only live and die; that flower with base infection meet; outbraves his dignity; Lilies that fester smell far worse than weeds.*

b) *"You" would change the meaning of a general praise and philosophical thought to a personal reproach which could give the rest of the sonnet an ironic meaning and criticise the addressee (a superior or a friend) for not giving all of what he may be able to give or for not appearing true to his feelings.*

Analysis

3 Analyse the structure of the sonnet and give each part a title.

Lösungsvorschlag   ***1st and 2nd quatrain: praise of restraint/contrast***
The first eight lines describe a contrast between a person in power or of a certain capability who does not make use of this ability.
Such persons can influence others yet do not give in to this temptation. (ll. 1–4)
Thus they are praised for keeping their composure, while the others can only use what they have received from nature. (ll. 5–8)

3rd quatrain: shift in focus
The image of the flower in summer which makes summer look beautiful is used, yet the flower itself does not think about its own importance; yet if this beautiful flower contracts a disease, it looks much worse than a healthy weed.

Couplet: conclusion/proverb
This is a reference to a proverb indicating the striking contrast between the sweetness of beauty and the danger of reality which might turn bitter.
The final lines use a strong metaphor to express the problem dealt with here, as sweet flowers should never smell badly.

Discussion

4 Do you believe the sonnet should be taken seriously or could it ...?

Lösungsvorschlag   **a)** *In line with a number of critical references, it is possible to say that both readings have some foundation. Taken seriously, ll. 1–8 seem to express nothing but praise. The way one interprets the very first word of the sonnet, however, could already open up the discussion as to whether this praise is to be taken at face value, as "they" could also be a hidden form of addressing "you". As the general topic of the sonnet is one of criticising the difference between "appearance and reality", this address could just as well be read as a harsh reproach to a friend or lover for not being open in his emotional behaviour or towards a superior for not reigning fairly.*

b) *Indirect criticism can be noticed when looking at the contrastive use of the word "others", as the opposite of this behaviour of concentrating on one's own restraint as a form of unspoilt beauty would be the behaviour of those who just use and spend those powers they have been given by nature, without any thoughts about having to make a good impression.*

The ambiguity that lies in this sonnet can be made out when looking at those phrases that can carry a positive as well as a negative meaning: "to temptation slow" (not lead to false action / not be moved to do anything at all); "to husband" (to use sparingly / to keep back).

2 | Shakespeare's language   Sonnet 94

Erweiterung   Die S vergleichen die vielfältigen Interpretationsansätze, die besonders im Bemühen um sprachliche Vereinfachungen entstanden sind kritisch mit den Auslegungen, die sich durch eine größere philologische Vorsicht auszeichnen. Einige (aus der Vielzahl von Quellen) eher kritisch zu würdigende Beispiele sind: http://nfs.sparknotes.com/sonnets/sonnet_94.html, http://en.wikipedia.org/wiki/Sonnet_94.html, http://british-poetry.suite101.com/article.cfm/shakespeare_sonnet_94.

Analysis   **5 *Compare the message of this sonnet to the other two sonnets presented here.***

Lösungsvorschlag   *The message of this sonnet might at first reading not seem to be as emotionally charged as the other two sonnets dealing with old age and the finality of death or the power of never-ending love. Yet the themes of truth and the reality of emotions seem to be just as close to the poet's heart regardless of whether one sees this poem addressed to a superior (a ruler or patron) or to a close friend or lover.*

Evaluation   **6 *Which of these sonnets is your favourite?***

Zusatzmaterial   → Klausurvorschlag 2 • Revision file 2

Lösungsvorschlag   Individuelle Antworten der S, bei denen eine begründete persönliche Positionierung deutlich werden sollte, die Gesprächsanlässe zu einer vertieften Beschäftigung mit den hier behandelten thematischen Bezügen bieten könnte.

Erweiterung   Weiterführende Literatur:
- Wulf Künne, *English and American Poetry Interpretations*, Stuttgart, 1986.
- Rex Gibson, *The Sonnets*, Cambridge, 1997.
- Ina Schabert, Shakespeare Handbuch, Stuttgart, 2009.
- Ben Crystal, *Shakespeare on Toast*, Cambridge, 2008.

Zum Abschluss von *Topic* 2 füllen die S noch *Revision file* 2 (Themenheft, Seite 60) aus. Ein Lösungsvorschlag befindet sich hier im Lehrerheft auf Seite 142.

| | Shakespeare's theatre   Didaktisches Inhaltsverzeichnis | **3** |

Topic 3: Shakespeare's theatre   pp. 20–27

Didaktisches Inhaltsverzeichnis
Bearbeitungszeitraum: 4–6 Unterrichtsstunden

Textsorte / Thema	Unterrichts-methoden	*Input boxes*	Kompetenzen	Textproduktion
[4◉] Lead-in: Shakespeare's theatre (118 words)				SB, Seite 20/21, LB, Seite 36–39
Combination of visuals and quotes/The theatre in Shakespeare's days	Kursgespräch		Orientierungswissen Bildbeschreibung/ -analyse Hörverstehen Gespräche führen	*Analysing the effect of stages* *Listening to historical information* *Analysing the role of theatre*
[5◉] Touring the theatre (957 words)				SB, Seite 22/23, Seite 40–42
Interview, map/The theatres in 16th-century London	Kursgespräch Online-Link: 601005-0006	*VIP file: James Burbage*	Leseverstehen Hörverstehen Gespräche führen Argumentieren	*Describing a theatre* *Listing elements* *Listening to an interview* *Summing up facts*
[6◉] [2🎞] What the Globe was really like, 2000 (992 words)				SB, Seite 24/25, Seite 42–47
Novel excerpt, interview, video clip/Life as an actor	Kursgespräch Online-Link: 601005-0007 Zusatzmaterial: Kopiervorlage 3	*VIP file: Nathan Field*	Leseverstehen Hör-/Sehverstehen Gespräche führen Argumentieren	*Collecting information* *Analysing the narrative perspective* *Making a list of pros and cons* *Listening to an interview* *Writing a diary entry*
[7◉] Producing a play (1002 words)				SB, Seite 26/27, Seite 47–49
Factual information/ Elizabethan playwright	Kursgespräch Zusatzmaterial: Klausurvorschlag 3	*Fact files: The Rose and the Globe – Theatre snacks*	Leseverstehen Hörverstehen Gespräche führen Argumentieren	*Writing down questions* *Listing aspects* *Writing out a daily schedule*

3 Shakespeare's theatre   Lead-in: Shakespeare's theatre

Unterrichtsverlauf

Photos/
Quotations/
Travel report

Lead-in: Shakespeare's theatre   pp. 20–21

HINTERGRUNDINFO

Entertainment in Shakespeare's time: *The nobility, the Queen and her court were often entertained by elaborate shows and spectacles. They loved dancing, jousting, hunting and even playing tennis. Ordinary people enjoyed bear- and bull-baiting, which were national institutions, overseen and encouraged by an office of the Court, and encouraged by ministers of the Church of England by royal order. The usual procedure for such events was to tie a bear or bull to a stake and let mastiffs (fighting dogs) loose on him, who would then bite the larger animal to death. Shakespeare must have felt pity for the animals, as he has Lear compare himself with them: "I am tied to the stake, and I must stand the course" (III, 7), he says upon realising that he has lost all means of changing his fate. Another form of entertainment was the public execution (see Topic 1, "Life in the suburbs", students' book, pp. 10–11). Thus we see that cruelties displayed on stage like in "Titus Andronicus", where Lavinia has her hands and tongue chopped off, would conjure associations of what Londoners witnessed in live performances every day.*

Travelling theatre companies: *Companies of wandering acrobats, comedians, and actors travelled with their cartload of gear (costumes, some props, food) from town to town. Whenever there was an event that drew large crowds, such as markets or Church festivals, they would be there, setting up their stage on the village green, in inn yards, or in baiting arenas. It was only by the beginning of the 16th century that these travelling entertainers started to perform real "plays" – stories containing several characters, and not only dealing with texts from the Bible or other religious books. The best place to go for all theatre companies was London, of course. In the 16th century, it was a vibrant, growing city, one of the largest and richest in Europe. Its streets thronged with traders and customers – a magnet for anyone who wanted to make a fortune. However, there was a lot of complaint about the players, too. By 1600, more than 30 buildings were either used permanently or occasionally for theatre performances in London. But the Puritans claimed that plays were an invention of the devil, and people living near the buildings in which performances took place complained about the noise caused by the playgoers, the music and the special effects. As a consequence, the city authorities set up all sorts of rules to keep players out of the city.*

Permanent theatres: *So it was only logical that the first permanent theatres were all built on land outside the city walls, as in Shoreditch (the Theatre, the Fortune, the Red Bull, the Curtain) or on Bankside (the Rose, the Globe, the Hope). Most theatres were in sinister areas, with skittle alleys, pubs and brothels close by.*

Effects, costumes and props: *Special effects were possible, but usually reserved for performances at the court. The actors used only few props: a crown for a king, an elaborate chair, a table or stools. Costumes were extremely valuable, often bought off servants who had inherited them form their masters, so wearing a theatre costume outside the playhouse was severely fined.*

Inside the theatrical world: *In this world, Shakespeare played the role of playwright, actor, part owner, and probably de facto director. The companies had 30 or more plays in their active repertoire at any one time, so the leading actor had to memorise 15,000 lines – plus dances, sword thrusts, costume change, cues, props and so on. As only a dozen actors were employed, plus maybe a handful of apprentice boys: doubling up was necessary, too. In "Julius Caesar", for instance, there are 40 named characters, plus unspecified numbers of "servants", "other plebeians", "senators, soldiers and attendants". These either had no lines at all or just a few, but they still had to know about the relevant props, cues, blocking, entrances and exits, and appear on time correctly attired. Clothing was a challenge, too. There were no zips, snap fasteners or velcro, and the expensive costumes had to be handled very carefully.*

Entrance fees: *The theatre's success in Elizabethan times was due to the low admission costs. A place in the pit could be bought for a penny, the same amount of money that a loaf of bread cost, so almost everyone could afford it.*

Thomas Platter *was a physician from Switzerland who travelled extensively in Europe in the years 1599 and 1600. His diary is a valuable source of information on culture, medicine and trade of the time. His report on a visit to the Globe on September 21, 1599, was published in 1909 in the magazine "Anglia". It has become an important document to give researchers a hint as to the dating of the opening of the Globe.*

Shakespeare's theatre   Lead-in: Shakespeare's theatre   3

"Henry V" is dated between March 27 and September 28, 1599. Like "Julius Caesar", it was in the repertoire of the newly opened Globe Theatre. It serves as a positive finale to the Lancaster trilogy in the War of the Roses, focussing on the theme of a united country under a strong leader. It is a play about patriotism and a glorious victory against the French archrival. "Henry V" may be seen to represent the ideal Elizabethan ruler. The quotations from the prologue are an appeal to the audience's imagination and reflect the problems of the presentation of reality on stage in an almost ironic tone, yet also offer the first textual reference to the shape of the Globe Theatre.

The **opening scenes** of Elizabethan plays were extremely important. In modern theatres, the audience knows how to behave: people who make too much noise are quickly hushed by those in the neighbouring seats, and they know by a number of various signals that the play is about to begin and thus become quiet and attentive. These signals did not exist in Shakespeare's time, so the players had to think of other ways of catching the audience's attention – and of keeping it. So conflicts must be introduced quickly, because conflict is at the heart of drama, the ingredient that keeps the audience on the edge of their seats, eager to know what happens next. Who will win the battles of war or love, jealousy or justice? In the opening scene of every play, Shakespeare uses language and creates situations in such a way so as to catch the audience's interest. The seeds of conflict are directly evident, or very strongly

implied. Consequently, the intimate relationship between actors and audience is particularly apparent in these opening scenes. Students can experience this intimacy by working with the scenes themselves.

The New Globe: In 1949, American actor and director Sam Wanamaker came to London for the first time. He was disappointed to realise that there was no memorial to Shakespeare and his theatre at the original site of the Globe in Southwark. The idea to create such a memorial never let go of him, so in 1970 he founded the Shakespeare Globe Trust in order to raise money for a faithful reconstruction of Shakespeare's famous theatre. Work on site began in 1987, but it was only in 1993 that the foundations were finished and construction of the building itself could begin – too late for Wanamaker, who died in December of that year. The theatre was finished in 1997 and opened with a performance of "Henry V". Today, the new Globe Theatre in London is not only a place where excellent performances of Shakespeare's plays can be watched. It also holds an extensive exhibition about Shakespeare and the theatre of his day, providing educational material and programmes for teachers, students and academics from all over the world. Sam Wanamaker was also a co-founder of the Shakespeare Globe Zentrum Deutschland *(SGC)*, which offers introductions, lectures and workshops on the Globe and Shakespeare in close cooperation with the ISGC (International Shakespeare Globe Centre) in London in order to make Shakespeare more accessible to German audiences.

Lernwortschatz	*theatre company, to tour the country, costume, elaborate, part, trap door, gallery, pit (BE), tiring room, storage*
Alternative	**Möglicher Einstieg über *opening scenes***

1. *Choose opening scenes from various plays. This technique works well with opening scenes from: "Macbeth", "Julius Caesar", "The Tempest", or "Hamlet". With weaker classes you may want to use the modern English version of the plays – the aim here is not to teach language, but effect, and it is a lot easier to shout commands in modern than in Elizabethan English.*
2. *Think of props: an old-fashioned garden lantern for "Hamlet", some old rags for "Macbeth", a table cloth for "Julius Caesar", a fan and raincoat for "The Tempest".*
3. *Distribute the scenes to the students and tell them to practise the first lines (it is not necessary to learn them by heart). They should be given a chance to choose the scenes themselves. Make sure they decide on how they want to convince the audience that the characters on stage are witches, that it is night time and bitter cold, or that the scene takes place on a ship in the middle of a storm.*
4. *If possible, change rooms: choose a large room (preferably without furniture). Tell them that they can start acting their scene as soon as they are ready. Their aim is to catch the attention of all the others in the room!*
   Alternative: Let them prepare their scene in group work as a homework assignment, so that they can think of things they would like to bring for the next lesson.
5. *Discuss: What is it that catches and holds the audience's attention, creates suspense? How do the actors know how to act and what to do?*

37

3 Shakespeare's theatre   Lead-in: Shakespeare's theatre

What kind of atmosphere is created?
How did the other students – their audience – react?

Erweiterung Publikationen, die das Thema an dieser Stelle vertiefen können:
- Ben Crystal, *Shakespeare on Toast*, Cambridge, 2008. (sehr knapp, pragmatisch und schüler-orientiert, dabei sehr präzise)
- Andrew Dickson, *The Rough Guide to Shakespeare*, London, 2005.
- Wendy Greenhill, *Shakespeare – Man of The Theatre*, Oxford, 2000.
- Francois Laroque, *Shakespeare – Court, Crowd and Playhouse*, London, 1993.
- Janet Ware, *101 Things You Didn't Know About Shakespeare*, Avon, MA, 2005.

Weitere Informationen zum elisabethanischen Theater sind im Internet zu finden. Hier eine Auswahl an geeigneten Links:
- http://internetshakespeare.uvic.ca/Theater/sip/index.html
- http://shakespeare.palomar.edu
- http://elizabethan.org/compendium/home.html
- http://internetshakespeare.uvic.ca/Theater/index.html
- http://teachersfirst.com (*cf. Shakespeare/Shakespeare's stage*)
- http://www.elizabethanenglandlife.com/index.html
- http://www.britainexpress.com/History/Elizabethan_life.htm
- http://www.uni-koeln.de/phil-fak/englisch/shakespeare/ (Hilda D. Spear, *The Elizabethan Theatre*)

Comprehension **1 *Look at the pictures of Shakespearean stages above. What effect ...?***

Die S können folgende Aspekte beleuchten:
- *a closer connection between actors and audience*
- *the audience might feel as if they were becoming a part of the world of the play*
- *the actors are surrounded on three sides, which has consequences for their acting*
- *the lack of a backdrop might animate the audience's imagination*
- *as there is no main curtain, everything visible on stage has a function and has to be used*
- *structural parts of the building such as pillars or the recess can be used as additional props*
- *the lack of artificial lighting results in the need to create atmosphere through words alone*

Lösungsvorschlag *The actors were surrounded by the audience. They could be seen more or less from all sides, and the groundlings were very close to the actors. This meant that there must have been a very close contact between actors and audience, resulting in both positive or negative effects, and the spectators themselves must have felt at times as if he were part of the action. The stage in the picture is bare, there is no backdrop and there are no props. So the audience has to imagine or be told by the actors' words and gestures where and when the action is taking place.*

Comprehension **2 [4⊚] *Listen to what a Swiss tourist in Shakespeare's day had to say ...***

Materialien → CD, Track 4

[4⊚] L präsentiert die Tonaufnahme von der CD. Diese Aufgabe kann auch als **Hausaufgabe** gestellt werden.

Lösungsvorschlag
- *Thomas Platter went to see "Julius Caesar" on the 21st of September. He also mentions a second play of apparently rather crude humour, but does not give the title.*
- *Entrance fees depended on the place in the theatre you wanted for yourself: those who were happy with standing in the pit paid a penny, a seat in the lower gallery cost another penny, and those who wanted the best seats plus a cushion paid three pennies.*
- *The performances usually ended with a dance. After one of the plays Platter went to see a group of four men. Two of them were dressed as women and went onto the stage and danced; after another play there were English and Irish dances.*

Shakespeare's theatre   Lead-in: Shakespeare's theatre   3

Analysis
3 What do the quotations from his plays tell you about ...?

Lösungsvorschlag

The quotations refer to monarchs and princes, wars and battlefields, life and death, and link all of them to the stage. It seems that Shakespeare's idea was to show the world on the stage, to tell stories about life that took his audience off to foreign places, to battlefields or royal courts, so that they might forget about their own lives for a moment and imagine the lives of kings and noblemen, heroes and villains, lovers and friends as if they were part of the action. The second quotation from "Henry V" ("Can this cockpit hold the vasty fields of France?") shows that Shakespeare was quite confident about achieving this aim, as the actors had the audience's imagination (and obviously the historical knowledge) to play with and rely on.

"All the world's a stage ...": For this quotation, which of course could be called the general motto for all Shakespearean drama, the students might come up with a number of examples from plays they might already have heard of.

Erweiterung

Shakespeare war außerordentlich erfolgreich, sein Konzept des Theaters, das in hohem Maß auf die Vorstellungskraft und Fantasie des Publikums aus allen Gesellschaftsschichten baute, funktionierte. Die S könnten ausgehend vom 2. Zitat aus *Henry V* diskutieren, inwieweit diese Vorstellungskraft heute noch von den Unterhaltungsmedien eingefordert wird, oder ob aufgrund der Vielzahl an Möglichkeiten, durch technische Effekte Wirklichkeit vorzutäuschen, diese Fähigkeiten des Menschen verlorengehen. Ausgehend vom 3. Zitat können die S noch besprechen, inwieweit dieser Ausspruch für ihre eigene Umgebung, ja für sie selbst relevant sein könnte.

Evaluation
4 What role do you think the theatre played in the lives of the people ...?

Lösungsvorschlag

There were permanent theatre buildings in London, and many theatre companies touring the country. The theatre, then, must have played an important role in the lives of the people who had few other form of entertainment. Books were expensive, newspapers and magazines did not exist, and only a minority of the people could read anyway. There was no TV, no radio, no Internet, no telephone or postal service that deserved such a name. So if you wanted to hear a good story, something to help you forget about the bleakness of life in Elizabethan times, the theatre was the place to go. Shakespeare's dramas were mass entertainment, the equivalent of today's soap operas. Besides, theatres were a thriving business. Apart from offering entertainment, the theatre also offered jobs: the companies needed players, apprentices, bookkeepers, tiremen to look after the clothes, stagekeepers and musicians. Applewives, bakers and pub owners profited from the theatre by selling their products to the crowds. It is hard to imagine Elizabethan life without it.

Erweiterung

Es gibt zahlreiche Möglichkeiten, die Beschäftigung mit dem Theater Shakespeares durch handlungsorientierte und kreative Aufgaben in kompetenzorientierten Unterricht münden zu lassen.

Beispiele hierfür sind:

- *Write a newspaper article on the events in late December 1598, when the Lord Chamberlain's Men dismantled the Theatre and started rebuilding it on the Bankside as the Globe.*

- *Write a newspaper article for the day the Globe opens in June 1599 with its first performance of "Julius Caesar".*

- *Create a handout that announces the first performance of a play in the newly built theatre, and in which you praise its particular qualities.*

- *Write an application to the Lord Chamberlain's Men. You would like to become apprenticed to one of the great actors in their troupe. What can you boast of?*

3 | Shakespeare's theatre   Touring the theatre

Interview | **Touring the theatre** | pp. 22–23

HINTERGRUNDINFO

The development of theatre stages: *One important source for the development of Elizabethan drama – apart from those of popular folklore and classic Greek drama – can be seen in a tradition reaching back to the Middle Ages. A very early form were cycles of religious scenes presenting Old Testament themes and supporting liturgical services on high religious holidays. Originally performed in churches by priests only, these plays underwent a process of secularisation, in which the presentation was placed in the hands of laymen, later to be organised by guilds of craftsmen. Along with this development, the representation of characters became much more individualised and the use of language became increasingly liberalised.*

These **mystery plays** *were quite often performed on open spaces from carts, sometimes with two storeys where the actors got dressed in the lower level and played on the upper level. Apart from stationary plays, processions of pageants became increasingly popular. While the mystery plays were abolished in the process of the Reformation as they were regarded as remnants of the old faith, the* **morality plays***, which had developed in a similar process, survived. These plays were mainly allegories of the fight of the forces of good and evil fighting for humanity. The centre of these plays was the ethical conflict of the individual torn between stock figures like virtue and vice, a setting later to be taken up and refined by the Elizabethan playwrights. (cf. "Richard III" vs. "Hamlet"). These plays showed three elements that were revolutionary to the further development of drama and became important characteristics in the plays of Shakespeare: they were written in English for the local community, with everyday affairs becoming increasingly important in showing God's involvement in human life, and they encouraged the whole range of dramatic skills from how to write dialogues and construct plots to the convincing portrayal of characters. The tradition of pageants and their increasingly secularised forms eventually led to the practise of groups of actors travelling the country, putting their carts alongside each other as a background for the presentation of their various acts. The groups received more and more invitations from innkeepers, who saw a good chance to attract further customers. The shape of these inn courts in the countryside was a decisive factor for the design of the stationary theatres which were built later.*
Drama was also used to display power. One of the functions of the early pageants can also be seen in the opportunity for the ruler to be able to impress his subjects. Such a famous occasion was the visit of Queen Elizabeth to Kenilworth Castle, where the Earl of Leicester had his own group of actors to entertain her with their performance. When these companies were not performing for the patron, they were touring the country. In the year 1573 the Earl of Leicester's Men performed in the Guild Hall at Stratford and William Shakespeare, still a young boy is said to have followed the show. Other places for performance were Great Halls of noblemen or universities, where a screen was put up on one side behind which the actors could get changed. These first indoor playhouses saw more refined performances to honour the host or to serve as a means of education. The advantages of these venues included the fact that actors were paid for their performance and they had a guaranteed number of spectators. The disadvantages included having to rely on the hospitality of inn-keepers or noblemen and the lack of storage space (they had to carry everything needed for putting on a play). The biggest obstacle for the actors, however, can be seen in the increasing reluctance of the authorities to permit public performances. From 1574 onwards London city authorities issued an increasing number of statutes and regulations culminating in the complete ban on outdoor theatres in 1596. Although a very small number of inns outside the city boundaries still saw performances, it is this policy which led to the building of new "public" open air theatres on Bankside as well as a number of small "private" indoor theatres. An example of the latter type is the Second Blackfriars which James Burbage bought in 1596 from the Master of the Revels, who until 1584 had owned parts of the old secularised Dominican monastery to lease them to some of the popular boy companies.

James Burbage, *supposedly born in Stratford in 1531, was a leading actor in the Earl of Leicester's Men and is said to have given Shakespeare his first part as an actor. They stayed friends throughout their lives and James' son Richard later became one of the principal actors in Shakespeare's company. Although the name of James Burbage is – like that of his rival Philip Henslowe – closely connected to the erection of the main open air theatres (the Theatre, later to become the Globe) he also had a very large influence on the development of the indoor theatres. He obtained the Blackfriars Theatre, which was home to the children of the Chapel Royal. After some dispute he started a boys' company under his own management at the Second Blackfriars, from where many actors joined the Lord Chamberlain's Men at*

the Globe after their voice broke. James Burbage died in the spring of 1597 so he never saw the new Globe	*Theatre (http://www.elizabethan-era.org.uk/james-burbage.htm).*

Lernwortschatz *involvement, pageant, to erect, custom-made, contagious, venue, to rise to prominence, lease, polygon, tier, diameter, recess, mole, (stage) props*

Materialien → Online-Link: 601005-0006

Comprehension **1 *Briefly describe the origin of The Globe Theatre.***

Hinweis auf die *VIP file* zu James Burbage.

Lösungsvorschlag
- *Religious processions turned into pageants.*
- *Some noblemen employed acting companies to tour the country.*
- *They started on improvised stages in inn yards or great halls.*
- *The inn yard dictated the shape and form of the later custom-made theatres in London.*
- *The companies moved outside the city walls to escape jurisdiction.*
- *In 1592 theatres were closed in the city due to diseases.*
- *When the lease to the Theatre was not renewed, James Burbage and actors pulled it down and erected it next to their rivals at the Rose and renamed it the Globe.*

Analysis **2 *List the stage elements and explain how they were used during a play.***

Alternative Diese Aufgabe kann auch als **Hausaufgabe** gestellt und von den S in Form einer Präsentation aufbereitet werden.

Lösungsvorschlag

State elements	How they were used
apron stage	*extended to the middle of the stage; the stage was only about one metre above the ground so the contact between the actors and the audience was very close*
galleries	*particularly those behind the stage were where the nobles sat who wanted to be seen; the actors had to play to them especially much*
doors at the back wall	*were needed to allow the fluent entrances and exits of the actors to secure an uninterrupted performance*
no painted backdrop	*meant that the setting of the play had to be created verbally*
a recess	*could have manifold purposes, e.g. as a tomb, a hidden bed, etc.*
a small gallery	*usually housed the musicians, who were vital to stress a certain atmosphere or play interludes and music for the final dances*
balcony	*when the windows of the middle gallery were opened, these spaces could serve for e.g. Juliet's bedroom or as a podium for speeches*
trap doors	*served as the entrance to the underworld or hell, also as graves*
heavens	*highly artistically painted, serving as the house of the gods*
room above the heavens	*a space for a trumpeter to start the play or for a canon which was used for sound effects; the roof was topped by a flag indicating that a play was in progress*

3   Shakespeare's theatre   What the Globe was really like

Erweiterung   Zusätzlich zu einer Beschreibung der Bühnenobjekte aus dem Text können die S die Zeichnungen des *Globe* von Seite 21 und 23 (Themenheft) oder eine selbstgewählte Rekonstruktion aus dem Internet für eine kurze Präsentation heranziehen. Möglich wäre hier auch ein kurzes Webquest zu *The Globe* als **Hausaufgabe** zu stellen. Nach einer umfangreicheren Recherche ist auch ein von den S selbst gestaltetes Quiz denkbar.
Nützliche Websites: http://www.3sixtydegrees.com/Globe.htm, http://www.britannia.com/history/londonhistory/histrose.html.

Comprehension   **3 [5◉] *Listen to this interview with Richard Burbage. Write a ...***

Materialien   → CD, Track 5

[5◉]   Die S hören das Interview von der CD.

Lösungsvorschlag   *Richard and William became lifelong friends. Richard's father James, the founder of commercial theatre, had brought the two together and when the lease of the Theatre ran out, the Burbages took it to pieces, transported it to Bankside, to offer it to the Lord Chamberlain's Men, a company named after their patron, to become their very successful playhouse: the Globe. Both Richard and William were actors and shareholders of their company. While Richard became one of the most important actors, William took to writing the plays and acting in some of the minor roles. All in all it became a great partnership between one of the greatest writers and one of the greatest actors.*

Comprehension   **4 [5◉] *What happened to the acting company when Queen Elizabeth died?***

Lösungsvorschlag   *When Elizabeth died, her successor King James I was even fonder of the theatre than she had been and took over the patronage and renamed the company the King's Men. The company was now part of the royal household and apart from their shares in the company were given large amounts of scarlet cloth and a tremendous increase in performances at court as the king enjoyed the plays and gave the company his royal approval, which made it even more famous.*

Novel excerpt/ Video clip

What the Globe was really like   pp. 24–25

HINTERGRUNDINFO

*The appearance of the interior of **Elizabethan playhouses and the Globe** is, despite extensive research, still not exactly known. Yet with the project of reconstructing Shakespeare's Globe at Southwark, which was the vision of the American actor Sam Wanamaker, knowledge about many more details of the Elizabethan stage and particularly the experience of how to act under such conditions has increased vastly. At the end of the 1980s Sam Wanamaker felt that it was a shame that the only remains of one of the most important Elizabethan playhouses was a brass plaque on a brewery wall. He developed his scheme to find enough support to rebuild the Globe using as many handcraft techniques of the Elizabethan period as possible. The original site of the Globe, where foundations could be found, could not be used because on top of it were other chartered buildings. After a long time it became possible to start rebuilding the theatre on the other side of the Rose, the remains of which can also be visited today. After the extensive cellar or foundation*

of the building had been finished in concrete, work on the actual theatre could begin. The Globe was built from 1988 bay by bay using freshly cut ("green") oak and putting the single beams together fixing them with wooden pegs. Not one single piece of metal was used to erect the hull of the "wooden O". This was possible due to the fact that when the wood is drying out in the course of time it shrinks slightly, making the joints extremely durable. Despite the very artistic construction by the architect Theo Crosby, the master carpenter Peter McCurdy still had to learn many of these techniques again which were so widely used in Shakespeare's times. The walls were made using a construction of wattle, a framework of woven sticks (usually made of willow), filled with lime and finished with plaster, to which a small amount of horsehair was added to increase flexibility. The roof was covered, like in Shakespeare's day, with thatch – making it the only modern building in London that had permission to be built in such a way. During the process of building

Shakespeare's theatre   What the Globe was really like   3

the Globe, which lasted until June 1997, the dream of reconstructing Shakespeare's theatre was supported by countless people and institutions around the Globe. When going to see a performance today three features of the stage may appear particularly striking. The massive columns on the stage were made from individual trunks of oak trees, one of which was donated by the Queen from Windsor Great Park. The magnificent tapestries that build the backdrop to the stage were handmade and donated by a group of women from New Zealand. Perhaps one of the most interesting facts of what can be achieved by schools may be the fact that the money (over £130,000) for building the beautifully painted heavens above the stage was raised by about 300 schools worldwide. In return for their donation, each "Globelink-school" received a little time capsule that could be filled with mementos from our time. These capsules were put into a little vault and sealed in the basement, which is used as exhibition space today. One day this space will be opened and the contents will be given to research to find out what it might tell about our period.

People who claim that the original Globe could hold up to 3,000 people are not vastly exaggerated as estimates on the slightly smaller Fortune Theatre have worked out a maximum of up to 800 groundlings and 1,500 seats available in the galleries. Philip Henslowe's diaries mention an average of about 1,000 spectators for the plays at the Globe.

The heavens are not only a very beautiful central feature of the stage, they also fulfil a very important dramatic function. As already mentioned above, one of the important sources of Elizabethan theatre can be seen in the morality plays with the fate of humanity being decided on stage. For the audience the references as to the fate of the character could not only be made out by his position on stage, where horizontally one side could be seen as good the other as evil, but also – more importantly within the concept of the Chain of Being – as being in a vertical connection under the influence of either the forces of evil underneath the stage or the blessing from the gods above it. Thus the artistic signs of the Zodiac, this "brave o'erhanging firmament, this majestical roof fretted with golden fire" ("Hamlet", II, 2), is of prime importance to the message of many plays. The overall structure above the stage, however, has a very practical function, too: to keep the actors and their magnificent costumes out of the weather. Today if bad weather or the noise from overhead planes spoils the pleasure of following the play for the groundlings, for Shakespeare the fact that his company performed in open daylight had important consequences for his writing. All the references to actions at night had to be referred to by words.

Additionally, not all members of the audience could read, so everything had to be conveyed to them by words. Speech was also vital for the setting as the Elizabethan stage did not use backdrops. As the apron stage thrusting forward into the middle of the yard did not allow a curtain, there were no breaks in the performance. All exits and entrances thus had to be worked out very thoroughly. So one of the main problems for tragedies was how to get any bodies of victims off the stage in order not to destroy the illusion of the performance. Thus victims are carried out by soldiers ("Hamlet") or murders might happen offstage ("Macbeth") or in the recess ("Othello"). Also the fact that the actors were surrounded by the audience on three sides at close proximity meant that the actors had to maintain a high degree of presence and connect with the audience because bored audiences could be quite rude and rough, culminating in unsuccessful actors having things thrown at them. The fact that the actors were surrounded by the audience as well as having to play to different social levels of society had a great effect on Shakespeare's writing technique. In every play we thus find elements of highly elaborate language next to fairly basic speech, sometimes becoming outright bawdy. Shakespeare had to bridge the gap from the crude to the sublime without losing the right balance. That he seems to be quite aware of this task and the problem of addressing every individual in the audience could perhaps be seen best with the help of two examples. When in "Julius Caesar" Mark Antony addresses the crowd with his famous words "friends, Romans, countrymen", what seems more natural than for the actor to actually bow to each of the three areas of the theatre in turn? That Shakespeare is even poking fun at this particular need to sometimes repeat words or actions so that the whole audience feels addressed can be seen in the hilarious scene from "A Midsummer Night's Dream", when Bottom in his performance of "Pyramus and Thisbe" is killing himself three times, thus "killing himself in a round" to use a phrase from Patrick Spottiswoode, the educational director of Shakespeare's Globe.

Nathan Field (1587–1619) was the son of a Puritan priest. He started his acting career with "The Children of the Queen's Revels" from 1600–1608. This group was one of the most popular companies of boy actors, which was founded by Richard Burbage to play at his indoor theatre, the Second Blackfriars. Field attended the prestigious St. Paul's School and as he was so successful, he was offered the opportunity to join the King's Men in 1609, playing alongside Shakespeare and Burbage and later becoming one of their leading players.

3 | Shakespeare's theatre   What the Globe was really like

Susan Cooper, *born in Buckinghamshire in 1935, attended Oxford University and became the first female editor of an Oxford student newspaper. After receiving her M.A. in English, she began writing a regular column in the "Sunday Times". Having married an American professor, she left England for the US in 1963 and started writing novels for children, winning several awards. She is probably best known for her classic fantasy series "The Dark is Rising". Despite her success with novels, she turned to writing screenplays and TV adaptations. After returning to the novel, she published one of her finest books in 2000, "King of Shadows", which she dedicated to her second husband Hume Cronyn.*

"King of Shadows" *is a youth novel in the style of a time travel story. Nat Field is a young student at an American youth theatre group in Cambridge, Massachusetts, led by the director Arby (R.B. – Richard Burbage!). They are casting boys for a production of "A Midsummer Night's Dream" to be performed at Shakespeare's Globe in London. Nat Field is accepted and is to play Puck. Like many members Nat is hosted by a family who are "friends of the Globe". After the first rehearsals on this unfamiliar stage Nat has a strange dream which makes him believe he is flying through space and down to earth again. When he wakes up, he realises that his bed has changed and has become a coarse mattress. After he gradually comes around again, he realises that his environment has changed. A boy, introducing himself as his fellow Harry, is holding his hand and asks if his fever has gone down. He is told that they were afraid that he might have had the plague. Only with great difficulty does Nat come to terms with the idea that he must have arrived at a different time. In what follows, the reader gets to know the different living conditions in Elizabethan housing and hygiene. When talking to Harry, Nat thinks about his lines from the play and finds out that he has taken the role of another boy in Shakespeare's day by the name of Nathan Field, who was rehearsing the part of Puck just like him. Harry tells him that they both live with Master Burbage and are to rehearse the play at the new Globe Theatre. It is the year 1599.*

The passage at hand has the two boys going to the Globe for the first time together. Harry explains many details of the building, such as the function of the flag flying on the roof and the history of transporting the playhouse from the north of the city to build it up again on Bankside. The following passages introduce the reader to Richard Burbage and to Will Kempe and his row with the company which led to his famous Morris dance from Norwich to London. The whole passage attempts to describe the scenery of the Globe within the framework of a theatre company rehearsal.

The further chapters of the book give a vast amount of detail surrounding the Elizabethan theatre in a similar way as the movie "Shakespeare in Love" achieved it by its special cinematic means. It also provides information on Elizabethan boy companies and the daily lives and pastimes of actors as well as the group of Shakespeare's rival playwrights. Ned receives first-hand information about the political connections and dangers acting companies might have run into and the system of royal patronage. Following the rehearsals, the reader becomes increasingly familiar with many plot elements of "A Midsummer Night's Dream" and is also made aware of a growing fondness Shakespeare develops towards one of his best boy actors. This relationship leads to Shakespeare writing a sonnet for Ned when the boy is having a sad moment while missing his father, who in his "real life" died before he joined the company. Towards the end we are told that Shakespeare was so impressed by this young actor that he wrote another part especially for him, namely that of Ariel in "The Tempest".

The end of the book has Ned waking up in a hospital bed and being reunited with his American friends, who eventually work out a theory why Ned Field had to be exchanged with a boy called Nathan Field from the days of Shakespeare.

Lernwortschatz *sledgehammer, crowbar, to cart, to christen, pit, to be preoccupied with, musty, indistinct, coil, thrusting stage, fusser, to rant, to rave, coaxingly, nimbleness, oblivious, tawny*

Comprehension   **1 Collect the information in the text about life in Shakespeare's time ...**

Lösungsvorschlag
- *to lease a piece of land here in Southwark (l. 2)*
- *the actors took The Theatre apart (l. 6)*
- *using the beams for a framework they built the theatre (l. 12)*
- *the theatre had an odd musty, grassy smell (l. 19)*
- *like those heads over London Bridge; reference to politically unstable times (ll. 23–24)*
- *central balcony at the back of a stage … [with a] climbing rope for a quick descent (ll. 30 ff.)*
- *the empty galleries, … the painted sky of the "heavens" and … the thrusting stage (ll. 35 ff.)*

44

- *clowns (l. 42)*
- *play once more, before a great lady (l. 55)*
- *acrobat (l. 59)*
- *yard – a dirt floor (l. 59)*
- *a layer of some sort of coarse grass (l. 60)*

Erweiterung Zur Ergänzung zum Thema *Shakespeare's life and his theatre* können diese *Websites* herangezogen werden: http://www.shakespeareontoast.com/
http://www.li-hamburg.de/fix/files/doc/shakespearelinks%202009.pdf
http://www.shakespeare4kidz.com/teachers
http://www.pbs.org/shakespeare/educators/.

Analysis 2 **Analyse the narrative perspective the author uses to …**

Lösungsvorschlag The author employs the view of a first-person narrator (Nat), who either directly describes his reactions and feelings (e.g. "an odd musty, grassy smell that I couldn't place,…", l. 19; "I'd begun to pretend that I was in the middle of a movie set in Elizabethan times, …", ll. 21–22; "I might have thought myself still in my own time if it hadn't been for Master Burbage at my side", ll. 33 ff.) or reports events and stories that he has heard or is being told (e.g. the report of the demolition and rebuilding of the Theatre/Globe, ll. 1–14; the description of going backstage, ll. 15 ff.). This is mixed with a very vivid dramatic mode in which other characters are talking directly to each other (e.g. Harry referring to his uncle the Master Carpenter, l. 3; the row between Kempe and Shakespeare, ll. 40 ff.; Burbage's reaction, ll. 64 ff.). In these parts the narrator gives the impression of being an outside viewer not seen by the speakers, a "fly on the wall". These two techniques on their own give the reader a very powerful connection to the plot. They are all the more effective when they are mixed. The positive effects of this artistic mix of narrative perspectives are increased by a high variety of vocabulary and descriptive adjectives and a constant change of descriptive and narrative elements, similar to those of the storytelling tradition.

Comprehension 3 [6⦿] **Make a list of the pros and cons of being a boy actor …**

> **HINTERGRUNDINFO**
>
> The idea of **women acting on stage** was thought to be immoral at the time. Neither training the skills of oratory nor those of professional entertainers were activities thought to be suitable for women. Women's roles were thus played by young boys who were between ten and 15 years old. In school plays the boys were used to playing male as well as female parts. From this basis the professional companies took on boys to play the women's roles. The boys were taken as apprentices of senior actors who trained them and gave them food and lodging. Although they were called apprentices, they usually did not stay with their masters as long as the seven years which was the normal time for service then.
>
> Little is known of what happened to the majority of boy actors after their voices broke and their period as actors had ended. Some were fortunate and became so famous that the professional companies took them on as regular members. Shakespeare often wrote for the special circumstances of his company. It is known that from 1596 to 1599 there were two particularly gifted boys in the company; a fact that might have inspired him to create such opposing pairs of characters as Hermia and Helena in "A Midsummer Night's Dream" or Rosalind and Celia in "As You Like It".
> (Andrew Gurr, "William Shakespeare", Harper Collins, 1995, pp. 78–81.)

Materialien → CD, Track 6

[6⦿] L spielt den Hörtext zweimal von der CD vor.

Lösungsvorschlag **Pros**
- learning the skill from a famous actor
- usually staying in his home
- good boy actors were very popular; when dressed as women, they had particularly demanding and rewarding parts to play

3 Shakespeare's theatre   What the Globe was really like

- many boys later had the chance to be taken on by the adult companies and some became famous actors
- they could then become a master and pass on the tradition

Cons

- they could only perform as boy actors until they voices broke
- as boys they usually only had small parts to play because even the female roles were not all that large
- they had to work very hard as there was a different play to learn every day, quite often in addition to school
- they were given an abundant number of jobs around the production
- when travelling, they had long journeys on dusty roads and had to look after a lot of goods
- they could be bought and sold by their managers like merchandise

Evaluation

4 [6⦿] *Creative writing: Listen to the interview with Nat Field.*

Hinweis auf die *VIP file* zu Nathan Field. In dem *diary entry* sollte der Unterschied zwischen dem Leben reisender Schauspieler und dem geregelten Tagesablauf in der Stadt deutlich werden.

Lösungsvorschlag   Individuelle S-Beiträge.

5 [2🖻] *If you visit London, will you want to attend a play …?*

Materialien   → Film 2 (First Night at the Globe Theatre) • Kopiervorlage 3 (Shakespearean insult sheet)

HINTERGRUNDINFO

This question is of course dependent on the **degree of enthusiasm** with which the students deal with the study of drama generally and that of Shakespeare in particular. Nevertheless, according to the different opinions seen in the video, one can assume that visiting the Globe would give the audience – to the extent that it is possible nowadays – an authentic experience of what it might have been like to visit the playhouse in Shakespeare's day.

Mark Rylance, then artistic director, compares it to standing in the bullfighting ring, just with the difference that this time emotions like "lust, anger, jealousy and rage" are being fought and the audience is witnessing this fight from close-up. Milling about like one of Shakespeare's groundlings can be a lot of fun (because one is not restricted to sitting quietly in a seat and letting the play pass one by). However, being a groundling also means standing (sometimes in the rain, sometimes in bright sunlight) for more than two hours. There are no seats in the yard and you cannot take any chairs with you. Despite efforts by the artistic staff of the Globe, some interviewees still raise doubts as to the theatrical quality of the performances and compare the Globe to a tourist magnet like Madame Tussaud's Wax Museum.

Apart from these critical voices, uttered before the opening, one has to realize that in the years that have passed since these interviews were made, the productions at the Globe have proved this fear to be unfounded, as most of the performances in the summer season are sold out, and not only to tourists. The Globe not only gives an idea about acting Shakespeare in his own environment and letting the audience participate in the process of the plays, the productions have also given numerous new insights into costume-making and particularly into the function of music accompanying the performances, insights that have enriched the overall knowledge about Shakespearean theatre tremendously.

Lösungsvorschlag   Individuelle S-Beiträge.

Erweiterung [2🖻]   Hier bietet sich der Einsatz von **Kopiervorlage 3** (Seite 106) an. Diese Übung aus dem Bereich der Dramenpädagogik mag zunächst befremdlich erscheinen, gibt aber einen recht guten ersten Kontakt mit der Sprache der *groundlings*. Mit Hilfe einer elektronischen Version der Werke Shakespeares kann diese Liste für jedes Stück individuell angepasst werden und bietet somit ein erstes Element des für die weitere Rezeption so wichtigen *ownership* des Sprachenmaterials durch die S. Darüber hinaus bietet das Internet eine Fülle derartiger Listen, es gibt

Shakespeare's theatre **Producing a play** | **3**

sogar sogenannte *Insult generator*. Selbstverständlich muss das soziale Klima der Klasse über die Anwendung dieser Übung aus dem Bereich der Dramenpädagogik entscheiden.

Vorschlag zur Durchführung: Die S stellen sich in zwei Reihen mit einigem Abstand gegenüber. Nachdem sie aus der Liste ihre bevorzugte Kombination aus einem Wort aus jeder Spalte zusammengestellt haben, geht ein erstes Paar nacheinander in die Mitte zwischen den beiden Reihen. S1 begrüßt S2 mit einem *insult*, S2 reagiert darauf. Als Erweiterung können sich die S vor der Begegnung gedanklich einen hohen oder tiefen Status der Person geben, die den *insult* dann ausspricht. Dies führt zu sehr vertiefenden Studien möglicher Charakterzüge.

Factual information

Producing a play   pp. 26–27

HINTERGRUNDINFO

***The Elizabethan entertainment industry**, as can be seen by the example of one of its focal points Southwark can be regarded as a mixture of modern cinemas, sports arenas, theme parks and theatres. It was the place for mass entertainment, which also shows that the Elizabethan society was quite familiar with the display of brutality as bear-baiting and dog fights drew crowds just as large as those in the playhouses. A playwright had to make sure to quench the audience's thirst for entertainment by constantly coming up with new productions. If a play lost its popularity, it was dropped from the repertoire. Much of what is known about Elizabethan theatres today is from Philip Henslowe's diary. Henslowe was the builder of the rival theatre The Rose, the foundations of which were discovered in 1989, only 200 yards away from the site of The Globe. Two companies were able to survive the time of the closures during the plague. The Admiral's Men with the famous tragedian Edward Alleyn played at the Rose while the Theatre hosted a new company known as The Lord Chamberlain's Men with Richard Burbage, the famous clown Will Kempe and William Shakespeare. Both companies offered a large number of productions. In 1594–95 the Admiral's Men alone played 38 different plays, non-stop for 49 weeks, six days a week.*

***The life of an actor** was quite hard. The members of the company had to learn six different plays in any one week. Sometimes they had more than one individual part. They were given strips of paper with* only their roles as the material was very expensive. They thus had to learn their cues, too, to know when to deliver their lines. Apart from this they had to be able to dance, sing, play an instrument, fence and to be physically fit for the stunts they also had to perform themselves. The company usually took on new members for non-acting jobs. If they were successful in first minor parts, they gradually might be given leading roles. The highest position an actor might achieve was to become a shareholder in his company, directly benefiting from a share of the profit from the productions. Only very few actors like Richard Burbage and William Shakespeare made it to this position, while the famous clown Will Kempe refused this status and left the company in scorn. Actors were usually paid for individual performances. Acting companies were mainly made of three social levels. Below the level of the shareholders were minor actors and hired personal like musicians or wardrobe keepers, in charge of the expensive costumes. The most important person on this level was the bookholder. He was responsible for the official script (in times of censorship a vital position) and also doubled as prompter. The third level of hierarchy consisted of the apprentices, who played the roles of children and women. Although their parts were quite demanding as they also had to learn female gestures and intonation, they were paid little, yet received room and board and got their training from more experienced actors.

Lernwortschatz   *preferably, shareholder, approved script, prompter, rung, peasant, jester, affordable, bear-baiting, bawdiness, elaborate, gore, brevity, wit*

Materialien   → CD, Track 7 • Online-Link: 601005-0007

Comprehension   **1** [7◉] ***Listen to this interview and write down some questions ...***

[7◉]   L präsentiert das Interview zweimal von der CD.

Lösungsvorschlag   • *How did the audience get to the Globe Theatre?*
• *What did the people do in bad weather?*

47

3   Shakespeare's theatre   Producing a play

- *What was the audience like and what were its attitudes?*
- *What was the consequence for the plays that there was no curtain in front of the stage?*
- *How did Shakespeare use the building of the Globe to help him tell his stories?*
- *What did Shakespeare have to consider about entertaining the whole audience?*
- *Why were Shakespeare's plays so popular in his time?*

Analysis

2   List the most important aspects of play production.

Lösungsvorschlag

- *The plays were produced in open daylight.*
- *Part of the audience had to stand in the open not sheltered by a roof.*
- *Plays were performed without breaks.*
- *The audience wanted to be entertained at all times.*
- *Humour was a very important factor for the success of a play.*
- *The social spread of the audience was considerable.*
- *The repertoire had to be large to please many different tastes.*
- *Any special skills of actors had to be capitalised upon.*
- *Costumes – at least for main characters – had to be very lavish.*
- *There were very few props available for the scenery.*
- *The architecture of the building had to be integrated into the play.*
- *Special effects, like the lowering down of angels or the appearance of a ghost, were very popular, as was the use of sound effects.*
- *Music was often used to create a certain atmosphere or to start or end the play.*
- *Swordplay was enthusiastically received.*

Erweiterung

In einem Beitrag zu *Groundling (Issue 2, issued by Shakepeare's Globe, 1999)*, der Zeitschrift für die im *Globelink* zusammengeschlossenen Schulen untersuchte Rex Gibson die Frage nach besonderen Aufführungsbedingungen und wie diese unser Verständnis von Shakespeares Stücken heute beeinflussen. Einige der genannten Aspekte werden hier kurz zusammengefasst:

- *There are quite a few scenes in Shakespeare in which the audience is addressed or is directly involved.*
- *In many other scenes there is audience acknowledgment or participation written in; one famous example being Anthony's speech in "Julius Caesar".*
- *Most evidently this is a prerequisite tool in the soliloquy (cf. "Richard III").*
- *Shakespeare had his theatre building in mind when he wrote his plays (cf. "Wooden O"; Hamlet speaks of the "brave o'erhanging firmament" surely addressing the heavens above the stage).*
- *Shakespeare mocks the whole business of acting in some scenes, which results in a "subtle complicity" between actors and audience (e.g. "Washing his hands in Caesar's blood, Cassius asks, 'How many ages hence shall this our lofty scene be acted over in states unborn and accents yet unknown?'" ("Julius Caesar", III, 1).*
- *When writing his plays, Shakespeare seems to have had the special geographical circumstances of the Globe in mind as the Elizabethan audience had a very sharp sense of direction and knew exactly were places lay when referred to in the text. The daily passage of the sun across the sky had a much stronger significance in its influence on people than is the case today.*
- *This sense of location and the fact that the Globe was a round building had an influence on the language of some plays when e.g. the witches in "Macbeth" speak their spell of "round and round the cauldron go".*
- *The Globe offers another fascinating feature due to its separation between the groundlings in the yard and the rest of the audience in various levels of the galleries. Although this separation stresses the strong emphasis of the Elizabethan society into a sharply divided hierarchy, the fact that the whole audience is brought together in their enjoyment of the plays gives the whole place a certain democratic feeling.*
- *In addition, there is the fact that the language of the plays is spoken into an open sky connecting actors and audience, giving this space an extra element of fascination.*

| | Shakespeare's theatre **Producing a play** | **3** |

Evaluation

3 *Write out the daily schedule of a typical Elizabethan actor.*

Lösungsvorschlag
- *wake at dawn, breakfast, go to the theatre*
- *learn fights and dances as required, check props and costumes*
- *perform around 2 o'clock, get your role for the next day*
- *find your props and costume and learn your role for the next day before it gets dark*
- *visit an ale tavern*
- *fall exhausted into bed*

Erweiterung
Nützliche *Websites*: http://www.shakespeareontoast.com/, http://shakespeare.about.com/od/interviews/a/performing_shax.htm, http://elizabethan.org/compendium/.

Analysis

4 *Explain the aspects an Elizabethan playwright ...*

Zusatzmaterial → Klausurvorschlag 3 • Revision file 3

Lösungsvorschlag
- *One of the most decisive aspects was the fact that the plays were produced in open daylight and a part of the audience had to stand in the yard regardless of the weather.*
- *The audience wanted to be entertained at all times. This could be done by performing a variety of types of plays (histories, comedies, tragedies, romances or a mixture of such elements) and by including additional magical or humorous effects on stage. The clown and the fool were very important roles as they had to break up the routine of the play and often sided with the crowd to deepen any emotion they might develop.*
- *The production also had to consider the social spread of the audience as the plays had to please the middle classes and the gentry in addition to catering to the rough tastes of the groundlings. Apart from producing continuous action, the dialogues had to be written in a very elaborate as well as a very direct style.*
- *The playwright also had to consider the strengths of his actors. He had to adapt the plays to their particular skills as it was sometimes these skills alone that would draw the crowds.*
- *As a big part of the costs for a production went into costume-making, fairly little money was spent on the scenery. This had important consequences for the playwright, too.*
- *As there was no central curtain in front of the stage, the back wall of the stage had doors through which the actors went from their tiring house onto the stage. As there was no curtain, there were also no intervals, and the play was presented in its entirety. This had great consequences for the playwright as well as the actors, who had to make sure that there were no moments without action. Otherwise, the audience might get restless. To be able to perform the action from a number of places on the massive stage, a number of structural elements were integrated into the play. Not only were all sides of the stage used, but also a gallery above the stage could serve as a balcony, an upper window or a battlement. The alcove underneath it could be used as a more private room, a cave or even a prison. Even the space above the heavens of the stage was used as it was topped by the flag indicating that a play was in progress. It also hosted the gear for any flying tricks or the "machinery". As with the reference to the gods above, the belief in ghosts coming through the trapdoor or out of the underworld was very popular. The massive columns at the front of the stage were also integrated into plays, for example as trees.*

Erweiterung
- *Some further details for the aspects in question which are not covered by the texts include:*
  – *Unlike today's moviegoers, Elizabethans went to hear rather than to see a play. If an actor wore a cloak, the audience knew it was an outdoor scene; if he carried a light, it was night time. When "Hamlet" starts with the words "Who's there?" everyone knew that it was night despite it being broad daylight in the theatre.*
  – *The important function of humour can also be seen in the fact that in almost every play there is either a significant part written out for a clown or a fool, or such comic relief is provided by the actors involved in the plot. The function of comic relief was vital to maintaining the interest of the audience and also to preparing them for tragic moments.*

- Zum Abschluss des *Topics* füllen die S *Revision file* 3 (Themenheft, Seite 61) aus. Ein Lösungsvorschlag befindet sich hier im Lehrerheft auf Seite 143.

49

4 | Shakespeare the dramatist   Didaktisches Inhaltsverzeichnis

Topic 4: Shakespeare the dramatist   pp. 28–45

Didaktisches Inhaltsverzeichnis
Bearbeitungszeitraum: 15–21 Unterrichtsstunden

Textsorte / Thema	Unterrichts-methoden	*Input boxes*	Kompetenzen	Textproduktion
Lead-in: Shakespeare the dramatist				SB, Seite 28, LB, Seite 52–54
Combination of visuals/ Shakespeare's plays	Kursgespräch Zusatzmaterial: Kopiervorlage 4		Orientierungswissen Leseverstehen Gespräche führen	*Summing up facts Pointing out differences*
The writing process (523 words)				SB, Seite 29, Seite 54/55
Factual information, visuals/Playwrights in Elizabethan era	Kursgespräch	*Word bank: Writing plays*	Orientierungswissen Leseverstehen Gespräche führen	*Summing up facts Pointing out differences*
***Richard III*: What happens in the play?** (376 words)				SB, Seite 30, Seite 56
Plot summary/ "Richard III"	Kursgespräch Gruppenarbeit Zusatzmaterial: Kopiervorlage 5	*Tip: The shape of drama Fact file: Genres*	Leseverstehen Gespräche führen Argumentieren	*Writing a short scene Acting out a scene*
[8 ⊚] [3 🖵] Richard's opening soliloquy – his discontent, his plot (233 words)				SB, Seite 31, Seite 57–59
Drama excerpt, video clip/Act I, opening scene i, soliloquy	Kursgespräch Gruppenarbeit Online-Link: 601005-0008 Zusatzmaterial: Kopiervorlage 6, Kopiervorlage 7	*Fact file: Soliloquy Word bank: Analysing film*	Leseverstehen Hör-/Sehverstehen Gespräche führen Recherchieren	*Dramatic reading Finding positive and negative expressions Analysing words and cinematic devices*
[9 ⊚] Richard woos Anne (622 words)				SB, Seite 32/33, LB, Seite 59–63
Drama excerpt/Act I, scene ii, dramatic dialogue	Kursgespräch Partnerarbeit Zusatzmaterial: Kopiervorlage 8, Kopiervorlage 9, Kopiervorlage 10	*Fact file: History plays*	Leseverstehen Hörverstehen Gespräche führen Argumentieren	*Dramatic reading Giving a comment Comparing dialogue and soliloquy Assessing acting skills*
Ward je in dieser Laun' ein Weib gewonnen?, 2007/2008 (363 words)				SB, Seite 34, LB, Seite 63
German journal article, quotes/A production of "Richard III"	Kursgespräch Partnerarbeit Gruppenarbeit		Orientierungswissen Leseverstehen Gespräche führen Argumentieren Mediation	*Discussing main aspects Comparing German translations of quotations*
[10 ⊚] Love: The balcony scene (421 words)				SB, Seite 35/36, LB, Seite 64–66
Drama excerpt, movie poster, photographs/ Act II, scene ii, dialogue	Kursgespräch Online-Link: 601005-0009 Zusatzmaterial: Kopiervorlage 11	*Fact file: Romeo and Juliet*	Orientierungswissen Leseverstehen Hörverstehen Bildbeschreibung/ -analyse Gespräche führen Argumentieren	*Writing a yellow press newspaper article Analysing imagery Writing a modern scene Acting out a scene Writing an ending Dramatic reading*

Shakespeare the dramatist Didaktisches Inhaltsverzeichnis 4

Textsorte / Thema	Unterrichts-methoden	Input boxes	Kompetenzen	Textproduktion
[11 ◉] Love: Saying farewell (326 words)				SB, Seite 37, LB, Seite 66–68
Drama excerpt, cartoon/ Act III, scene v, dialogue	Kursgespräch Zusatzmaterial: Kopiervorlage 12	*Fact file: Romeo and Juliet*	Leseverstehen Hörverstehen Bildbeschreibung/ -analyse Gespräche führen Argumentieren	*Analysing tools Pointing out opposites Analysing a cartoon Writing personal letters Comparing scenes*
[12 ◉] Conscience: Macbeth's guilt (226 words)				SB, Seite 38, LB, Seite 68–70
Drama excerpt, photograph/Act I, scene vii, soliloquy	Kursgespräch Online-Link: 601005-0010	*Fact file: Macbeth*	Orientierungswissen Leseverstehen Hörverstehen Bildbeschreibung/ -analyse Gespräche führen	*Outlining aspects Analysing reasons Describing and assessing a picture*
[13 ◉] Order and disorder: Macbeth disrupts stability (431 words)				SB, Seite 39/40, LB, Seite 70–72
Drama excerpt, photographs/Act II, scene iv, dialogue	Kursgespräch	*Fact file: Macbeth*	Leseverstehen Hörverstehen Gespräche führen	*Summing up a scene Making a list Analysing aspects Writing a plot summary*
[14 ◉] The supernatural: Hamlet learns the truth (312 words)				SB, Seite 40/41, LB, Seite 73–78
Factual information, drama excerpt/Act I, scene v, dialogue	Kursgespräch Online-Link: 601005-0011 Zusatzmaterial: Kopiervorlage 13, Kopiervorlage 14	*Fact file: Ghosts and the supernatural*	Leseverstehen Hörverstehen Gespräche führen	*Summing up facts Analysing themes and atmosphere*
[15 ◉] The supernatural: Hamlet and Gertrude (598 words)				SB, Seite 42/43, LB, Seite 78–81
Drama excerpt/Act III, scene iv, dialogue	Kursgespräch	*Fact file: The chain of being*	Leseverstehen Hörverstehen Gespräche führen	*Pointing out arguments Examining the tone of language Discussing facts*
Working with a scene				SB, Seite 44, LB, Seite 81–83
Drama workshop/Acting out a scene	Kursgespräch Gruppenarbeit Partnerarbeit	*Fact file: The spoken word*	Hör-/Sehverstehen Gespräche führen	*Dramatic reading Creative textwork Speaking in dialogues Choral speaking Acting out a situation Creating a slide show*
Did someone else write Shakespeare?, 2004 (386 words)				SB, Seite 45, LB, Seite 84–86
Handbook excerpt/ Authorship	Kursgespräch Zusatzmaterial: Kopiervorlage 15, Klausurvorschlag 4, Klausurvorschlag 5	*VIP file: Sir Francis Bacon*	Leseverstehen Gespräche führen Recherchieren	*Outlining arguments Structuring a text Preparing a role play Finding out facts*

4 Shakespeare the dramatist   Lead-in: Shakespeare the dramatist

Unterrichtsverlauf

| Photos | **Lead-in: Shakespeare the dramatist** | p. 28 |

HINTERGRUNDINFO

The canon: *William Shakespeare was not very interested in making money out of books. He published two of his long poems, but none of his plays; others did that for him. About half of his plays were published as quarto editions while he was still alive, but the others remained unpublished until 1623, when his friends decided it was time to preserve his plays for posterity. They tracked down and edited 36 plays for the First Folio Edition and divided them into three categories: tragedies, histories, and comedies. This division is now disputed by scholars. They categorise some of the later comedies, in which Shakespeare blends tragedy and comedy, as romances (for example "Cymbeline", "Pericles", and "The Winter's Tale"), and some of the others that elude categorisation as problem plays ("All's Well That Ends Well", "Measure for Measure", and "Troilus and Cressida"). Despite his friends' efforts, two of Shakespeare's plays are lost: "The History of Cardenio", a late play based on a story from Cervantes' "Don Quixote", and "Love's Labours Won", mentioned as one of Shakespeare's recent works by a late 16th-century writer. Two other plays did not find their way into the First Folio of 1623, but survived as quarto editions – "Pericles, Prince of Tyre", added to the Third Folio, and "Two Noble Kinsmen", which was not added to the complete works until three centuries later. Shakespeare did not always work alone; some of his plays were written with a collaborator (most notably John Fletcher). One of these plays ("Edward III", his eleventh history) was only recently admitted to the Shakespeare corpus. But he also collaborated on the works of others – an unfinished play about Thomas More by Anthony Munday is an example of such collaborations. Shakespeare's canon consists of 39 plays in all. Taking into account that he also wrote four narrative poems, the sonnets and other poetry, one can safely say that he was an extremely prolific writer. The complete canon with the dates of publishing or writing can be found here:* http://shakespeare.palomar.edu/canon.htm*.*

The sources: *In a world were copyright had not been invented yet and plagiarism was not considered even a minor offence, Shakespeare was free to borrow from all available sources. As a boy at Stratford grammar school, he had become acquainted with the classics such as Ovid and Plutarch, but he must have continued to read extensively for the rest of his productive life. For his Roman histories like "Julius Caesar", "Anthony and Cleopatra" or "Timon of Athens" he drew heavily on "Plutarch's Lives"; and for the English histories mainly on "Holinshed's Chronicles of England, Scotland and Ireland". Other sources were Cinthio's collection of stories called "The Hecatommithi", which he used for some of the comedies, and popular tales like "The Tragicall Historye of Romeus and Juliet" by Anthony Brooke. He did not mind borrowing from his colleagues, either. It seems that for "Hamlet" he not only relied on a Norse legend composed by Saxo Grammaticus in Latin around 1200 AD, but also on the so-called "Ur-Hamlet", a play by Thomas Kyd. "The Troublesome Raigne of Iohn King of England" had also been published and performed by the Queen's Men before Shakespeare wrote his own version, for which he might have consulted John Foxe's "Book of Martyrs", too. Shakespeare often used minor sources to improve the plot he had found in one of the sources mentioned above, like "The Mirror of Magistrates", a tale of twenty princes – parts of it went into "King Richard III", "King Lear" and "Henry IV, Part 2".*

The plays for which it is a bit more difficult to track down the sources are his comedies. He seems to have used Boccacio's "Decameron" and a novel called "Rosalynde: Euphues Golden Legacie", written by Thomas Lodge, for "All's Well that Ends Well". The source for "The Merchant of Venice" was a tale in an Italian collection entitled "Il Pecorone; or, The Simpleton", written in 1378 by Giovanni Fiorentino. Some of the comedies, however, seem to have sprung entirely from his imagination: no literary sources are known for "A Midsummer Night's Dream" or "Love's Labour's Lost".

So when it comes to plots, Shakespeare was not necessarily a great inventor. What made him unique was his ability to interweave plots and newly invented sub-plots, to breathe life into characters by giving them penetrating soliloquies, to use his powerful way with words to blend what material he had into something entirely new, brilliant and fascinating. Detailed information on the sources Shakespeare used for his plays can be found here: http://www.shakespeare-online.com/sources/*.*

The topics: *One of the reasons why Shakespeare is still performed so often is that he deals with universal topics, relevant to our lives today as much*

52

4 Shakespeare the dramatist   Lead-in: Shakespeare the dramatist

as they were relevant in his time. One is conflict: quarrels between families ("Romeo and Juliet"), between brothers and sisters ("Twelfth Night"), fathers and children ("King Lear"), husbands and wives ("All's Well That Ends Well"), dynastic struggles ("Richard III") or, in the comedies, conflicts caused by love. Another topic is change. Shakespeare presents arrogant youths that turn into lovers, kings and tyrants that fall from power, heroes who gather new insights and change their ways, the change from life to death. The topic of order and disorder is presented on various levels. It shows the consequences of disorder for persons, as when Lear goes mad, on society (for example civil war, as in "Richard III"), and on nature, where such disorder is often reflected in the weather (the thunderstorm in "King Lear" or as a foreboding at the very beginning of "Macbeth"). One of the most intriguing topics, though, is the difference between appearance and reality. So many of his characters wear masks of honesty, are "smiling villains", disguising their true feelings behind a mask of madness, and many of the plays thrive on the treachery of their main characters.

A special reason for the continued fascination with Shakespeare today is the great potential of **timelessness** his plays convey. Shakespeare made very liberal use of his varied sources in his capacity as one of the greatest storytellers in world literature, taking up relevant themes of his time but also dealing with elementary human emotions and conflicts. To deal with these topics effectively, Shakespeare had to use ideas easily understood by his audience. Thus, central ideas like that of "man fighting against the forces of the world and the cosmos around him" were expressed using images

like that of the "chain of being", the "fall of princes", the correspondence between "microcosm and macrocosm" or the theory of the bodily "humours". Although these concepts show an emancipation process e.g. from ancient beliefs in the gods, they themselves were replaced in the course of the history of ideas. Despite modern psychology the ideas behind these concepts are not outdated because the problems today are still very much the same deep down. It is this question of how to make these timeless truths appear fresh to every new audience which is the central task for the playwright. It is remarkable that most of the main themes in Shakespeare are dealt with in all types of genres. Even in plays that do not lend themselves to comedy there have to be comical elements (e.g. the porter scene in "Macbeth" or the gravedigger scene in "Hamlet"), while most of the aforementioned themes can also be found in the classic comedies. Quite frequently, Shakespeare does not present or discuss a special thematic reference in one play only, but refers to a number of them within a particular play. This topic focusses on the most important themes and tries to show how Shakespeare discussed these issues within the context of his plays. It is furthermore noteworthy to recognise the development which a single thematic element takes from a quite simple treatment in an early play to a highly complex one in the plays towards the end of Shakespeare's career.

A very helpful **source** of comprehensive information on Shakespeare's plays and poetry is Leslie Dunton-Downer and Alan Riding's "Essential Shakespeare Handbook", London, 2004.

Comprehension

1 All these pictures show scenes from Shakespeare's plays.

Lösungsvorschlag

*Clockwise from top left: The picture from Romeo and Juliet can be matched to **love**. **Power** is probably best shown in the top picture from "Richard III". Here he has the crown already and is leading his army against the usurpers toward the end of the play. The first picture of Lady Macbeth shows her screaming, maybe at the audience, and perhaps because of her guilty **conscience**.*
*Ambition can also be linked to the picture of Macbeth, who is visited by **supernatural** forces, but his downcast eyes indicates that he also has qualms of **conscience** and finds it hard to resist temptation at the same time. The picture of Lady Macbeth in which she is crowning herself shows her **ambition**, of course.*

Analysis

2 Which plays do you think the scenes were taken from?

Lösungsvorschlag

The pictures are from (clockwise from top left): "Romeo and Juliet", "Richard III", and "Macbeth". They show the balcony scene, Richard before he goes to battle, Lady Macbeth (maybe in her sleep walking scene), then Macbeth and the three weird sisters and finally Lady Macbeth crowning herself.

4 Shakespeare the dramatist   The writing process

Evaluation   **3 [👥] *Choose one of the pictures and invent a storyline around it.***

Zusatzmaterial   → Kopiervorlage 4 a–d (Drama families)

Lösungsvorschlag   Individuelle S-Beiträge.

Alternative   *A good way of introducing the students to the plays is to let them work with the "drama families" (**Kopiervorlage 4 a–d**, pp. 107–110). For this exercise, plot summaries that tell the story from the perspectives of various characters in the play are cut up. The students are each given a slip of paper, Lady Macbeth, for instance, or Prince Hamlet, or Shylock, each slip telling the most important aspects of the story from that character's point of view. The tasks are as follows:*

1. *Find the members of your family by asking each other questions about where you live, what you do for a living, or your name.*
2. *Arrange all members in the classroom in a way that tells as much as possible about the plot.*
3. *Explain who you are and what your role in the play is – remember: the others should be able to understand the plot on the basis of what you say!*

Some classes will only read out their parts, others will change the texts to make it more like a real play and add gestures and movements to their roles. If your class likes acting, you can bring props they might find useful (a white sheet for a ghost, for instance), hand out a more detailed plot summary (they can be found here: www.sparknotes.com/shakespeare) and give them some time to prepare their "production" of the play.
You should plan a double period for this exercise, but it is worthwhile, since afterwards the students will have enacted one short version of a Shakespeare play and seen up to three more, depending on the size of the class.
Further discussion might include the following aspects: Which play would you like to see? Which plot would you turn into a film? What setting would you choose for the drama/film if you were the director?

Factual information

The writing process   p. 29

HINTERGRUNDINFO

*Discussing the questions a **dramatist** must consider when writing a new play might lead to a deeper understanding of the particular play and the themes being studied. Studying the manifold sources, the working conditions and Shakespeare's literary influences might also change the students' focus of interest from the more historical and factual in the early topics of this book to an appreciation of the plays themselves. The fact that Shakespeare used many classic as well as popular sources and worked in contemporary issues plus the thought that plays quite often may have resulted from an exchange of ideas or professional co-operation might also take away some of the impetus of the speculations about Shakespeare the person and lead to a more deepened interest in the structures and artistic qualities of the plays themselves.*

Lernwortschatz   *maxim, infant, tavern, fame, fortune, contemporaries, craze, merely, despotic, reluctant*

Erweiterung
- Eine Auswahl aus der Fülle der Materialien zur Vertiefung der thematischen Aspekte:
  Ina Schabert, Shakespeare Handbuch, Stuttgart, 2009.
  Roland Petersohn/Laurenz Volkmann (Hrsg.), Shakespeare – Didaktisch (I), Tübingen, 2006.
  Leah Scragg, *Discovering Shakespeare's Meaning*, Harlow, 1994.
  Fintan O'Toole, *Shakespeare is Hard, but so is Life*, London, 2002.
  Germaine Greer, *Shakespeare – A Very Short Introduction*, Oxford, 1986.
  Rex Gibson, *Teaching Shakespeare*, Cambridge, 1998.

- Weniger wissenschaftlich, eher für die Hand der S geeignet:
  Leon Garfield, *Shakespeare Stories I + II*, London, 1994.
  Terry Deary, *Top Ten Shakespeare Stories*, London, 1989.
  Geraldine McCaughrean, *Stories from Shakespeare*, London, 1999.
  Humphrey Carpenter, *Shakespeare Without the Boring Bits*, London, 1994.

Shakespeare the dramatist   The writing process | 4

Humphrey Carpenter, *More Shakespeare Without the Boring Bits,* London, 1997.
Andrew Donkin, *William Shakespeare and his Dramatic Acts,* London, 2004.

- Nützliche *Websites* zum Thema:
  http://www.bbc.co.uk/drama/shakespeare/
  http://www.bbc.co.uk/drama/shakespeare/60secondshakespeare/index.shtml
  http://www.imdb.com/title/tt0147788/

Brainteaser

1 *Summarise what the text says about the writing process: ...*

Lösungsvorschlag

What the text says about the writing process
Dramatists of the Shakespearean age did not have the opportunity to travel extensively, nor did they have the help of modern media to give them a plethora of information for their plots. Yet life around them was far from dull and although they had no direct contact with the rulers, the royal families were a more popular topic of talk than they are today. It was a time of storytelling with the material coming from popular books, oral tradition or gossip. One very important factor was the exchange of ideas with fellow writers, watching their plays or acting in them. When a play was finished, it was sold to a company. The company edited it to their performance requirements and had it licensed. For fear of a rivalling company stealing a finished production, full scripts were rarely printed.

What sources were used?
- *stories from popular books or oral tradition*
- *mythology and historical reports (Holinshed's chronicles; 1587)*
- *popular plays used as role models*

How were the sources used?
Shakespeare merely used the information as a source, a platform from which he then changed the story to serve his dramatic purposes. (e.g. "Richard III", whose appearance was over dramatised to make him appear the cruel ruler Shakespeare – and Tudor mythology – wanted him to be)

What influenced writers?
- *exchange of ideas with fellow writers to receive a first response about a new concept*
- *a successful invention of a type of play could lead to follow-ups of the same genre*
- *popular opinion*

Evaluation

2 *Point out the differences between writing a play in Shakespeare's ...*

Lösungsvorschlag

Individuelle S-Beiträge, die die grundlegenden Arbeitsbedingungen zur Zeit Shakespeares mit den Möglichkeiten moderner Informationsbeschaffung und Medieneinsatzes vergleichen sollten.

Erweiterung

Die S bereiten ein Gruppenprojekt zur folgenden Aufgabe vor und präsentieren ihre Ergebnisse:
At one of the Friday tavern meetings, Shakespeare discusses an idea for a new play, e.g. "Richard III", with his colleagues. Use the information in this text and other sources to imagine the scene. Which questions and problems would the playwrights have to consider?

4 | Shakespeare the dramatist   Richard III: What happens in the play?

| Plot summary | **Richard III: What happens in the play?** | p. 30 |

HINTERGRUNDINFO

"Richard III" is not only one of the most popular plays by William Shakespeare on today's stages and in the cinema, it is arguably also one of the most suitable plays to be studied in the classroom. Although it is an early play marking the end of the cycle of eight history plays, it already dramatises many of the issues and features of mature Shakespearean drama. Additionally, it offers the opportunity to study elements of all genres; moreover, they can be looked at in a more pure form as Shakespeare tended to increasingly blend the moods more intricately in the course of his growing skills as a playwright. Many thematic elements that can be seen quite openly in earlier plays are taken up again as the basis for later plays. It was taken for granted that the Elizabethan theatregoers were familiar with this development.

The following scenes not only were selected to cover the most important themes of "ambition", "disguise", "love", "power", "public office", but also to give opportunities for an active approach to text interpretation in the class in the three forms of individual-, pair- and group-work. Before focussing on individual aspects of the scenes, it might be necessary to gain a general idea about the gist of the rather complex plot and the basics of the historic background necessary to understand the course of the play. This should not become an aim in itself but a means to "whet the appetite" and facilitate the following work with the play itself. Although the play lends itself to a number of individual preferences in the analysis of key issues, there are some core themes which are in the centre: "the Machiavellian gain of power with the help of plotting and treason", "the character of a typical villain and his tools of disguise", "the concept of divine retribution and the fall of princes", "real vs. false emotions", "fortune and superstition". At the beginning the students are given a number of basic choices of plot elements to create interest in some of the themes of the play which will be taken up in the course of study.

Eine hervorragende Hilfe zur detaillierten Arbeit mit *Richard III* in Verbindung mit dem Internet bietet: http://www.zum.de/Faecher/E/BW/exr3.htm. Weiterhin zu einzelnen Stücken: http://internetshakespeare.uvic.ca/Library/plays/R3.html.

| Brainteaser | **1 *What parts of the plot sound most interesting to you? Why?*** |

Hinweis auf den Tipp zu *The shape of drama* und die *Fact file* zu *Genres*. Ausgehend von der *Fact file* können die S Beispiele von ihnen bekannten Dramen sammeln und versuchen, diese den jeweiligen Genres zuzuordnen.

Lösungsvorschlag Individuelle S-Beiträge.

Alternative Nach einem kurzen Blick auf die Titel der thematischen Aspekte kann L fragen, welche Aspekte der Meinung einzelner S nach in diesem Stück fehlen. Es könnte sein, dass der anfängliche Schwerpunkt auf historische Bezüge nicht bei allen S motivierend wirkt und insbesondere das Fehlen von romantischen Elementen bemängelt wird. In einem solchen Fall gilt es, die Ansätze zu diesen fehlenden Elementen besonders herauszuarbeiten und zu betonen.

| Evaluation | **2 [👥] *Work in four groups and write a short scene for one part ...*** |

Zusatzmaterial → Kopiervorlage 5 (Themes of Shakespeare)

Es sollte darauf geachtet werden, dass alle Passagen des Plots in den Gruppen bearbeitet werden. Die Vorbereitung der Gruppendialoge sowie das Einüben der einzelnen Rollen kann aus Gründen der Zeitökonomie als **Hausaufgabe** gestellt werden.

Lösungsvorschlag Individuelle S-Beiträge.

Erweiterung Ergänzend bietet sich hier der Einsatz von **Kopiervorlage 5** (Seite 111) an, um den S einen Eindruck von der thematischen Vielfalt des Stückes zu vermitteln.

| | Shakespeare the dramatist   Richard's opening soliloquy – his discontent, his plot | **4** |

Drama excerpt   **[8◉] Richard's opening soliloquy – his discontent, his plot**   p. 31

HINTERGRUNDINFO

Soliloquy: The most important aspect of the stage convention of the soliloquy is that the audience gets first-hand information regarding the thoughts of the speaker, which is used to channel their further expectations. They are thus free from thinking about a possible further cause of action and rather are free to concentrate on the way in which the story carried on and the reaction of the other characters, who are

without knowledge of the reasons. This discrepancy between knowledge and ignorance is a vital source of dramatic tension. Shakespeare has developed his soliloquies to more and more artistic and complex forms of drawing characters in his later tragedies, namely in "Othello", "Macbeth" and "Hamlet".

Lernwortschatz   *discontent, son, wrinkled, adversary (fml), amorous, rudely stamped, nymph, deformed, villain*

Materialien   → **CD, Track 8** • **Online-Link: 601005-0008**

Eine sehr gute Hilfe zur Vertiefung dieser *soliloquy* stellt auch das Filmskript zu Al Pacinos *Looking for Richard* besonders in Verbindung mit der Bearbeitung des Dokumentarfilms dar: http://www.script-o-rama.com/movie_scripts/l/looking-for-richard-script-transcript.html.

Brainteaser   **1 *This opening scene sets the stage for the whole play.***

[8◉]   Hinweis auf die *Fact file* zu *A soliloquy*. Danach wird die Szene von der CD präsentiert.

Lösungsvorschlag
- *The War of the Roses is over ("the winter is made summer"); the House of York has won ("victorious wreaths").*
- *Rather than wartime marching and fighting, the preoccupation of the king and his followers in times of peace are dancing, music and courting ("he capers nimbly to the lascivious pleasing of a lute").*
- *Richard has been physically deformed since birth ("deformed, unfinished, sent before my time into this breathing world"), does not feel (is not) handsome enough to be able to join the festivities ("I, that am curtailed of this fair proportion, … have not delight to pass away the time").*
- *Richard vows to become the villain as he hates the "idle pleasures of these days".*

Erweiterung   Denkbar ist die Nachbearbeitung dieser Aufgabe durch eine (Internet-)Recherche zu *The War of the Roses* oder *The Tudor Myth*. Neben einem historisch-landeskundlich orientierten Ansatz ist es an diese Stelle auch reizvoll, die Bedeutung der Eingangsszene für Shakespeares Tragödien näher zu untersuchen. Gerade die Eingangszenen der in diesem Topic mit Textbeispielen vertretenen Dramen veranschaulichen, wie bedeutsam sie für den Handlungsverlauf und die weitere Atmosphäre der Tragödien sind. Ein solcher eher systemisch orientierter Ansatz lässt sich organisch mit den Anregungen zu einer aktiven Drameninterpretation nach dem Vorbild Rex Gibsons verbinden. Damit kann dem Problem des Zeitmangels zur Behandlung ganzer Dramen begegnet werden und es eröffnen sich neue Möglichkeiten, die gleichsam nachhaltig und von hohem inhaltlichen Anspruch sein können (siehe dazu: Rex Gibson, *Teaching Shakespeare*, Cambridge, 1998, Seite 150 ff.).

Analysis   **2 *Find keywords in the soliloquy that give you information about …***

Lösungsvorschlag   *There are three main stages in the development of moods given in the text:*
- *First, Richard gives a rough sketch of the emotions during and after the war:* **Winter** *of* **discontent** *vs.* **summer**; **clouds** *have emptied themselves into the ocean; not wounds but* **wreaths** *on the brows;* **arms** *have become* **monuments**; **stern alarms** *changed to* **merry** *meetings;* **dreadful** *marches have changed to* **delightful** *events; the* **grim** *face of war has changed, the* **wrinkles** *are* **smoothed**; *the king does* **not ride on his armed horse** *to fight the* **fearful adversaries** *but follows amorous intentions (***"he capers in a lady's chamber to the lascivious pleasing of a lute"***).*

57

4 Shakespeare the dramatist Richard's opening soliloquy – his discontent, his plot

- Second, Richard himself is not good-looking (**"not shaped for sportive tricks"**, **"not made to court"**, **"rudely stamped"**, **"want love's majesty"**, **"curtailed of this fair proportion"**, **"cheated of feature"**, **"deformed, unfinished, sent before my time ... scarce half made up"**, **"lamely and unfashionable that dogs bark at me"**.
- Third, Richard hates this world of merriments and courting and decides to have his will in a different way: **"I have no delight** ... unless to **spy** my **shadow** in the **sun"**, "therefore since I **cannot prove a lover** to **entertain** these **fair well-spoken days**, I am **determined** to prove a **villain**, and **hate** the **idle pleasures** of these days".

Dramatic reading

3 Read the soliloquy aloud with various emotions. Which seem most effective?

Zusatzmaterial → Kopiervorlage 6 (Richard's thoughts)

Individuelle Bearbeitung durch die S. Sie sollten ausdrücklich darin bestärkt werden, sehr individualistisch und kreativ mit dem Text zu arbeiten. Eine anfänglich recht ungeordnete Phase des Unterrichts ist an dieser Stelle im Hinblick auf die spätere Auseinandersetzung mit dem Text eher förderlich. Vergleiche hierzu Rex Gibson, *Teaching Shakespeare* (Cambridge, 1998) bzw. James Stredder, *The North Face of Shakespeare* (Cambridge, 2009).

Erweiterung
- Auch bei lernstarken Gruppen empfiehlt es sich, vor dem individuellen Lesen eine Übung zur Förderung des entwickelnden dramatischen Lesens voranzustellen, bei der zunächst jeder S nur ein Wort des Textes, dann eine Zeile oder eine Sinneinheit laut liest. Hierbei fallen gleichzeitig schwierige Begriffe auf, die anschließend kurz geklärt werden.

- Hier bietet sich als Ergänzung der Einsatz von **Kopiervorlage 6** (Seite 112) an.

Analysis

4 [👥] In groups, watch a film version of this scene. Analyse the ...

Hinweis auf die *Word bank* zu *Analysing film*. Es gibt bislang drei filmische Bearbeitungen von *Richard III*: *King Richard III* (Lawrence Olivier, 1955), *Richard III* (Ian McKellan, 1995), *Looking for Richard* (Al Pacino, 1996). Für allgemeine grundlegende Informationen zur Filmbearbeitung siehe www.IMBD.com. Die jüngste filmische Bearbeitung des Stoffes (2008) ist derzeit noch nicht als DVD erhältlich. Bei der Bearbeitung der Aufgabe in Gruppen sind verschiedene Methoden möglich: Denkbar ist die Beschränkung auf eine Filmszene, bei der sich einzelne Gruppenmitglieder bei der Analyse der filmischen Mittel arbeitsteilig nur auf einen Aspekt der Aufgabe beschränken und dann ihre Ergebnisse der Kleingruppe vorstellen. Nach Absprache mit der Gruppe erfolgt eine Präsentation vor der Klasse. Daran schließt ein weiterer Durchgang mit einer anderen Bearbeitung an. Bei leistungsstarken Lerngruppen ist auch ein kontrastives Präsentieren verschiedener Bearbeitungen unter Bezug auf die diversen Aspekte der filmischen Analyse möglich (siehe dazu: Thomas Tepe (Hrsg.): Filmanalyse, 2004, Klett-Nr. 577463).

Comprehension

5 [3🎞] Choose one of the interviewee's opinions and continue ...

Materialien → Film 3 (Estimating the Bard) • Kopiervorlage 7 (Opinions about Shakespeare)

[3🎞] Die S schauen den Videoclip entweder als **Hausaufgabe** oder im Unterricht an.

Lösungsvorschlag *Some of the arguments mentioned on the video clip as a basis for discussion*
- *The English speaking world "breathes" Shakespeare, he's a "man for all time".*
- *His phrases are common parlance and his plays are "poured over" at school and are bound in service to "-isms" from Marxism to Structualism.*
- *At the heart of the fascination, the play is the thing.*
- *You can't put him on a high enough pedestal. Every actor wants to play Shakespeare.*
- *It's alright, but it's quite difficult to understand sometimes.*
- *Shakespeare says in a very beautiful way the things that seem ugly in everyday life.*
- *Thelma Holt: "We cannot have too much Shakespeare, we cannot have too much of a work of a genius. Can we have too many Rembrandts? But bad Shakespeare, of course, we do not want; we want good Shakespeare."*

Shakespeare the dramatist   Richard woos Anne | 4

- *A few voices say this obsession – bardolatry – has gone too far.*
- *Professor of Literature: "I think we over-emphasize the work of Shakespeare, there's a great danger that everybody else gets pushed into the background and there are some first-rate dramatists writing at the same time: Christopher Marlowe is one, Ben Jonson is another. There are people whose plays aren't very often played and ought to be."*
- *Critically acclaimed in his day, it was with the rise of the Romantic Movement that Shakespeare began to be unquestionably deified.*
- *Another literary critic: "After the Romantics, early 19th century, great period for Shakespeare, beginning of really serious bardophilia, wonderful language, terrific characterisation, super plots, great moral sense, wonderful parts for great actors and that was the 19th century and it established Shakespeare as a person we love and adore, even though nowadays we see him in a more complex light."*

Erweiterung Zur Vertiefung des Verständnisses und zur Festigung der Kernkompetenz Hören kann der Videoclip auch mit **Kopiervorlage 7** (Seite 113) vorbereitend bearbeitet werden.

Drama excerpt | [9⊚] **Richard woos Anne** | pp. 32–33

HINTERGRUNDINFO

*If the **first scene** explained the background to the plot ("what?") and laid the foundation to the reasons ("why?") that might lie behind Richards actions, this passage gives a first powerful insight into Richard's methods ("how?"). The theme of conscience, or rather the lack of it, is taken up again ("I'll have her but will not keep her long"). Despite his physical inferiority, Richard seems to have the upper hand psychologically, yet Anne – despite being seemingly superior – softens towards the end of the dialogue in the full knowledge of the fact that as a widow she would have to rely on the strong support of a husband to secure her family. Thus it can be argued that the dialogue is a good example of the battle of the sexes in which true feelings fall victim to scheming plans and outward show. This is quite a strong thematic counterpoint which might be explored in an active approach in the classroom.*

Lernwortschatz *to adore, to woo, to provoke, to stab, executioner, to bid (fml), rage, to enclose (fml), curse, marvellous, to lament, inflection*

Materialien → CD, Track 9

Visualising | **1 Find out about the history of the Tudor dynasty and draw a family tree ...**

Vor oder während der Bearbeitung dieser Aufgabe kann L einen kurzen Überblick auf die Familienverhältnisse Richards geben.

HINTERGRUNDINFO

Edward III *was a Plantagenet. His grandson Richard II became king after him. Richard was forced to abdicate by his cousin Henry, Earl of Derby, a son of John of Gaunt, who was a political heavyweight in England in the 14th century. So this Henry became Henry IV of England, and when his father John died, he also inherited the title "Duke of Lancaster". He was succeeded by his son Hal – this was Henry V, the one who won the battle at Agincourt. When Henry V died, his son Henry became King of England – Henry VI. He was rather unsuccessful both in political and military matters, and often ill – mentally and physically – so that some noblemen started to scheme against him. The most ardent among these was Richard Plantagenet, Duke of York, who had just as much right to the throne as Henry VI himself. Henry's grandfather had seized the crown although his cousin Edmund Mortimer, Earl of March, was next in succession after Richard II's abdication, and Richard Plantagenet was a nephew of Edmund and his heir. This conflict led to the outbreak of the War of the Roses: The House of Lancaster, whose heraldic symbol is a red rose, against the House of York (white rose). Here is were the family tree begins: this Richard Plantagenet, Duke of York, died in battle, but his son Edward became Edward IV of England, and his brother Richard is the scheming villain in "Richard III".*

59

4 Shakespeare the dramatist — Richard woos Anne

Lösungsvorschlag The Earl of Richmond, winner of the battle against Richard, is to become Henry VII, father to Henry VIII. Richmond's claims to the throne were tenuous, as they mainly rested on a female link. However, Henry and his son Henry VIII founded the Tudor dynasty that was continued by Elizabeth I during Shakespeare's times. The Tudors were highly interested in their lawful reign, so with the beginning of the reign of Henry VII they tried to portray Richard III as a usurper who had usurped the English throne, and so they had many "histories" written to prove this.

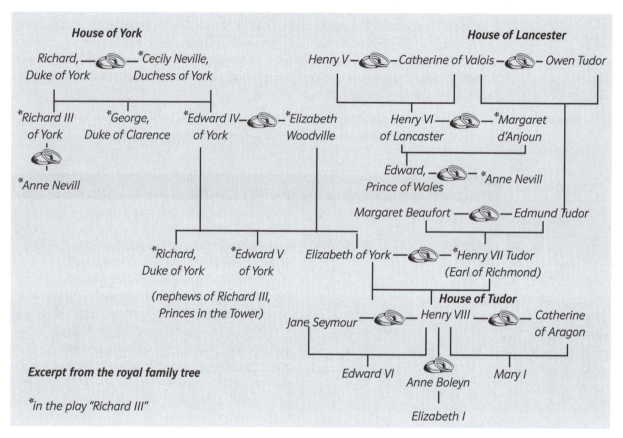

Excerpt from the royal family tree

*in the play "Richard III"

Erweiterung Sir Thomas More, *History of Richard III* (1513–18); Polydore Vergil, *Historia Anglia* (1534).

Dramatic reading 2 [👥] **First on your own, then with a partner, read the dialogue aloud.**

HINTERGRUNDINFO

"The principles of successful school Shakespeare" were laid down by Rex Gibson with the Shakespeare and Schools Project at the University of Cambridge in 1986. The following compilation lists the most important aspects of this approach, which have led to fundamentally different aspects not only in the creation of new textbooks on Shakespeare but also for work in the classroom (compiled and quoted from: Rex Gibson, "Shakespeare and Schools", No. 24, Summer 1994):

- "Shakespeare's plays have to be treated as scripts". This insight attempts to turn teachers away from the traditional over-analytical approach of looking for right and wrong answers and neglecting the motivating potential of drama.
- "School Shakespeare has to be learner-centred" to give the students an opportunity to find meanings for themselves. Rather than forcing preconceived ideas that have to be learnt, it is much more rewarding to offer students exercises such as letting them look for alternative endings.
- "School Shakespeare is social." This is an activity that is shared where students work in pairs or small groups to exchange their impressions on the subject matter. For example, sharing the language of a soliloquy is a "kind of internal conversation".
- "School Shakespeare celebrates imagination" and takes advantage of the students' interest in the power of the images in the play. A good way of putting this maxim into practice is to let the students build tableaux from given lines of information about a certain scene. Photos of these tableaux could then be used for further creative exercises.

Shakespeare the dramatist   Richard woos Anne   4

- "School Shakespeare is physical." Hamlet's advice to the players, "to suit the action to the word and the word to the action" is one of the most important factors for producing successful Shakespeare productions at school.
- "School Shakespeare is exploratory." Shakespeare's works defy any ready-made answers of right and wrong and rather ask for a "free-wheeling exploration of possibilities". At the opening of "Romeo and Juliet" a task to the students could be to enact their own versions of the scene, as Shakespeare deliberately wrote to leave many questions on universal issues of man open to be dealt with and discussed.
- "School Shakespeare addresses essential themes." The list of themes addressed in Shakespeare is long and every lesson will have to make sure to help the students understand these central themes or special qualities of the plays being studied. The need to give the studentspersonal ownership of parts of the play is a vital prerequisite.

- "School Shakespeare involves choice and variety." One should try to ensure that the students can respond in a variety of ways to the material, that there is a certain choice of different topics as well as methods and activities to chose from.
- "School Shakespeare celebrates plurality." An important piece of advice is "Forget Shakespeare, think of Shakespeares". There is no definitive version of a Shakespeare play, so the aim must always be to look at a play from a variety of angles.
- "School Shakespeare respects negative capability." Rex Gibson's creed was "You don't have to know it all – nobody does!" This must set energy free to be able to explore and express ideas of individual or group creativity.
- "School Shakespeare should be enjoyed." This final statement is probably the most important, even for students who are not native speakers. Shakespeare's prime task was to entertain and not to lecture. This is sometimes all too often forgotten in our classrooms today.

Lösungsvorschlag   *Some emotions that could be brought up: initially Richard is sly and submissive, he even quite bluntly admits to having murdered Anne's husband only to change his tone immediately and confess to be in love with her. He is putting psychological pressure on her by offering her to speak her verdict over him. Anne naturally answers quite hatefully and does not want to converse with Richard, admitting that she does not trust his intentions. The middle section of the scene sees a very powerful exchange of verbal attacks, almost like a fencing match, where the tension is extremely hightened due to the quick repartees of both speakers. When Anne nevertheless takes Richard's ring, the mood changes again, which can be seen in Richard's use of sweet imagery (ll. 37 ff.). The audience is yet in for another change in the emotional climate after Anne has left the stage and Richard in his soliloquy once again shows his real face to the audience, thus already giving a hint as to the price Anne will have to pay for having been gulled into believing Richard in this scene.*

Erweiterung   Die S sollten, nachdem sie sich individuell mit dem Text vertraut gemacht haben, ermutigt werden, mit dem Textmaterial zu experimentieren. Ein wichtiger Grund für die intensive sprachpraktische Vorbereitung ist, dass die S den Eindruck gewinnen sollen, den Text quasi zu ihrem Eigentum zu machen und somit die begründeten anfänglichen Hemmnisse im Umgang mit der Sprache Shakespeares zu überwinden. Gerade in der Methode des spielerischen Experimentierens liegt eine große Möglichkeit, die verschiedenen emotionalen Tiefen der Texte zu erkunden und die S für eine weitere Arbeit an den Texten zu motivieren.

Analysis   **3 Who or what is meant by "love" in its four instances in lines 23–24?**

Lösungsvorschlag   *Richard tries to persuade Anne that her real feelings are not hateful as she will think differently when she has some time to think things over. He admits that in order to gain her affection ("thy love") he killed her husband ("thy love"). However he also warns her that if she rejects him she will be responsible for the death of an even greater ("truer") love, his real affections. The last line could also be a hint by Richard towards Anne that he might even be prepared to give up his aspirations to become king for her love.*

Evaluation   **4 Point out the phrases in this excerpt having to do with love and hate.**

Lösungsvorschlag   **Love:** *"'twas thy beauty that provoked me" (l. 12); "'twas thy heavenly face that set me on" (l. 14); "or take up me" (l. 16); "Then bid me kill myself, and I will do it" (l. 19); "This hand, which for thy*

61

4   Shakespeare the dramatist   Richard woos Anne

love did kill thy love, Shall for thy love kill a far truer love." (ll. 23–24); "Then never was man true."
(l. 29); "Vouchsafe to wear this ring." (l. 35); "thy breast encloseth my poor heart" (l. 38); "for both
of them are thine" (l. 39).

Hate: *"contempt" (l. 2); "revengeful heart cannot forgive" (l. 3); "dissembler; though I wish thy*
death" (l. 17), "I have already" (l. 20); "To take her in her heart's extremest hate, With curses in her
mouth, tears in her eyes, The bleeding witness of her hatred" (l. 46–48); "no friends, but the plain
devil and dissembling looks" (l. 50).

Erweiterung   Weitere gut geeignete Unterrichtshilfen zu dieser Passage bietet der Online-Service der
Folger Library, Washington unter: http://www.folger.edu/eduLesPlanDtl.cfm/?lpid=818 oder
www.folger.edu.

Comment

5   Comment on the differences between the dialogue ...

[9 ⊚]   Die S können bei der Beantwortung individuelle Schwerpunkte setzen. Einige mögliche Aspekte zeigt der Lösungsvorschlag. Vor dieser Aufgabe bietet sich der Einsatz der Tonaufnahme auf
der CD an.

Lösungsvorschlag   *In the dialogue Richard sees the necessity to wear his mask well as otherwise his plan to gain*
Anne's favour would fail. The gradual change of mood in Anne's replies shows how successful
Richard goes about his plans. The form of dialogue is necessary here to show the audience the
degree of opposition Richard has to overcome and the development of his success. As the
soliloquy follows the dialogue, the audience might even ask itself whether Richard's words may
have some true core as he might feel the effects of his loneliness. If there are any beliefs in
romantic traces in Richard's character, they are soon brutally dispersed with as soon as Anne
leaves the stage. This scene shows very strikingly how effectively Shakespeare used his dramatic
tools as he directs even the expectations of the audience with this stage convention where the
character speaks the truth in order to keep the tension up.

Evaluation

6   Describe Richard's line of argumentation with regard ...

Zusatzmaterial   →   Kopiervorlage 8 (The meanings of *Richard III*)

Hinweis auf die *Fact file* zu *History plays*.

Lösungsvorschlag   **a)** *Richard shows a complete arsenal of psychological skills, beginning his speech with flattery*
("lips were made for kissing"), followed by submissiveness ("I lend thee this sword") and
overdone humbleness ("humble beg thy death"). He even tries to incite Anne into action ("Nay
do not pause"), thus showing his mental superiority gambling on the idea that she will prove
unable to act. He even goes so far as to tease her ("Nay, now dispatch") which then leads to his
logical alternative that if she does not kill him she has no reason for not liking him ("or take up
me"). When Anne protests that she has already wished his death, Richard claims that these
thoughts don't count because they were irrational and quite understandable under the
circumstances. But Anne is of sane mind now and he threatens her that she might even be held
responsible for causing more severe damage if she remains inactive. Richard succeeds in having
Anne exchange quibbles with him, thus seemingly giving her a forum to try out her rhetorical
powers and proving to be a match for him. As the exchange of arguments does not show a clear
winner, Richard even shows signs of the true husband he promises to be, a sentiment with
which Anne leaves the stage.

b) *In the following, Richard even boasts of having won Anne in a somewhat sportive contest.*
This stands in some contrast to his mood in the first soliloquy where his disposition was more
sombre. In this second soliloquy one might even see some traces of cynicism.

Erweiterung   Hier bietet sich als Ergänzung **Kopiervorlage 8** (Seite 114) an.

| | Shakespeare the dramatist   Ward je in dieser Laun' ein Weib gewonnen? | **4** |

Evaluation

7 Watch a film version of this scene.

Zusatzmaterial   → **Kopiervorlage 9 (Tools of language)** • **Kopiervorlage 10 (Richard the politician)**

Individuelle Auswahl und Schwerpunktsetzung der S. Hierbei sollte aber in jedem Fall auf die Unterschiede durch Filmadaptationen aus verschiedenen Zeiten (z. B. Olivier vs. McKellan) sowie die Art von filmischen Umsetzungen (z. B. Besonderheiten einer Dokumentation wie Al Pacinos *Looking for Richard*) eingegangen werden.

Lösungsvorschlag   Individuelle S-Beiträge.

Erweiterung
- Zur Vertiefung weiterer Aspekte bei einer Erarbeitung größerer Abschnitte von *Richard III* kann **Kopiervorlage 9** (Seite 115) herangezogen werden.

- Nachdem am Beispiel einer *soliloquy* und eines Dialoges inhaltliche Schwerpunkte von *Richard III* untersucht wurden, können mit der Krönungsszene (**Kopiervorlage 10**, Seite 116) weitere inhaltliche Bezüge erarbeitet werden. Die abgedruckte Szene ist eine Schlüsselszene sowohl für das Verständnis der Doppeldeutigkeit Richards als auch für die globale Intention des gesamten Stückes. Am Beispiel dieser Passage kann u.a. auch auf die Konzepte des *fortune's wheel* sowie des *divine right* eingegangen werden.

German journal article

Ward je in dieser Laun' ein Weib gewonnen?   p. 34

Discussion

1 [👥] Mediation: Imagine you were taking part in an exchange programme ...

Der Text entstammt dem Programmheft einer Aufführung von *Richard III* der *University Players* Hamburg aus dem Jahr 2007.

Lösungsvorschlag   *Individual answers, yet the idea could be brought up, as to whether the stance of this article is*
- *a particularly German one, or*
- *one that is taken by younger rather than older people, or*
- *the fact that this individual view in the article is expressed by a female writer and could thus also lead to a discussion on aspects of gender.*

Analysis

2 [👥👥] The text refers to a number of rather pointed statements ...

Lösungsvorschlag   *Some aspects from the article that could be discussed*
- *Beautiful women tend to chose weak spouses as the latter prove to be more tolerant.*
- *Partners who are capable of flirting well choose this capacity to hide their real emotions.*
- *Power makes people sexy.*
- *When someone assumes power, someone else must lose it.*
- *Today, gaining power is often done through mental rather than physical means.*
- *If power makes people attractive, women have to accept a certain degree of ruthlessness in their partners.*

Analysis

3 Compare the German translations of these quotes from Richard III.

Lösungsvorschlag   *The comment on the translations of these sentences could criticise the fact that many German productions still refer to the classic translation of Shakespeare by Schlegel/Tieck rather than trying to present the content in a translation that is closer to modern German without trying to present the language of Shakespeare as an icon of culture, the changing of which is claimed by some to be a sacrilege.*

Erweiterung   Jede der drei Aufgaben ist dazu geeignet, die Grundlage einer *formal debate* zu bilden.

63

4 Shakespeare the dramatist   Love: The balcony scene

| *Drama excerpt/ Photos* | **[10 ⊚] Love: The balcony scene** | pp. 35–36 |

HINTERGRUNDINFO

The play starts with conflict right away: *The Chorus introduces the "ancient grudge" in the prologue, and some Capulets exchange insults with Montagues in the street. The escalating brawl can only be stopped by the Prince of Verona, who forbids a public disturbance. Old Capulet invites Paris to a party, encouraging him to woo Juliet, and when Romeo learns that the girl he is in love with, Rosaline, is among the guests invited to the party, he decides to go himself. The Montagues wear masks, but Romeo's voice is recognised: again, they are headed for trouble with the Capulets. The fast-paced act ends with a devastated Romeo, who learns that the girl he has just fallen head over heels in love with is a Capulet. The prologue to Act 2 builds suspense by laying out the difficulties facing Romeo and Juliet and by indicating that there may be a possibility to overcome them: "But passion lends them power, time means, to meet,/Temp'ring extremities with extreme sweet" (II. Prologue 13–14). Act II is the happiest and least tragic act in the play, with a focus on the positive and romantic aspects of young love. Because of its beautiful poetry, the present scene, the so-called balcony scene (it is often staged with Juliet on a balcony, though the stage directions only say that she is at a window above Romeo), is one of the most famous scenes in all of theatre.*

Language: *The balcony scene is probably so famous not only because of its romantic implications, but for the wonderful way in which Shakespeare manages to let rhythm and sound contribute to the scene and make the passion with which the two young lovers meet here palpable for the audience.*

Dominic Dromgoole, *the Artistic Director of the Globe Theatre and a passionate Shakespearean describes in "Will and Me. How Shakespeare Took Over My Life" how one particular line from this scene got hold of him when he was a teenager: "Romeo, Oh Romeo. Wherefore art thou, Romeo?" He explains that "[T]he magic of that line is peculiarly trans-gender, ageless and international … However badly it is attacked, it defies destruction. Its basic tool is a bold and open use of big, wide vowel sounds … It's someone throwing the window of their heart wide open. Try and say it without sounding as if you're full of longing and yearning. The very physicality involved in forming the sounds creates the emotions it describes." (Dominic Dromgoole, "Will and Me. How Shakespeare Took Over My Life", London, 2006, p. 51.)*

Lernwortschatz	*beloved, passionate, family feud, fatal, envious, to sneak, orchard, bold, glove, mortal, to deny, to text, striking, presumably*
Materialien	→ **CD, Track 10 • Online-Link: 601005-0009**

Evaluation	**1 *When Shakespeare was around 30 years old, he wrote …***
Zusatzmaterial	→ **Kopiervorlage 11 (The cornerstone is the metre)**
[10 ⊚]	Hinweis auf die *Fact file* zu *Romeo and Juliet.* L präsentiert den Textauszug von der CD. Die S werden vorher darauf hingewiesen, dass eine Heirat aus Liebe in vielen Kulturkreisen auch heute noch keine Selbstverständlichkeit ist. Insbesondere in der arabischen und südasiatischen Welt, in denen Frauen oft eine untergeordnete Rolle spielen, werden Kinder als Besitztümer ihrer Eltern betracht, die Ehepartner von den Eltern ausgesucht und Ungehorsam gegenüber dieser Entscheidung mit dem Tod bestraft. Ein Hinweis auf die sogenannten „Ehrenmorde" hier in Deutschland, die meist eine Folge der Autonomiebestrebungen einer jungen Frau sind, kann hilfreich sein.

Lösungsvorschlag	***Teen killings in Verona – vengeance as a motif?***
	Police stand by as young boys slay
	Yesterday the body of another young Veronese citizen, Mercutio M., 16, was found on the beach near Verona harbour. Police officers declared that death was brought about by a shotgun wound, but refused to give any more details.
	Mercutio M.'s death is another peak in a series of outbursts of violence between teenagers on Veronese streets. The city authorities are at a loss as far as an explanation for this violence is concerned.

Shakespeare the dramatist   Love: The balcony scene   4

"It seems there are two rivalling groups fighting each other, but we do not exactly know why. We are absolutely appalled at the ferocity with which these youngsters are at each other's throats," Verona's mayor, Dario Prince told reporters. "Our hearts go out to the families of the young men who were killed. I rely on our police to find the murderer."

Chief Constable Jerome Vespucio said at a press conference, "We have done everything we could to prevent further violence with twice as many policemen patrolling the streets at night, but of course we can't be everywhere." Mercutio M's death could have something to do with another violent incidence that occurred on Tuesday in which Tybalt C., 17, was killed.

"I can't understand why the police didn't interfere much earlier," a friend of the family told us. "They could have prevented these terrible crimes if they had arrived a bit earlier and stepped in. They never seem to be there when they are needed!"

The MP for Verona, Don Monsanto, responded with the usual concern, stating that "everything was being done to get the youngsters off the streets, and that "anti-violence training programs in schools and youth clubs were sure to show their effect in the near future."

Erweiterung   Die berühmte *balcony scene* eignet sich (neben den Auszügen aus den Selbstgesprächen *Richards* oder *Macbeths* sehr gut zu einer vertiefenden Einführung in die Bedeutung des Rhythmus für verschiedene Ausdrucksintentionen Shakespeares. Bei einem ersten Blick auf die *balcony scene* werden die S vermutlich die große Regelmäßigkeit des Versmaßes feststellen. Sehr schnell wird z. B. in Zeile 8 auffallen, dass *envious* das Versmaß sprengt. In gleicher Weise würde eine Untersuchung der Satzzeichen in der Rede *Macbeths* (Themenheft, Seite 38) sehr schnell deutlich machen, dass Zeilenende und Satzende an keiner Stelle übereinstimmen. Dass es sich hierbei jeweils nicht um einen technischen Fehler handelt, sondern dies ganz bewusst als Mittel des Ausdrucks eingesetzt wird, kann anhand von **Kopiervorlage 11** (Seite 117) erarbeitet werden.

Analysis   ## 2 Look at the imagery in lines 5–10. Explain how it adds to the scene.

Lösungsvorschlag   *When Romeo speaks these lines, he is hiding in the Capulet's orchard after the party and sees Juliet leaning out of a window (II. i. 44–64). Though it is late and the night dark, Juliet's beauty makes Romeo imagine that she is the sun, turning the darkness into daylight, and making the moon envious of her brightness and beauty. Shakespeare here uses the contrast between night and day, light and dark which is a motif that runs through the play. The imagery adds to the romantic tone of the scene, but it is also a foreshadowing of the conflicts to come.*

Evaluation   ## 3 Imagine the same scene took place today. Juliet would ...

Lösungsvorschlag   Juliet is on the balcony outside her room. She has been trying to contact her friend for a while, but she doesn't answer the phone. Now Juliet's phone has just rung, and it is her friend Viola.

Juliet: *Hi, Viola, what have you been up to? I've been trying to reach you for ages! Oh, not your battery again. Your telephone is never charged when I need you. Well, anyway, you know we had this party at our house tonight? I met the most amazing boy there! He is absolutely gorgeous!*

Romeo: (below the balcony, hears this and thinks to himself) *Oh no! I'll bet she fell for that stupid guy she was dancing with when I first saw her!*

Juliet: *Ssh, Viola, wait a minute, I think there is someone down there. No, it was just a cat. All right, so I met this great boy, and – Yes I know I'm supposed to fall for Paris, but just because my parents made me dance with him doesn't mean I like him, right?*

Romeo has trouble suppressing his joy.

Juliet: *So I talked to this charming, good-looking boy, and I really think I'm in love with him.*

Romeo grabs his mobile phone and starts texting like a madman.

Juliet: *Yes we kissed. Isn't that romantic? The only trouble is I think he is a Montague. At least I heard someone say so at the party. But even if that's true, I don't know how he could get in, my parents simply can't stand them. But names aren't important anyway, are they? Couldn't he change his name? Yeah, I suppose you're right; changing names*

4 Shakespeare the dramatist Love: Saying farewell

doesn't solve a problem. Wait – I think there is someone down there now – I'll ring back later, bye!

Evaluation

4 How do you think the scene continues? What might Romeo say …?

Lösungsvorschlag Romeo steps into the open and looks up at Juliet, who suddenly discovers him.

Juliet: (with a gasp and terribly embarrassed) *What are you doing down there? And how long have you been standing here?*

Romeo: (smiling) *Long enough to hear you say that you want me to be your love. May I come up?*

Juliet: (steps back and hesitates, but only a moment) *You may if you can, but don't make a noise. We don't want to alarm my parents!*

Romeo climbs up and jumps onto the balcony, where he immediately pulls Juliet into his arms.

Juliet: *Did you hear everything I said? That is so embarrassing!*

Romeo: *I don't know for how long you have been talking to yourself about me, but I heard enough to feel quite flattered.*

Juliet wriggles herself loose, but Romeo holds her and draws her back into his arms. As she tries to protest, he kisses her.

Romeo: *I love you, Juliet. You are the most beautiful and wonderful girl I've ever met.*

Juliet: *I love you too, Romeo!*

They kiss again.

Nurse: *Juliet? Juliet! Are you there?*

Romeo: *Who's that?*

Juliet: *That's Nurse. She's looking for me. You have to go now, Romeo! Hurry!*

Romeo: *When will I see you again? I can't leave without having something to look forward to!*

Juliet: (urgently) *I don't know, I can't think of anything right now, But I'll send nurse with a message. Where can she find you?*

Romeo: *At the market place, at noon. I'll be waiting there. I love you, Juliet! Bye!*

Juliet: *And I love you, my Romeo. Now hurry!*

They part with a kiss.

Evaluation

5 Choose a line, sentence or short section here that you find …

Lösungsvorschlag Individuelle S-Beiträge.

Erweiterung Ergänzender Vorschlag zur Arbeit mit den Fotos auf Seite 36 (Themenheft):
- *Describe and compare the pictures from various productions of "Romeo and Juliet".*
- *Try to think of ways in which the actors in the pictures would say their lines.*
- *Discuss which of the productions would you go to see if you had the choice.*

Drama excerpt

[11◉] Love: Saying farewell   p. 37

HINTERGRUNDINFO

*Once again the combat between **day and night** or, more generally, between light and dark is the motif that runs through the scene. Juliet attempts to change the world through language: she pretends that the lark is truly a nightingale and the breaking dawn only a meteor. Whereas in the balcony scene Romeo saw Juliet as turning night into day, here it is the other way around: day is night. But just as they were unable to cast off the feud that separates their families, they cannot change time. Reluctantly, they separate, and the scene ends on a glum note: "more light and light – more dark and dark our woes".*

Lernwortschatz *due, nightingale, lark, on tiptoe, misty, exhale, newlywed, out of tune, pomegranate, discord*

Materialien → CD, Track 11

Shakespeare the dramatist   Love: Saying farewell

4

Comprehension

1 Explain what Romeo and Juliet are disagreeing about here.

[11 ◉] L präsentiert den Textauszug von der CD. Hinweis auf die *Fact file* zu *Romeo and Juliet.*

Lösungsvorschlag *Romeo knows that he has to leave. By no means must he be caught in Juliet's bed: not only because he is a Montague, but also because nobody knows that they are secretly married and Juliet is promised to Paris. In addition, Romeo has been exiled from Verona for having slain Tybalt, and will be killed if he is found within the city walls. Romeo knows that he has to leave; he has noticed dawn breaking in the East, but Juliet does not want to let her husband go so soon. She knows what what challenges face her once he is gone.*

Analysis

2 Analyse the tools Romeo uses to change Juliet's mind.

Lösungsvorschlag *At first Romeo tries to persuade Juliet by telling her that what they both heard was the lark, an early morning bird, and not the nightingale, and by emphasising that he has already seen the sun breaking through the clouds in the East. He even refers to the danger that staying in her bed implies: "I must be gone and live or stay and die". But Juliet is not willing to give in yet. She persists that the light Romeo has seen is not the daylight and that he can stay. So Romeo pretends to give in to her and invents another explanation for the light he has seen to support Juliet's point of view. He says what he expects from staying – death – and that he does not mind dying because it is a consequence of Juliet's wish. Only at this point does Juliet realise her own selfishness and now urgently implores her lover to leave.*

Analysis

3 Romeo and Juliet *is, to a great extent, about the clash of opposites: ...*

Lösungsvorschlag *The most obvious opposite is the one between night and day. Whereas in the balcony scene Juliet was in Romeo's eyes the sun who turned night into day with her dazzling beauty, and Shakespeare stressed the opposite between this beauty and the pale, envious light of the moon, the enemy of the two lovers now is an envious sun (l. 7) because it separates them. The second opposite is the one between life and death: staying means certain death, but togetherness for another moment, leaving means life and separation. The symbolism of light and dark is stressed in the concluding lines, in which Romeo links the motif to their own fate: again a foreshadowing of the sorrows to come.*

Evaluation

4 Look at the cartoon of a modern Juliet and Romeo sending ...

Die S können diskutieren, was an der Situation von Romeo und Julia aus heutiger Perspektive anders wäre: Wie verfahren die Gerichte im Fall eines Totschlags aus Notwehr? Würde Julia sich gegen eine Zwangsheirat zur Wehr setzen müssen? Aus welchen Gründen würde Romeo sich beeilen müssen, Julias Schlafzimmer zu verlassen, und wie würde sie versuchen, ihn zu halten? Anhand der so zusammengetragenen modernen Aspekte können die S eine völlig neue Szene in modernem Englisch schreiben und vorspielen.

Lösungsvorschlag Individuelle S-Beiträge.

Analysis

5 Compare the love in this scene to that in the wooing scene from Richard III.

Zusatzmaterial → Kopiervorlage 12 (Juliet as an example of the question of gender)

Lösungsvorschlag *The wooing scene in "Richard III" starts with Anne expressing her hatred, not her love for Richard, so the basic theme of the scene is Richard's effort to persuade Anne that her real feelings are not hate and that she will see him in a different light once she has had time to think things over. But when Anne has left, Richard reveals his true feelings: he does not love her, but wishes to conquer her and do with her as he pleases: "I'll have her, but will not keep her long." Although the scene is resonant with phrases having to do with love ("thy lips were made for kissing", "true love", "vouchsafe to wear this ring", "my poor heart"), it is quite clear that neither*

67

4 | Shakespeare the dramatist Conscience: Macbeth's guilt

Anne nor Richard feels any love for the other. In the scene from "Romeo and Juliet" it is obvious that the two protagonists are passionately in love with each other. They have just spent the night together and are now reluctant to separate ("Therefore stay yet; thou need'st not to be gone", l. 16, "I have more care to stay than will to go", l. 23). Besides, they call each other "love" (l. 5, l. 7) and "my soul" (l. 25) and bemoan their fate, which forces them apart ("More light and light – more dark and dark our woes", l. 36).

Erweiterung
- Zur Vertiefung kann hier **Kopiervorlage 12** (Seite 118) eingesetzt werden.

- Es gibt zahlreiche Möglichkeiten, *Romeo and Juliet* kreativ im Unterricht zu bearbeiten. Hier ein paar Vorschläge, die sich auch dann umsetzen lassen, wenn die S nur mit diesen beiden Szenen und dem groben Handlungsverlauf vertraut sind:

  – *Juliet writes a letter to an agony aunt in which she explains her difficult situation: she has fallen in love with a young man that her parents do not approve of; instead they want to marry her off to someone else. What does the agony aunt answer?*

  – *A team of journalists report on teen killings in the streets of Verona. They interview neighbours, passers-by, families and friends of victims, town officials, and church representatives. What are their attitudes? What do they suggest? Create a radio or TV documentary or an article for a magazine.*

  – *Romeo's and Juliet's parents meet accidentally. They start quarrelling immediately, the Prince of Verona tries to step in and calm them down. Write the scene and act it out.*

Drama excerpt | **[12⊚] Conscience: Macbeth's guilt** | p. 38

HINTERGRUNDINFO

*Shakespeare's **"Macbeth"**, with only 2477 lines, is one of his shortest plays, a little more than half the length of "Hamlet". The first recorded performance of the play is 1611 in the Globe, but it must have been written well before that date, as some references to current events suggest. In fact, the whole play reflects the climate of conspiracy, show trials and fear that dominated London at the time. The memorable chiasmus "Fair is foul and foul is fair" that the witches pronounce at the end of the first scene of the play is the leitmotif of "Macbeth", and at the same time a sharp criticism of the period and the government.*

blurred. Phantoms of the imagination haunt the castle ("Is this a dagger which I see before me?", "Yet here's a spot", Banquo's ghost) and the Scottish heath becomes a witches' haunt. "Macbeth" is considered one of Shakespeare's finest plays. It may be hard to keep track of the large cast of characters with the sometimes confusing similarity between Scottish names, and for modern readers the supernatural forces may have lost some of the magic they conjured for Jacobean theatregoers, but Macbeth's riveting soliloquies and Lady Macbeth's terrifying imagery continue to captivate readers and audiences alike.

***Before the action begins,** Scottish troops have fought successfully against the army of Norway, which was supported by a Scottish traitor, the Thane of Cawdor. Macbeth has proved his courage and valour in this battle and is rewarded with the title of the traitor, who is executed. Macbeth's tragic descent begins here: the witches who open the play predicted that he would become Thane of Cawdor and king afterwards. His wife's and his own ambition spur him on, so that he murders Duncan to become king, then he murders his friend Banquo and other Scottish noblemen and their families in order to stay king. The noble war hero turns into a tyrannical murderer, who in the end gets what he deserves; in a hand-to-hand fight, Macduff kills Macbeth. Throughout the play, appearance and reality become*

*In the play, Lady Macbeth enters **at the end of the soliloquy** and is told that Macbeth does not want to go on with their plan. She is furious, calls him a coward and questions his love for her. Macbeth tries to shut her up, but she rages on, telling him that he is not a man, and with some of the most chilling lines of the play claims that she herself would stick to what she had promised to do – even if it resulted in killing her own baby. She sweeps away Macbeth's doubts with her ferocity, and impressed by his wife's conviction and determination he resolves to commit the deed. In one of her lines she says to her husband "We fail? / But screw your courage to the sticking place and we'll not fail." The picture might be taken at this moment, with Lady Macbeth "screwing" her husband's head in the right position.*

| | Shakespeare the dramatist   Conscience: Macbeth's guilt | **4** |

Lernwortschatz *conscience, guilt, judgment (also: judgement), justice, deed, to bear/bore/borne, meek, virtue, to stride/strode/stridden, intent*

Materialien → CD, Track 12 • Online-Link: 601005-0010

[12 ◎] Statt den Monolog von der CD vorzuspielen, kann er auch von den S paarweise vorgetragen werden. Dabei übernimmt jeweils ein S eine Zeile. Shakespeare verdeutlicht die innere Zerrissenheit Macbeths auch dadurch sprachlich, dass er ihn in diesem Monolog fast ausschließlich *run-on lines* sprechen lässt. Dies wird besonders deutlich, wenn die S sich beim Vortrag der Zeilen abwechseln. Sie sollten jedoch zuvor Gelegenheit haben, den Monolog in Ruhe für sich zu lesen und Aussprachehürden zu beseitigen. Hinweis auf die *Fact file* zu Macbeth.

Brainteaser   **1 *One of Shakespeare's most important themes was conscience.***

Lösungsvorschlag *A person's actions and thoughts are governed by moral and ethical principles, and the motivation for actions that derives logically from these principles is what we call conscience. It cannot be the same for everybody, as the principles which form the conscience are different. The greatest differences can be noted between different cultures. For example, for some religious groups it is perfectly all right to stone a woman to death for committing adultery. No one would even think of making adultery an official crime in our society, however, let alone of stoning someone to death for having committed it. But there are also differences within a society. For most people in our society, adultery is something you should not do, others have no moral qualms at all if they cheat on their partners; it is a part of their lifestyles. Conscience is not a static force. It is continuously shaped and reshaped with what we learn and with decisions we make. The more often we listen to it and accept new rules, the stronger it will become; the more often we decide against our conscience, the more obscure it will become.*

Erweiterung • Rex Gibson sieht in dem vorliegenden Redeauszug eine hervorragende Möglichkeit, die Gewissensnöte Macbeths für S dadurch erfahrbar zu machen, dass jeweils zwei S sich die Hand geben und die jeweiligen Argumente hin und her bewegen, als ob sie Holz sägen würden. Hierbei werden die jeweiligen Gedanken gleichzeitig ausgesprochen.

• Weiterhin bietet es sich an, das dramatische Potential dieser Szene, das durch die besondere Fülle von rhetorischen Mitteln wie *imagery, repetition, lists, antithesis* und *compulsing rhythms* geprägt ist, für eine szenische Darstellung nach eigenen Vorstellungen zu nutzen. Als Vorübung kann der Text kopiert und die Stilmittel von den S farbig markiert werden (siehe Rex Gibson, *Teaching Shakespeare*, Cambridge, 1998, Seite 75 ff.).

Comprehension   **2 *Outline the main aspects of Macbeth's speech.***

Lösungsvorschlag *Macbeth is trying to make up his mind whether to kill Duncan or not. One of the prophecies of the witches has come true; he is Thane of Cawdor, and the only way to fulfil the second prophecy and become king of Scotland is to kill the present king. In this speech Macbeth grapples with his conscience, considering all the facts that speak against committing regicide. He comes to the conclusion that the only motivation he has for killing the king is his own ambition.*

Analysis   **3 *Analyse the way in which Macbeth's conscience works. List the reasons ...***

Lösungsvorschlag *At the beginning of his soliloquy Macbeth considers the risk that killing the king implies: he cannot be sure of the outcome because he cannot maintain control of all the consequences ("If th' assassination could trammel up the consequence", l. 3). He is afraid of earthly judgement ("But in these cases, we still have judgment here; that we but teach bloody instructions, which, being taught, return to plague th' inventor", ll. 7–10). Besides, he realises that Duncan is a good king ("this Duncan hath borne his faculties so meek, hath been so clear in his great office, that his virtues will plead like angels, trumpet-tongu'd, against the deep damnation of his taking-off", ll. 16 ff.). Macbeth is Duncan's relative and his subject, and perhaps most importantly, Duncan is his guest – all of which are good reasons to protect him rather than to murder him, which he*

69

4 Shakespeare the dramatist   Order and disorder: Macbeth disrupts stability

knows is "a horrid deed" (l. 24). What does not count for him at all is the afterlife and heavenly judgement: "we'd jump the life to come" (l. 7).

Analysis

4 Explain the last sentence of the soliloquy. What does it tell us ...?

Lösungsvorschlag

Macbeth realises that the driving force for his actions is his ambition ("I have no spur to prick the sides of my intent", l. 25) and is quite clear about the qualities of this force. It is "vaulting" and "o'erleaps itself, and falls on th'other" (ll. 27–28), which means that it makes him rush to take decisions that might lead to disaster. It seems that at the end of his soliloquy Macbeth has realised that this ambition is an insufficient justification for murdering the king and is resolved not to commit the deed.

Evaluation

5 This photo shows Macbeth and his wife right after ...

Lösungsvorschlag

The picture shows Macbeth grinding his teeth, open-mouthed, eyes closed, as if he was in pain or deeply troubled, with Lady Macbeth standing behind him and clutching his head with both her hands, her eyes focused on her husband. It seems as if Macbeth has just told her something that she is not happy with (perhaps that he does not want to kill the king) and now she is trying to change his mind (he must commit the deed so that she can become queen).

Erweiterung

Die S können einen Monolog für Lady Macbeth schreiben, in dem sie über das eben Erlebte nachdenkt – wie schwierig es war, Macbeth auf ihren Weg einzuschwören, welche Schwächen ihr Mann hat, inwiefern diese Schwächen dem Ziel noch im Weg stehen werden, was ihre eigene Rolle sein wird. Um ihnen die Aufgabe zu erleichtern, kann ihnen der Monolog Macbeths in modernem Englisch vorgelegt werden (im Internet zu finden unter http://nfs.sparknotes.com/macbeth/page_40.html).

Drama excerpt/
Factual
information

[13 ◉] Order and disorder: Macbeth disrupts stability   pp. 39–40

HINTERGRUNDINFO

The Elizabethans' world picture *was, despite the fact that theirs was an age of learning and discovery, to a large extent a simplified version of the complicated medieval picture. The universe was arranged in a fixed system of hierarchies, but subject to modification by humans' sins. Elizabethans pictured this hierarchy in the form of a chain of being that stretched from God's throne at the top down to the lowest elements of creation (rocks). On this level, there is mere existence, the inanimate class: liquids, the elements and metals, which again are hierarchically ordered. Water, for instance, is nobler than earth, gold nobler than brass. On the next level there is life, the vegetative class, in which the oak is nobler than the bramble. Then comes the sensitive class: life and feeling. This leads up to humanity, a state of being that has life, feelings, and understanding, and is surpassed only by the purely rational or spiritual creatures, the angels. The Elizabethans were terrified that this order might be upset, obsessed as they were by the fear of chaos, which to them meant anarchy on a cosmic scale. Visible signs of disorder like uproar in nature or unnatural behaviour of animals appalled them*

because of their suggestion that the hierarchical order of the world itself was upset. Shakespeare often refers to this idea in his plays. In "Troilus and Cressida", Ulysses says: "O, when degree is shaked / Which is the ladder to all high designs, / Then enterprise is sick! How could communities, / Degrees in schools and brotherhoods in cities, / Peaceful commerce from dividable shores, / The primogenitive and due of birth, / Prerogative of age, crowns, sceptres, laurels, / But by degree, stand in authentic place? / Take but degree away, untune that string, / And, hark, what discord follows!"
The speech is a fine example of the Renaissance preoccupation with order, and reveals what Shakespeare himself thought about it: acting without regard to authority or order has horrific, terrible consequences. It will bring about the downfall of the usurper, but society as a whole will suffer first. For more information on the Elizabethan world picture see Eustace M. Tillyard: "The Elizabethan World Picture" (Pimlico Books: London, 1998) or http://web.cn.edu/KWHEELER/Tillyard01.html for Tillyard in a nutshell.

70

Shakespeare the dramatist   Order and disorder: Macbeth disrupts stability   4

"Macbeth" in its historical context – a time of unrest: The connections of "Macbeth" to the Gunpowder Plot and Garnet's trial are useful in dating the play, but read from the point of view of the playwright, who according to new research in all likelihood was himself a Catholic, the play contains numerous, albeit allegorically veiled allusions to the disastrous situation for Catholics in England during the early reign of James I. In the 1590s many English Catholics looked to James I, son of a devout Catholic mother, with hopes and expectations, since he had promised relief for the Catholics. But James went back on his word. When he became King of England in 1603, he proclaimed that the severe anti-Catholic penal laws would remain unchanged. His book on witchcraft, "Daemonology", was used to intensify the hunt for "witches" in Catholic areas, and after the Gunpowder Plot measures against Catholics became even more draconian. In "Macbeth", the protagonist is initially a hero, but becomes the embodiment of evil. When Duncan in Act I, Scene 4, says of the traitor that

"There's no art / To find the mind's construction in the face: / He was a gentleman on whom I built / an absolute trust" he can not know that the same is true of his "valiant cousin" Macbeth, and Catholics who had set their hopes on James I may have thought that it was a fitting description of their present king. One of the few references Shakespeare makes to his religious beliefs in his plays can be found in this scene. The characters on stage are introduced as "Old Man" and "Ross"; later Macduff joins them. However, the Old Man is addressed as "father" by Ross and Macduff. "Father" is a title of reference for church dignitaries such as monks and priests, and fittingly enough this father sends both on their way at the end of the scene with a blessing: "God's benison go with you; and with those / That would make good of bad, and friends of foes." Seen from a Catholic point of view, there is a priest complaining on stage about the uproar in nature, which is a reflection of the chaos in society, and blessing those who intend to improve that situation.

Lernwortschatz   *to disrupt, stability, score, to entomb, obedience, sovereignty, to comprise, enlightened, to consist of, manifestation, decisive, to ponder sth, option*

Materialien   → CD, Track 13

[13 ◉]   Bevor der Textauszug von der CD präsentiert wird, erfolgt ein Hinweis auf die *Fact file* zu Macbeth. Außerdem können bereits hier die beiden *Fact files* zu *Ghosts and the supernatural* (Themenheft, Seite 40) und zu *The chain of being* (Themenheft, Seite 43) hinzugezogen werden.

Comprehension   ### 1 Summarise the scene.

Lösungsvorschlag   *In this scene, Ross and an old man discuss the strange and portentous events of the past few days. Although it is daytime, it is dark outside – an owl was seen killing a falcon – and Duncan's beautiful and well-trained horses turned wild and even ate one another. Macduff joins them and is asked if he has any information on who killed Duncan. He answers that suspicion has fallen on the chamberlains, who must have been paid off by someone, most likely by the two princes, Malcom and Donalbain, since they have fled. Regarding Ross' conclusion that in that case Macbeth will probably be the next king, Macduff answers that Macbeth has already been named and gone to Scone to be crowned. Ross will follow him there and attend the coronation, whereas Macduff intends to return home to Fife.*

Analysis   ### 2 Make a list of the examples of disorder Ross and the old man talk ...

Lösungsvorschlag   **Examples of disorder**
- *although it is daytime, it is very dark outside (ll. 7–11)*
- *a falcon, a bird that hunts in daytime, was attacked and killed by an owl, a nocturnal hunting bird which usually preys on mice, not on other birds*
- *Duncan's horses, known as obedient and beautiful creatures, have turned against each other and against their masters*
- *the common elements are that some natural laws seem to have been reversed, and that hierarchical orders are turned upside down: the falcon "towering in her pride of place" is a noble bird, superior to the owl, and the horses, servants of men in wars now "make war with mankind"*

71

4 | Shakespeare the dramatist Order and disorder: Macbeth disrupts stability

Analysis **3 *Analyse the way in which Shakespeare links order and ...***

Lösungsvorschlag *The murder of King Duncan has destabilised society and caused confusion. It is uncertain who really killed the king, or who ordered the murder, and the coronation of Macbeth is only possible because the prince who would have succeeded his father has fled. The orderly way of things has been disrupted by the regicide. In this scene Shakespeare links disorder in society to disorder in nature. The confusion in society caused by the murder is reflected in nature. The noble falcon "tow'ring in her pride of place" was killed by an owl, as Duncan, the noble king, was killed by a murderer who chose the dark night for his deed. The description of the horses turning against each other and refusing to obey might be seen as a foreshadowing of the conflicts between the Thanes that ensue from Macbeth's usurpation. The fact that it is dark even though it is daytime is a hint at the dark times that lie ahead.*

Evaluation **4 *In another one of Shakespeare's plays,* Troilus and Cressida, ...**

Wenn auf die *Fact file* zu *Ghosts and the supernatural* noch nicht eingegangen wurde, wird sie jetzt von den S in Stillarbeit gelesen.

Lösungsvorschlag ***Aspects the students might mention***
- *Macbeth is crowned, but some Thanes have doubts about the rightfulness of this coronation and threaten him, a conflict that will ultimately lead to the outbreak of civil war.*
- *The princes who have fled organise an army to take back what is rightfully theirs.*
- *Macduff's decision not to take part in the coronation but to go back to Fife instead might be seen as a first act of revolt against the new king, so that he could play a vital part in the fight against Macbeth.*

Erweiterung Die dramatische Entwicklung vom Helden zum Tyrannen, die Macbeth durchläuft, bietet zahlreiche Möglichkeiten der weiteren kreativen Bearbeitung im Unterricht, die sowohl einen kommunikativen und handlungsorientierten Ansatz verwirklichen als auch die Relevanz der Thematik für unsere Zeit verdeutlichen. Mögliche Erweiterungen sind:

- In Form einer Sondernachrichtensendung wird über die Situation in Schottland berichtet. Eine Nachrichtensprecherin im Studio fasst die bisherigen Ereignisse zusammen, Interviewpartner im Studio (z.B. Ross, Macduff) werden zu ihren Eindrücken und ihrer Einschätzung der Lage befragt, Reporter vor Ort befragen einfache Leute (*Old Man*) und versuchen eine Stellungnahme der neuen Würdenträger zu ergattern (Lady Macbeth, Macbeth).
- Szenen werden dazu geschrieben, die im Drama selbst nicht auftauchen: *Macduff* berichtet – zu Hause angekommen – seiner Frau von den Ereignissen und diskutiert die weitere Vorgehensweise mit ihr.
- Die bisherigen Ereignisse oder die selbst geschriebene Zusammenfassung des weiteren Verlaufs des Dramas wird aus der Perspektive einer einzelnen Person zusammengefasst: wie sieht z.B. Lady Macbeth ihre Rolle in dem Drama? Wird sie von Selbstzweifeln und Selbstvorwürfen geplagt, oder schiebt sie die Schuld an der Katastrophe ihrem Mann in die Schuhe? Wie sieht eine Hofdame die Entwicklung am schottischen Hof?
- Die S gestalten eine eigene Nachrichtenseite, in der über die Krönung berichtet wird. Welche Schwerpunkte werden gesetzt? Wie kritisch ist die Berichterstattung? Was für Bilder zeigen das neue Königspaar?

Drama excerpt **[14⊙] The supernatural: Hamlet learns the truth** — p. 41

HINTERGRUNDINFO

Ghosts appear in only four plays by Shakespeare: "Richard III", "Julius Caesar", "Hamlet" and "Macbeth". This could lead to the conclusion that the element of the supernatural might be of minor importance. Quite to the contrary, not only are references to supernatural beings and popular beliefs in superstitions abundant in his plays, but Elizabethan society was also very interested in metaphysical questions. In the history of drama this can be seen in the renewed interest in translations of plays by Seneca as well as the tradition of the morality plays. Seneca often started plays with a ghost functioning as a messenger to inform the audience by means of an expository flashback as well as an analysis of the tragic hero's entanglement between "guilt and revenge", followed by a prophesy about the further course of the action. In classic drama the ghost scene thus had a very important function to guide the audience in its expectations about the outcome of the play as well as to provide a means of condensing the dramatic action. Elizabethan drama, however, was more interested in the presentation of characters in action rather than that of an overuling moral principle. In this development the ghost scene was increasingly used in the process of presenting the connection between the cause of sin and its necessary repentance. The Elizabethans were much more interested in the question of whether the ghost demanding revenge might be a manifestation of the devil rather than a divine minister. This is one of the reasons that ghost scenes developed into a much more dramatic mode. The ghost scene in its narrower sense offered the playwright a number of important functions for his dramatic art, yet it took a gifted playwright, as such a scene could also become utterly unconvincing and ridiculous even for spectators during the Elizabethan Age. This period is one of a gradual liberation from medieval thought. The Reformation in England did not result in old beliefs disappearing completely. This can be seen in the fact that next to the constant threat of a return to Catholicism which still held the idea of a necessary "purgatory", the belief in good or evil ghosts was still maintained. According to protestant belief, the existence of any supernatural wonder or any form of angel or benevolent spirit had finished with the creation of the first church by the Apostles. Any form of supernatural apparition, good or bad, must therefore be a manifestation of the devil. This position was taken by no one less than King James I, who in his "Daemonology", one of the most important publications on the question of the supernatural of the period, very strongly supported the Protestant position. No wonder that it is in "Hamlet" that we find the question concerning the character of the ghost to be worked out in such great detail and influence on the plot.

It is significant for the period that Elizabethans managed to keep the belief in the old world order such as that of "cosmic correspondences" or the "chain of being" despite new scientific findings, increasingly focussing on a more anthropocentric world view. Shakespeare found himself on the verge of a new era of thought concentrating on the conflict between humankind and nature. One of the central ideas is that natural behaviour is seen as being virtuous, and a shortage of it will lead to destruction. Another conflict lies in the confrontation in which a supernatural force takes a threatening stance and makes it impossible for people to distinguish clearly between good and evil, virtue and vice, as can be seen best in "Macbeth". This lack of clarity is a key to the dramatic function of a ghost scene where the nature of a ghost lies – according to popular folklore – in its lack of physical definition. Any danger that might be coming from such a lack of clarity is made even stronger by the notion that a ghost might act of its own accord and be able to offer shelter or cause destruction. This is a significant parallel to the question of "moral ambiguity" which was very important in Shakespeare's time. The second element taken up from popular superstition is the belief that ghosts would only appear in the middle of the night when they were covered by darkness and their victims' presence of mind was restricted due to their lack of sleep. In Shakespeare's ghost scenes the motif of dream and sleeplessness is significant.

One of the strongest arguments for the playwright to use a **ghost scene** thus lies in the chance of plurisignation of reality for the audience. For them a ghost could be a manifestation of a higher link in the chain of being or that of a demonic power – a living dead person – breaking into the human world from a hostile environment. Elizabethans were still open to a belief in popular superstition and Shakespeare made sure to cater for their tastes yet used these elements to serve a function in the dramatic framework. The extent to which this aim was put into practice can be seen when comparing the four plays with ghost scenes. At the beginning of his career Shakespeare used the isolated ghost scene which was made popular by the genre of the revenge tragedy, started by Thomas Kyd's "Spanish Tragedy". Such a development can be seen from the

4 Shakespeare the dramatist The supernatural: Hamlet learns the truth

repetitive chorus of Richard's victims to the mental torture of Macbeth, whose guilty conscience inside his mind alone conjures up the vision of Banquo's ghost, not only convincing the guests at the banquet but surely also the audience.

Lernwortschatz *to be bound to do sth, to be doomed, to be confined, to fast, quill*

Materialien → CD, Track 14 • Online-Link: 601005-0011

Als Einstieg wird noch einmal auf die *Fact file* zu *Ghosts and the supernatural* (Seite 40) verwiesen. Denkbar ist auch ein Vorgriff auf die *Fact file* zu *The chain of being* (Seite 43).

Comprehension

1 *What information does the ghost give Hamlet?*

Zusatzmaterial → Kopiervorlage 13 (Feel the rhythm and power)

[14 ◉] Die S hören den Dialog bei geöffneten Schülerbüchern und klären danach das Globalverständnis. Während einer zweiten Präsentation von der CD machen sie sich stichwortartig Notizen zu den Inhalten der Szene. Alternativ kann das Verfassen einer kurzen Inhaltsangabe auch als schriftliche **Hausaufgabe** gestellt werden.

Lösungsvorschlag *The ghost claims to be the spirit of Hamlet's father, whose fate it is to walk at night until someone revenges the crimes that were committed during his lifetime. The ghost indicates that he might be able to reveal some details of the nature of purgatory, yet does not want to tell his son because the details are so terrible that they would frighten young Hamlet. This lack of clarity might prepare Hamlet and indeed the audience for the order the ghost then gives. Hamlet is to revenge the murder of his father. Murder in itself is a terrible act, yet this murder is, according to the ghost's message, even more hideous. This deed was the murder of a just king, murdered by his brother while he was sleeping, unaware of any mischief that might befall him. The centre of the realm (here: the ear, the organ that takes up language) was used to kill the second highest link in the chain of being. The homicidal brother then became the new king, marrying Hamlet's mother, an act which is later called "incest". Hamlet senses a call to action to set the system of justice right again, not knowing whether he can trust this apparition.*

Erweiterung
- Die Textausgabe von Rex Gibson bietet eine Reihe von Übungen zur szenischen Interpretation dieses Textauszugs an. Zur Vorbereitung einer möglichst eindringlichen Vertonung dieser schaurigen Szene sollten die S mit der Stimme experimentieren, um Geräusche aus dem Purgatorium zu erzeugen. Als visueller Impuls für die Auseinandersetzung mit der Vorstellung des Purgatoriums können Bilder von Hieronymus Bosch dienen. Die Reaktion Hamlets auf die Rede des Geistes kann von den S in Partnerarbeit in der Form von Tableaux umgesetzt werden (siehe R. Andrews/Rex Gibson, *Hamlet*, Cambridge, 1994, Seite 44).

- Hier bietet sich ergänzend der Einsatz von **Kopiervorlage 13** (Seite 119) an.

Analysis

2 *Analyse the various themes touched upon in this passage.*

Diese Aufgabe kann entweder im Unterrichtsgespräch oder in häuslicher Vorbereitung bearbeitet werden. Auch ein arbeitsteiliges Vorgehen mit Hilfe von Rechercheaufgaben zu einzelnen thematischen Aspekten ist denkbar.

Lösungsvorschlag *The value of this particular scene can be seen in the fact that it touches upon a variety of different themes. To mention just a few:*

Reality vs. appearance
The use of a ghost scene coincides with one of the key themes of drama, the question of whether the presentation on the stage is real or not. Do I take it to be the truth and can thus allow myself to be fooled? Originally a means of informing the audience about the fate of the protagonist, the rising degree of verisimilitude in the presentation of the drama fails to provide any more clarity to the audience members when they have to decide about the question of dramatic irony. The fact that a ghost is presented in a life-like fashion could also be used to

leave the audience in doubt as to its nature rather than to give them more information and thus a greater amount of knowledge than the characters. This deliberate lack of information in the spectators is used by the playwright to create a higher degree of tension.

Superstition
This scene shows that despite the influence of humanism, the Elizabethan period was still full of people who believed wholeheartedly in superstitions.

The supernatural
The confrontation of a human being with supernatural forces and his dependency on them is probably older than the history of drama. When on stage, the actors could refer to these powers either in the beautifully painted heavens with the zodiac signifying the realm of the gods or in the space underneath the stage which could be entered through the trapdoor. In "Hamlet" the ghost's origin is hinted at when Hamlet refers to it as a "sad old mole", indicating its origin as being underneath the stage.

Death
As the passage is taken from a tragedy, it naturally deals with the topic of death, yet here it receives extra emphasis as an example of regicide. The topic of murdering a king has a special relevance when seen in connection with the traditional concept of the chain of being.

The chain of being
This image represents the traditional view of a hierarchical structure of creation from the inanimate elements and animals to humankind as the height of creation, with royalty as its top, functioning as a link to the gods. In this scene the concept of humanity's sins culminates in the fact that the current state is rotten to its core as the new young king himself has murdered the old and just king.

Revenge
"Hamlet" is one of the most famous examples of the genre "revenge tragedy" initiated by Kyd's "Spanish Tragedy". Yet Shakespeare takes the development of the theme of revenge in "Hamlet" a lot further as here the protagonist himself has to commit a murder to take revenge, relying solely on his assessment of the ghost's reliability. His tragic flaw is heightened by the fact that whatever action he takes he will be a victim. Remaining inactive would cause shame to his family, yet killing the king burdens him with a capital sin which can only be answered for by his own death.

Ambition
The theme of ambition can be seen at the very end of the passage with reference to Claudius, who killed old Hamlet in order to wear the crown and have Hamlet's mother Gertrude become his wife.

Love
The theme of love can be traced in this passage to the love between father and son which the ghost of Old Hamlet shows in his attempt to spare Hamlet too many cruel details of his present state, to his question regarding young Hamlets ever having loved his father' and to Prince Hamlet's willingness to take revenge.

Power
The theme of power of course is discussed when a king is involved as a character. In this scene it is not only the power of royalty and respect caused by a royal father, but the power of the supernatural fighting against the unlawful gain of power.

Order and disorder
"Something is rotten in the state of Denmark" has become a set phrase in modern English as well as in German. This scene focuses on the idea of a balanced system of power turned into chaos as a result of the violation of the "divine right of kings" a concept very well known in times after the reformation.

Guilt
Whatever the protagonist undertakes, he will be guilty. Later in the play Hamlet refers to this dilemma when he sees himself as both "scourge and minister" to the actions of the gods,

4   Shakespeare the dramatist   The supernatural: Hamlet learns the truth

depending on his perception of the ghost as an "honest ghost" or an "incarnation of the devil". Shakespeare is well aware of the problem of giving away his personal preference regarding this question. From this it seems noteworthy that he seems to have been more interested in presenting a dramatic conflict rather than a theological dispute.

Erweiterung

Most of the above themes could be extended by looking at further examples of references from the whole play, e.g.

- *The theme of "death" could also be discussed in connection with the question of suicide raised at Hamlet's famous soliloquy as well as by studying the character of Ophelia.*
- *The revenge motif finds a plainer parallel in the play itself in Laertes' desire to revenge the death of Ophelia.*
- *The contrast between love vs. lust in the above scene indicated by the ghost's reference to the unlawful gain of the crown can be discussed at greater depth in the following scene, as well as by contrasting the relationship between Hamlet and his son to the treatment Ophelia receives from her father Polonius.*

Analysis

3 Analyse the atmosphere of the text and how it is achieved.

Zusatzmaterial   → Kopiervorlage 14 (Tossing lines)

Lösungsvorschlag

The atmosphere of the text

The scene is full of suspense throughout. Before analysing the text, one must consider that the setting is on an windy outdoor guard-platform in the middle of the night. The ghost has already been seen by Horatio and Marcellus, but it did not speak them. According to folklore which the Elizabethan audience would have been well aware of, ghosts can only be seen and can only talk to those for whom they have a direct message. The fact that in this scene the ghost speaks for the first time is in itself an important factor for creating tension. Unlike other ghost scenes, in which the apparition delivers his message in the form of a monologue, the fact that this scene is interrupted by short exclamations from Hamlet heightens the level of authenticity.

The dialogue starts with Hamlet boldly charging the "thing" that crosses his way and is preparing to leave. He addresses the ghost directly by ordering it to speak, claiming to be ready to hear the ghost's message. With the first question the ghost informs Hamlet and the audience what the main topic of this scene and indeed the whole play is about: revenge. The ghost asks one of the most important questions regarding the protagonist. Will Hamlet be able to carry out this duty? From the very beginning the ghost scene sets the focus on the question of how the hero will perform, rather than what the course of action will be like.

Language tools that create a highly charged atmosphere

- *The choice of words stressing fear, e.g. "doomed", "fast in fires", "foul", "harrow up thy soul".*
- *Intensified by powerful*
  - *images of fear, e.g. "freeze thy blood", "make your eyes start from their spheres", "your knotted hair open up and stand on end like quills upon the porpentine",*
  - *images used by Hamlet to underline his quick resolution to act, e.g. wings as swift as meditation or the thoughts of love", contrasted by the ghost with*
  - *images of inaction, e.g. "duller than the fat weed that roots itself on Lethe wharf", to indicate the amount of criticism waiting for him in case Hamlet fails to respond to this task.*
- *The ghost heightens the tension by repeatedly indicating the degree of secrecy involved with his visit and making vague references to the place he has come from, e.g. "I am ... confined", "I am forbid to tell the secrets", "prison house", "I could a tale unfold", "it must not be".*
- *Contrasts, e.g. "lightest word" vs. "eternal blazon", "thy dear father" vs. "murder most foul", "father's spirit" vs. "ears of flesh and blood".*
- *Hyperbole, e.g. "each particular hair to stand on end", "eternal blazon", "didst ever thy dear father love", "most unnatural murder", "murder most foul, as in the best it is".*
- *Rhetorical questions and phrases, e.g. "if thou didst ever thy dear father love", "wouldst thou not stir in this".*

Shakespeare the dramatist   The supernatural: Hamlet learns the truth   **4**

- *Repetition and anaphora, e.g. "List, list, o, list", "Revenge his foul and most unnatural murder. Murder! Murder most foul, as in the best it is; But this most foul, strange, and unnatural."*
- *Exclamations, e.g. "O God!", "Murder!", "O my prophetic soul!"*

After the intensive dialogue between father and son in which the ghost has discovered Hamlet's readiness for action, the scene culminates in the ghost finally telling the protagonist and the audience the details about his death. These details are significant foundations for the assessment of all further action to come. The ghost starts by ordering his son to listen carefully. He then uses an extremely strong and telling image by referring to the "whole ear of Denmark" as the centre. This image reflects the belief of the time of the correspondence between "macrocosm and microcosm". The ear of the king was not only a gateway for the process of murder, but it is the ear (i.e. the centre) of the state that is foul. Thus the whole society is corrupt and must be corrected.

This strongly charged verdict is accompanied by significant, almost religious vocabulary; ("serpent" to kill "sleep", the "prophetic soul" of the "noble youth" has always feared receiving this terrible information) and images (e.g. the same snake is now the new king). A final important aspect which may be overlooked is the fact that there is no difference between the language of the ghost and that of Hamlet. By gradually moving away from a fixed form, which was closely rhetorically structured (as we can see e.g. in "Richard III"), this scene emancipates itself from the established tradition of ghost scenes of its time. The higher the degree of verisimilitude in the presentation of the ghost, the higher is the acceptance by both Hamlet and the audience to see it as an acting character and thus to believe what it says.

Connected with the atmospheric quality of the scene are the ghost's different functions for the play. In this scene three main functions can be made out. Like traditional ghost scenes it has a referential function as it supplies the plot with necessary background information. Secondly, it is its emphatic quality which maintains the connection to the audience by making them shudder, thus maintaining the dramatic tension. In this respect the ghost scenes in Hamlet show quite a remarkable development only to be surpassed perhaps by the appearance of Banquo's ghost in "Macbeth". A third important aspect in favour of integrating a ghost scene, apart from that of a high degree of expression, is its appellative function, which is made particularly strong here through the order the ghost gives to Hamlet to act.

Generally speaking, the more different functions a single scene offers to the complexity of the play, the more valuable it becomes as a tool for the playwright. This is one of the reasons for the popularity of ghost scenes in classic and Renaissance drama.
(siehe M. Pfister, Das Drama, München, 1982, Seite 151 ff.)

Erweiterung

- Als Ergänzung bietet sich hier der Einsatz von **Kopiervorlage 14** (Seite 120) an.

- Ein guter Weg, den S die Bedeutung von Eingangsszenen zu erschließen, besteht darin, den Dialogtext kopiert in einzelne Streifen zu schneiden und an die S zu verteilen. Die Gruppe sitzt oder steht im Kreis, die S sprechen ihre Zeile und werfen dabei einen Gegenstand (z. B. einen Ball) einem Mitschüler zu, der daraufhin seine Zeile spricht und den Gegenstand dem nächsten zuwirft, usw. Diese auf den ersten Blick banale Übung hat eine Vielzahl von Stärken. Durch die Elementarisierung des Textes werden Textprobleme sofort erkannt und können behandelt werden. Die S üben spielerisch die Aussprache und die Struktur des Textes.

- In einem weiteren Schritt können auf Folie vorbereitete Streifen des Textes von den S in die richtige Reihenfolge gebracht werden. Nach einer Weile ist den S so der ganze Text gut bekannt und „gehört ihnen" im Sinne der Funktion von *ownership*. Jetzt können signifikante Aspekte einer Interpretation erörtert werden. Ähnlich wie in vergleichbaren Eingangsszenen besteht ihre Funktion auch hier darin, das Thema zu bereiten, z. B. die Angst vor dem Übernatürlichen, die Dunkelheit und Kälte usw. hervorzuheben. An dieser Szene kann auch der Wechsel in der Anredeform thematisiert werden. Ein solcher Wechsel in der Anredeform deutet immer auf etwas Besonderes in der Szene hin. Der deutlichste Beleg hierfür ist Lady Macbeth, die Macbeth zunächst mit dem vertrauten *thou* anredet, sobald sie aber Zweifel an der Entschlusskraft ihres Gatten hegt, zum förmlicheren *you* wechselt. Dieser Hinweis, wie auch eine Fülle weiterer pragmatischer Hilfestellungen besonders zur Sprache Shakespeares, finden sich bei Ben Crystal, *Shakespeare on Toast*, Cambridge, 2008.

4   Shakespeare the dramatist   The supernatural: Hamlet and Gertrude

- Ein ganze Reihe von Übungen, die auch für nicht englische Muttersprachler geeignet sind, um eine kreative szenische Interpretation dieses Textauszugs vorzubereiten, bietet James Stredder, *The North Face of Shakespeare*, Cambridge, 2009, Seite 187 ff.

Drama excerpt   **[15 ◉] The supernatural: Hamlet and Gertrude**   pp. 42–43

HINTERGRUNDINFO

*This second encounter between **Hamlet and the ghost** of his father is another very significant scene for the whole play as it is marks a decisive climax for the whole plot. The ghost ordered Hamlet to take revenge but to spare his former wife, Hamlet's mother. After the play-in-a-play has convinced Hamlet that the ghost has spoken the truth, he had one chance to kill his step-father while Claudius was praying. Hamlet decided against it and shortly after was punished for this by accidentally killing the spying Polonius. The main difference of this ghost scene to that in Act I is that now a second character, Gertrude, is present. According to folklore, ghosts only appeared to those they were allowed to contact, so Gertrude is not able to see or hear the ghost and takes Hamlet reaction to the appearance of the ghost as proof that her son has gone mad. (This further development in the presentation of a ghost scene, the idea that ghosts do not appear in any significant form but are able to torture the mind of*

the victim is finally brought to perfection in "Macbeth".) The plot structure is thus even more complex than that of the earlier ghost scene as it mixes elements of dialogue with the appearance of monologue. The purpose for the ghost to appear again at this point in the plot is to renew his order for Hamlet to take revenge because the prince seems too hesitatant and at the same the ghost wants to prevent him from killing his mother in an outburst of uncontrolled rage. The main scope of this scene, apart from the questions connected with the supernatural is that of the ethical conflict between "love" and "lust". In very strong words Hamlet appeals to his mother to leave her new husband by criticizing her for having low moral standards, manifested by her marrying his uncle to satiate her craving for sex and power. Although having killed Polonius, Hamlet himself is already beyond a point of no return, he nevertheless still tries to save his mother.

Lernwortschatz   *vice, shreds, tardy, to chide, capable, temperate, to trespass*

Materialien   → CD, Track 15

Analysis   **1 *Point out the arguments on both sides of the dialogue.***

[15 ◉]   L präsentiert den Dialog von der CD. Erneuter Hinweis auf die *Fact file* zu *The chain of being*.

Lösungsvorschlag

Hamlet	Gertrude
• *The royal bed is stained, the kingdom is corrupt. It is not love that you show, it is lust. (ll. 6–8)*	• *Don't hurt my feelings, I am your mother and this is too much to bear. (ll. 1–4, l. 18)* • *Has no answer but despairs. (l. 17)* • *What is wrong with you? (l. 35)*
• *Claudius is not only a murderer, he is the very opposite of a divine king; he is the manifestation of vice. (ll. 12–17)* • *(to the ghost) Do not scorn me for not having revenged you yet. (ll. 24–27)* • *(to Gertrude) Can't you see how sad your former husband is? (ll. 44 ff.)*	• *Has no answer but despairs. (l. 17)* • *What is wrong with you? (l. 35)*
• *(to the ghost) Your sadness might hinder me from my action that needs courage. (ll. 46–49)* • *(to Gertrude) Look at my father in his royal clothing! (ll. 55 ff.)*	• *Who are you talking to? I don't see or hear anybody but us. (ll. 50–54)*

Shakespeare the dramatist   The supernatural: Hamlet and Gertrude   **4**

Hamlet	Gertrude
• *I am not ecstatic! My pulse is as calm as yours. Test me! I can give you much stronger words that usually result from madness. (ll. 63–67)* • *Do not give in to that "flattering unction" lust and the corruption of morals. Repent the past and avoid any further wrongdoings. (ll. 68–74)* • *Forgive me for being so strict, but morals are topsy turvy now. (ll. 75–77)*	• *You are mad and madness can create visions! (l. 59)*

Analysis

2 *Examine the tone of the language used by the three different speakers.*

Lösungsvorschlag

The tone of this passage is manifold and might perhaps be analysed best by following the three speakers through their utterances one by one.

Gertrude sets the early tone of the passage with her words of fear and injury ("thou turn'st my eyes into my very soul", "I see … spots … [that] will not leave their tinct". She begs her son three times to stop his accusations ("no more") as his "words are like daggers".

Hamlet accuses his mother very harshly using extremely aggressive language ("rank sweat" of an "enseamed bed, stewed in corruption"), comparing it to a pigsty and thus his mother to a pig. He shows his hatred of Claudius, calling him a "murderer and a villain! A slave", "a vice of kings" (referring to the medieval morality plays), a plain cutpurse (thieves were hanged in Shakespeare's day). Suddenly, when he mocks King Claudius ("a king of shreds and patches"), his tone changes abruptly and he shows fear, invoking the angels ("you heavenly guards") to help him against the returning ghost (for the audience he is thus building up the corresponding pair of heaven and hell).

Meanwhile, *Gertrude* changes her tone to that of motherly pity for her son ("Alas, he's mad!").

The ghost starts to speak in a very authoritative tone ("do not forget … blunted purpose") yet quickly changes into an almost loving and caring tone, not commanding but asking Hamlet to help the desperate Gertrude to "step between her and her fighting soul". This change makes the ghost appear to be almost human as he is shown as the loving husband that he was.

When *Hamlet* dutifully obeys the order to look after his mother, she responds in the same caring voice asking him why he is behaving the way he is. She is puzzled and, practically as if she were giving stage directions herself, describes Hamlet's wild actions and appearance. Her mild and loving questions as to his state are not answered; rather to the contrary Hamlet still appears to be very agitated, referring to the dreaded sight of the ghost. He is, however, not only afraid of the ghost but also full of pity, being reminded of his father's sufferings by his endlessly sad expressions. He tries to remind himself not to become melancholic but rather carry on with his task. A short dialogue with Gertrude after these passages of extreme emotions seems to convey a much more neutral tone, exchanging information in an almost matter-of-fact style. This seems to be the calm before the storm, though, as Hamlet almost appears to be relieved to see the ghost disappear when he returns to urge his mother to change her ways.

Afterwards, *Gertrude* tries to explain her son's agitation as being a result of wild thoughts.

Hamlet first argues with his mother that he is just as calm and sane as she is. Directly after this reasoning he returns to imploring Gertrude with extremely powerful images to change her ways. In this passage Hamlet appears to be in full command of the situation giving power to his point of view with phrases that appear to be almost taken from a sermon, ending by putting the opposing values that Gertrude has to choose from in direct opposition to each other.

Erweiterung

• Die Szene wird aus der Perspektive Gertrudes analysiert. Wie verhält sie sich? Ist sie glaubwürdig in ihrer Reaktion? Diese Änderung der Perspektive kann auch als *creative writing* umgesetzt werden, wobei Gertrude ein Tagebuch führt und dort ihre Gedanken niederschreibt. Eine ähnliche Möglichkeit bietet sich bei Macbeth an, indem Lady Macbeth eine Antwort auf den Brief ihres Mannes entwirft.

4 Shakespeare the dramatist The supernatural: Hamlet and Gertrude

- Als Erweiterung ist ein Vergleich der weiblichen Rollen der anderen Szenen und der Unterschiede zwischen Lady Anne, Juliet, Nurse, Gertrude, Lady Macbeth denkbar. In dieser Reihenfolge wird sehr gut die zunehmende Form der Emanzipation der weiblichen Rollen sichtbar. Dabei kann auch auf die Bedeutung und Leistung der *boy actors* eingegangen werden, derart unterschiedliche und komplexe Charaktere zu spielen.

Brainteaser

3 Discuss whether you believe this political scene helps ...

Lösungsvorschlag

This task may at first seem odd in respect to the above passage. One of the first questions might be "In what way is this scene political?" Yet looking a bit more closely one could come up with some of the following aspects: The scene puts two different sets of values in opposition. The old system of order, with its divine right of kings, with real affection, true love, the concept of honour and the respect for family values has been defeated by the new state if disorder, including corruption, usurpation, murder, overwhelming sexual desires and common chaos in the state.

To Hamlet the world looks like
- *Moral values are sacrificed for personal gain.*
- *Political assassinations are an accepted tool to attain power.*
- *The new set of values for the ruler is that of self gratification and self-interest (in this there is a parallel to other plays like "Richard III", "Macbeth" and "King Lear").*
- *The queen (Hamlet's mother) is siding with the winner, a concept that underscores the belief in power as being "sexy".*
- *True love and friendship have been replaced by mercenary behaviour. Aside from Hamlet's criticism of Gertrude, his opinion is made stronger when put into the larger context of the play by his depressing experience with Rosencrantz and Guildenstern, but much more powerful with that of Ophelia, whom he really loved and who was misused by her father Polonius to spy on him.*

In addition to the task of putting the murderer of his father to justice, Hamlet sees his main task to be that of an advocate for
- *the divine order of kings, (which also according to Protestant ethics had to be obeyed as long as the ruler proved to be just),*
- *family values with intact hierarchies and structures,*
- *true love.*

Faced with such a mammoth task of taking revenge and restoring order without taking up guilt, the protagonist is shown as the tragic hero who despairs, makes tragic errors and eventually has to pay for them with his life.

Apart from being Shakespeare's only revenge tragedy about the grief of a father, "Hamlet" also is a highly political play when considering that in Elizabethan England spying was virulent. "Hamlet" was written in 1601, only two years before the death of Queen Elizabeth. In such a political climate, where the monarch was considered to be situated directly under God, the Protestant Elizabethan code of conduct required the subjects to obey authority and to be rewarded in a later life. Shakespeare seems to have been quite bold when in "Hamlet" he not only deals with the key theme of "reality and appearance" but even uses this theme to show the power of dramatic art in the process of detecting "foul play". When Hamlet says: "The play's the thing / Wherein I'll catch the conscience of the king" (II, 2), he really seems to be talking about the ethical power of theatre. At the very beginning of the play Hamlet has already expressed his personal beliefs when he answers his mother's question "Why seems it so particular with thee?" with "Seems madam? nay it is, I know not seems" (I, 2). From this very beginning the audience assumes that Hamlet will only be playing the madman in order to be able to fathom out the degree of evil and guilt. Hamlet thus is hero and victim at the same time. This is the highly political topic of the play as a whole.

How imminent the threat to the question of obeying authority was can be seen in the fact that the Gunpowder Plot by Guy Fawkes against James I was uncovered only two years later. In the same year Shakespeare wrote "Macbeth" under his new monarch, who was from Scotland.

Shakespeare the dramatist   Working with a scene

4

To answer the question of political relevance of this content might depend on the personal views held by the students. It should, however, be taken for granted that topics such as those of favouring personal gain to that of unquestionable ethical conduct have lost nothing of their political impetus over the past 400 years, as can be seen in the reaction large parts of the population have when asked for their opinion (or prejudice) towards contemporary politics.

Erweiterung   Der Kontext kann szenisch durch ein Untersuchungsgericht erweitert werden, bei dem es um die Frage geht: *Why did Hamlet hesitate?* Als Vorübung kann eine Übung dienen, bei der ein S in der Mitte des Kreises Fragen beantworten muss, die mit *Why…?* beginnen. Diese können zunächst noch losgelöst vom Kontext des Stückes formuliert werden. Bei der nachfolgenden Untersuchung ist dann ein S der Untersuchungsrichter und stellt einzelnen S gezielte Fragen. Diese Fragen müssen dann vom Anwalt des betreffenden S – dem jeweils rechts neben ihm stehenden S – beantwortet werden. Antworten in eigener Sache oder die Unfähigkeit, für seinen Mandanten zu sprechen, werden mit dem Ausschluss aus dem Verfahren geahndet. Aufgrund dieses Ausschlussverfahrens eignet sich diese Übung vor allem für kleinere Gruppen (siehe James Stredder, *The North Face of Shakespeare*, Cambridge, 2009, Seite 96 ff.).

Eine umfangreichere szenische Übung, die den Dialog zwischen Hamlet und Gertrude in den Kontext des gesamten Stückes stellen könnte, stellt die Verbindung von Tableaus mit vorbereiteten Rollenkarten dar. Den S werden Charakterkarten mit kurz gehaltenen Informationen zu ihren Rollen gegeben. Diese Informationen geben den S Anhaltspunkte für den Bau von Skulpturen. Ein S ist der Künstler, erstellt Statuen und stellt sie in Beziehung zueinander. Als Information hierfür dient ihm lediglich das Material der Rollenkarten, die jeder einzelne S in Händen hält, oder in Form von selbstklebenden Etiketten an sich trägt. Nachdem die Tableaus gestellt worden sind, erhalten die S den Auftrag, sich zu bewegen und miteinander zu sprechen. Das Ergebnis ist eine improvisierte Szene – ohne vorherige Kenntnis des Stückes – die die S zu einer vertiefenden Bearbeitung motivieren soll.

Eine Variante besteht darin, dass L die Tableaus als Ergebnis direkter Befragungen der einzelnen S zusammenstellt, wodurch die S sich ihrer Bedeutung im Stück bewusst werden. Der Einsatz von Tableaus als Mittel zur Visualisierung kann klassischerweise natürlich auch dazu dienen, nach der Besprechung des Stückes die wesentlichen Szenen noch einmal zu rekapitulieren. Wenn Tableaus fotografiert werden, können diese dann wieder in andere Formen, wie z. B. kommentierte Bildergeschichten umgesetzt werden. (Zur Umsetzung einer Reihe von Übungen in diesem Zusammenhang siehe u. a. James Stredder, *The North Face of Shakespeare*, Cambridge, 2009, Seite 166 ff.).

Workshop exercises

Working with a scene   **p. 44**

HINTERGRUNDINFO

*The focus of this page is working on a Shakespearean text with a **dramatic or physical approach**. Although it could also be seen as an introduction to the topic of Shakespeare the dramatist in general, it serves here as a connection to the following pages dealing with the question of relevance and the modern perception of Shakespeare today. The exercises on this page are chiefly based on the didactic principles set up by the Shakespeare and Schools project started by **Rex Gibson** in the 1980s. As early as 1980 practical approaches were already in use mainly due to the pioneering work of **Cicely Berry**, formerly Voice Director at the Royal Shakespeare Company, Stratford. Berry fears that the rather careless usage of the English language today, limiting it to its*

function of a "lingua franca" is endangering its imaginative power. Keeping the excitement of the themes alive by actively speaking Shakespeare in the classroom is a means to counterbalance this tendency. Students are to speak the texts to provoke reactions from others. This opens up a chance for them to be involved in the story of the characters from their own personal experiences.

*One of the main creeds of this concept is to enable the student to gain some "**ownership**" of the text. The first aim is to take away the student's fear of the difficult language. This is the main reason for the rather detailed procedure presented on this page. Although it may seem very time-consuming at first,*

81

4 Shakespeare the dramatist   Working with a scene

it can be said that the more the students are familiarised with this technique, the more rewarding their work will be in later stages of text work, as a higher degree of understanding increases intrinsic motivation.

James Stredder points out that for many people Shakespeare seems to be too hard to tackle. There is, however, a very sound basis for using techniques from the teaching of drama in order to make the plays of Shakespeare more rewarding for the classroom. Using the classroom as a stage results in the involvement of the whole class and makes use of the social forces that lie in the peer group, and of course it also does justice to the fact that the plays were written to be acted.

A systematic and comprehensive approach to developing a physical response to the text for non-native speakers is offered by the following three levels of exercises. The first level starts with imitating small elements of language, which are not directly text based, in a way of "listening and speaking", so that the skill of reading does not hinder a spontaneous response. The second phase of approaching the texts actively would be to read a few words, memorise them and speak them out to a

partner or audience. The third level is "learning and acting", in which short segments of language are put into dramatic contexts derived from the plays. The main focus is always to let the students use parts of the script and experiment with them rather than have them read or memorise long passages without asking for any direct response.

Summing up the arguments of the key proponents of the dramatic approach, one can easily see that such a change of the didactic concept – to see the texts mainly as scripts – also automatically sets the focus on the basic question of the plot and its development, rather than any additional fields of research around the concept of Shakespeare in general. This change in focus away from teaching about Shakespeare and his plays in a more academic way to helping the students make a direct connection to the issues of the plays maybe one answer to meeting the hard yet rewarding challenge that Shakespeare's texts are for students today. As the practical consequences of this didactic school of thought are also dependent on the individual texts studied, it is worthwhile to consult the publications by Rex Gibson, Cicely Berry and James Stredder.

Lernwortschatz   *repetitive, imaginative, to alternate, to deduce*

Grundlegende Literatur zu diesem Thema:
Cicely Berry, *From Word to Play*, London, 2008.
Cicely Berry, *The Actor and the Text*, London, 1992.
Rex Gibson, *Teaching Shakespeare*, Cambridge, 1998.
James Stredder, *The North Face of Shakespeare*, Cambridge, 2009.
James Stredder, Shakespeare spielen – das Klassenzimmer als Bühne, in:
Roland Petersohn/Laurenz Volkmann (Hrsg.), Shakespeare – Didaktisch (I), Tübingen, 2006.
Mark Almond, *Teaching English with Drama*, London, 2005.

Einige grundlegende Internetadressen zum Thema:
http://nationalstrategies.standards.dcsf.gov.uk/node/113512
http://www.rsc.org.uk/learning/
http://www.shakespeares-globe.org/globeeducation/
http://www.ssf.uk.com/

1 [👥👥👥] *Warming up in groups: Start by reading …*

Hinweis auf die *Fact file* zu *The spoken word* als Einleitung zu den Übungen.

Die an dieser Stelle vorgestellte Methode aufbauender Schritte zur Gewöhnung an die schwierigen Ausgangstexte geht von einer Behandlung im Klassenraum aus. Gut geeignet wäre an dieser Stelle auch ein Ort, der größere Bewegungsfreiheit zulässt. Nachdem der Text zunächst im (Stuhl-)Kreis gelesen wird, ergibt sich zum Abschluss der ersten Phase die Möglichkeit, den Text chorisch zu lesen und dabei durch den Raum zu gehen. Die Bewegung im Raum bewirkt eine automatische Rhythmisierung des gesprochenen Textes.

Shakespeare the dramatist **Working with a scene** | **4**

2 *On your own: Read the text aloud while walking through the room.*

Die Übungen zu **b)** stellen eine Erweiterung der ersten aktiven Begegnung mit den Texten unter **a)** dar. Diese Methode intendiert eine stärkere emotionale Auseinandersetzung der S als Grundlage für die spätere Analysearbeit. Das Ausführen von wiederholenden körperlichen Tätigkeiten ist eine erprobte Methode, um sich die Texte besser einprägen zu können. Das laute Sprechen, zunächst noch ohne einen Gesprächspartner, soll sukzessive die Scheu vor emotionalem Sprechen abbauen helfen. Nachdem die Hemmschwelle auf diese Weise etwas herabgesetzt wurde, sollte jetzt versucht werden, mit dem Text kreativ zu experimentieren.

Erweiterung Eine Vielzahl von alternativen Übungsangeboten zu *active reading* finden sich bei James Stredder, *The North Face of Shakespeare*, Cambridge, 2009, Seite 138 ff. Eine besonders reizvolle Übung ist die *prompter technique* (Seite 140), bei der zwei S hintereinander gehen, wobei der hintere S dem vorderen Textstücke zuflüstert, die dieser dann laut ausspricht.

3 [&&] *With a partner: Stand opposite each other and alternate ...*

Nachdem der Text weitgehend in Einzelarbeit gesichert ist, wird ihm im Folgenden als dramatischem Text Rechnung getragen. Zunächst noch mit geringen Bewegungen, die nur unterschiedliche Effekte aus dem Grad der Entfernung der Dialogpartner hervorrufen, wird die Arbeit an den Texten zunehmend interaktiver und bewegter. In einem nächsten Durchlauf wird jetzt die Passage in verteilten Rollen gelesen. Durch das Wiederholen der vorangegangenen Zeile wird die sprachliche und inhaltliche Verbindung zwischen den einzelnen Zeilen für die S körperlich erfahrbar unterstützt. Der letzte Schritt dieser Übungseinheit ist bereits ein erster Interpretationsversuch. Der von den Dialogpartnern jetzt recht flüssig (auch szenisch) vorgetragene Text bewirkt bei den Zuhörern (ähnlich wie bei Shakespeares Zuhörerschaft) eine direkte Reaktion auf bestimmte Reizwörter. Diese wiederum tragen das Gerüst einer ersten gemeinsamen Interpretation.

4 [&&&] *In a group: Divide up the parts and prepare ...*

Das chorische Sprechen einer Passage durch die Gruppe stellt den vorläufigen Höhepunkt der Übungssequenz dar. Hierbei treten neben der reinen Textarbeit jetzt auch Elemente der Sozialbeziehungen innerhalb der Lerngruppe in das Blickfeld. Nachdem der Text in seinen Grundzügen von allen gesichert ist und mit verschiedenen Varianten des Ausdrucks experimentiert wurde, wird jetzt versucht, diese ganz bewusst zu intendierten Effekten einzusetzen. Diese Phase stellt die komplexeste und anspruchsvollste Arbeit am Text dar. Nach der praktischen Arbeit folgt in den nachfolgenden Phasen die Auswertung vor dem Hintergrund der gemachten eigenen Erfahrungen. Es wird erwartet, dass die jetzt gemachten Feststellungen deutlich intensiver ausfallen, als das ohne szenische Arbeit der Fall wäre. In einem letzten Schritt können die Szenen im Zusammenhang oder in Form von Standbildern zu ausgewählten Zitaten visuell nachgebildet und ggf. mittels einer Foto-/Videokamera aufgezeichnet werden. Die Form der Fotoserie von Standbildern eignet sich sehr gut bei einer abschließenden Einheit zur Behandlung eines kompletten Stückes. Hierbei können den Fotos nachträglich Kommentare zugefügt werden.

Handbook excerpt — **Did someone else write Shakespeare?** — p. 45

HINTERGRUNDINFO

The authorship debate: Shakespeare was without a doubt a genius. He excelled in poetry and drama alike, could draw from an enormous body of material for his creativity, and in his writings shows an insight into people's hearts that is unparalleled in English literature. The question is, though, how did a simple country lad from rural Warwickshire without any university education do it? Where did he learn his craft? These are some of the puzzling questions that fuel the ongoing debate about the authorship of his plays. People who argue against Shakespeare as an author, the **"Oxfordians"**, point out that no manuscript survives, that there are very few references to him by others during his lifetime (as compared to some lesser writers) and that the surviving references do not link him with the theatre, much less playwriting.

They conclude that someone else must have written the plays and have come up with a number of candidates. One of them is Francis Bacon, Elizabethan essayist and statesman. His references to the bible and the ancient classics are similar to those found in some Shakespeare plays, but his style and expression vary greatly from that of Shakespeare's, and besides, considering his own voluminous output, one can hardly imagine him having written another 39 plays and over 150 poems. The second candidate on the list is Christopher Marlowe. He had a university education and made a brilliant start in London as a playwright. However, he died in 1593, well before Shakespeare wrote most of his plays, which would make him the ultimate ghost-writer. His fans claim that he did not really die, but, being a government spy, faked his death, went to Italy and started penning poetry and drama under the name of Shakespeare – hence the Italian settings for so many plays.

Number three is Edward de Vere, 17th Earl of Oxford, who gave the group of anti-Shakespearians their name. The Oxfordians argue that he was a well-educated and well-travelled nobleman, contemporary of Shakespeare, and that there are similarities between the Earl's life and the extant plays. He, too, died before Shakespeare wrote some of his greatest masterpieces; however, his untimely death does nothing to put the Oxfordians off. The Earl, they say, wrote the plays before his death and told his friends to put them on stage or publish them afterwards, with a couple of references to current events included to make them sound up-to-date. Those who defend Shakespeare, otherwise known as **"Stratfordians"**, do not accept these arguments. Their most important piece of evidence is the First Folio edition, in which his friends and former colleagues John Heminge and Henry Condell published the plays under his name. The affectionate preface to the First Folio stresses his virtues, both as a writer and friend. Another piece of evidence is Ben Jonson's poem, also published in the First Folio, "To the memory of my beloved, The author Mr. William Shakespeare". The best remembered lines of which are probably the following ones:

"My Shakespeare, rise! I will not lodge thee by
Chaucer, or Spenser, or bid Beaumont lie
A little further, to make thee a room:
Thou art a monument without a tomb,
And art alive still while thy book doth live
And we have wits to read and praise to give."

Would these friends and colleagues of Shakespeare have lied? Would they not have exposed themselves to ridicule? After all, it is hard to believe that such a hoax as publishing all these plays under a false name would have worked in a city where many who had known the playwright and seen his plays were still alive. For more information on the debate see: http://shakespeareauthorship.com/howdowe.html (Stratfordians) and http://www.shakespeare-oxford.com/ (Oxfordians).

Delia Bacon (1811–1859) was the first scholar to devote her life to her doubts about the authorship of Shakespeare's works. After a series of blows – a failed relationship, an unsuccessful attempt at opening her own school, falling ill with cholera and malaria – she made Shakespeare the centrepiece of her life. She was absolutely convinced that he was a hoax and a fraud, and was determined to prove it. Somehow she managed to convince the American poet Ralph Waldo Emerson of her ideas, who supported her and in the person of his wealthy friend Charles Butler found someone to provide her with the necessary funds for a journey to England. According to her theory, a secret Elizabethan society with such prominent members as Walter Raleigh, Edmund Spenser, the Earl of Oxford and Francis Bacon wrote the plays in order to promote radical political ideas. To her, Shakespeare was nothing but a deer poacher and stable boy. Once in England, Delia refused to accept any advice on how to proceed. She never consulted any original Shakespearean resources and left Carlyle's letter of recommendation to the British Museum untouched. To her mind, proof for her theory that Bacon, her favourite candidate, really wrote the plays was to be

Shakespeare the dramatist Did someone else write Shakespeare? 4

found either in the plays themselves or in Shakespeare's grave. She spent an entire two years reading the plays time and again, trying to find clues for her theory in the texts. Her search for clues against his authorship in the plays remained fruitless. When she had run out of money, Delia decided to write to the American consulate at Liverpool and ask for help. The consul there happened to be Nathaniel Hawthorne, who paid her debts and praised those parts of her book on her theories which she had sent him (without, however, forgetting to ask her when she would deal with the historical documentation). Eventually he even wrote a foreword to "The Philosophy of the Plays of Shakespeare [sic] Unfolded", although he did not believe any of her theories. She never forgave him for saying so in the foreword. While waiting for the publication of the book, her mind turned to the second place in which she hoped to find proof for her theory: Shakespeare's grave in the Stratford parish church. She became obsessed with the idea of digging up his bones, so much so that she

repeatedly came into the church at night with a lantern to stare at the altar and the tomb. She only gave up when she fell ill. Instead of bringing her instant fame and money, the book turned out to be a disaster. Her long diatribe (682 pages!) against Shakespeare went down poorly with the critics and with the readers, and it was only later that Mark Twain showed himself impressed by it, and even Walt Whitman and Henry James came to believe her theories. Too late for Delia, though. Her physical and mental health began to deteriorate, so that she spent the rest of her life in an asylum, where she died in 1859. Her book can be found online here: http://onlinebooks.library.upenn.edu/webbin/gutbook/lookup?num=8207.

Helpful websites are: http://scandalouswoman. blogspot.com/2008/04/delia-bacon-woman-who-hated-shakespeare.html, http://www. absoluteastronomy.com/topics/Delia_Bacon, http://womenshistory.about.com/od/writers19th/a/delia_bacon.htm

Lernwortschatz   *to wield, contemporary, candidacy, craft, Bard of Avon, prosper, fake, fondness, perpetuate, gossipy, envious, outburst, hoax, to expose*

Comprehension   **1 *Outline the arguments the author names both for and against ...***

Lösungsvorschlag

For Shakespeare's authorship

- *His friends published the plays under his name, speaking of him with fondness and admiration in the preface.*
- *Many of his plays were written after the other candidates had died.*
- *There are as many as 50 references linking Shakespeare to his plays.*
- *As early as 1592 a writer named Robert Greene enviously refers to Shakespeare in one of his writings.*
- *Such a hoax would not have worked in a gossipy town such as London.*

Against Shakespeare's authorship

- *He had no university education: how could he have had such a large vocabulary?*
- *It is unlikely that a man from a provincial town could have known so much about so many topics, let alone court etiquette.*
- *No manuscripts exist.*
- *There are fewer references to him than to lesser contemporaries.*
- *The plays might have been written by someone else who published them under the pseudonym of Shakespeare.*

Erweiterung   Zur dieser, in der letzten Zeit von einer Reihe von Stimmen wieder neu entfachten Fragestellung, gibt es eine Fülle von lebhaften und nicht immer emotionslosen Beiträgen. Diese beweisen, dass neben dem beinahe zeitlos starken Interesse am Werk Shakespeares, das nicht zuletzt durch die nicht endende Zahl von Bearbeitungen in den verschiedensten Medien belegt ist, d.h. neben der Beschäftigung mit dem künstlerischen Werk es noch weitere Bereiche gibt, für die die Frage nach der Bedeutung Shakespeares wichtig ist. Es kann hier nicht darum gehen, in die komplexen Argumentationsstrukturen der Parteigänger der einzelnen Lager einzusteigen. Für die S kann allerdings die Frage, ob es für die Beurteilung des Werkes wichtig ist, von wem es geschaffen wurde, oder ob diese Frage neben dem Werk nur sekundären Charakter hat, die Auseinandersetzung um *literary appreciation* fördern. Damit dies nicht in einem

4 | Shakespeare the dramatist   Did someone else write Shakespeare?

akademischen Vakuum geschieht, kann diese Frage in einer Diskussion nach den Regeln einer *formal debate* geschehen.

Comprehension

2 Structure the text and find headlines for the paragraphs.

Lösungsvorschlag

The text is neatly structured and can easily be divided into three parts: introduction, main part and conclusion.

- **1st paragraph** – *introduction: Why it is unlikely that Shakespeare wrote the plays? (ll. 1–7)*
- **2nd paragraph** – *main part: The candidates: who really wrote the plays? (ll. 8–22: Arguments that speak for Sir Francis Bacon, ll. 8–14; Arguments in favour of Edmund de Vere, ll. 15–22)*
- **3rd paragraph** – *conclusion: The First Folio as the strongest argument in favour of Shakespeare (ll. 23–31)*

Evaluation

3 Prepare a role play in which Shakespeare's friends, ...

Zusatzmaterial

→ Kopiervorlage 15 (The authorship debate – role play)

Hinweis auf die *VIP file* zu Sir Francis Bacon.

Erweiterung

- Ergänzend kann **Kopiervorlage 15** (Seite 121) eingesetzt werden. Das Arbeitsblatt enthält Rollenkarten für eine *authorship debate*.

- Auch hier bietet sich die Möglichkeit der Gestaltung einer *feature story* z. B. für eine Zeitschrift an. Beispiele dafür finden sich im Internet z. B. unter http://www.spiegel.de/spiegel/print/d-67768129.html oder http://news.bbc.co.uk/local/oxford/hi/people_and_places/history/newsid_8380000/8380564.stm.

- Auch eine Gruppenarbeit ist möglich, dabei wird jeder Gruppe einer der Kandidaten zugewiesen. Der Arbeitsauftrag kann lauten:
  - *Collect biographical information on the candidate.*
  - *Point out arguments why your candidate is the most likely author of Shakesepare's plays.*
  - *Present your results to the class (poster, PowerPoint Presentation).*

Research

4 [▣] What did Delia Bacon, a Boston teacher, have in mind ...

Zusatzmaterial

→ Klausurvorschlag 4 • Klausurvorschlag 5 • Revision file 4

Lösungsvorschlag

When Delia Bacon spent a night in the parish church in Stratford, she intended to dig up Shakesepare's tomb. She thought she would find some proof in it that Shakespeare did not write the plays himself. Her favourite theory was that Francis Bacon, the philosopher and statesman, had buried some evidence of his own authorship – a manuscript, a token – in the grave along with Shakespeare.

Erweiterung

Zum Abschluss des *Topics* füllen die S *Revision file* 4 (Themenheft, Seite 62) aus.
Ein Lösungsvorschlag befindet sich hier im Lehrerheft auf Seite 144.

Not for an age, but for all time Didaktisches Inhaltsverzeichnis

Topic 5: Not for an age, but for all time pp. 46–52

Didaktisches Inhaltsverzeichnis
Bearbeitungszeitraum: 8–10 Unterrichtsstunden

Textsorte / Thema	Unterrichts-methoden	Input boxes	Kompetenzen	Textproduktion
Lead-in: Not for an age, but for all time				SB, Seite 46/47, LB, Seite 88/89
Combination of visuals/ Shakespeare for all time	Kursgespräch Partnerarbeit		Orientierungswissen Bildbeschreibung/ -analyse Gespräche führen	*Describing and assessing pictures*
Is Shakespeare still relevant today?, 2008 (467 words)				SB, Seite 48, LB, Seite 89/90
Interview/Are Shakespeare's plays timeless?	Kursgespräch Partnerarbeit	*VIP file: Jennifer Lee Carrell*	Leseverstehen Gespräche führen Argumentieren	*Pointing out features Planning a film based on a play*
Ourselves in Shakespeare, 2007 (407 words)				SB, Seite 49, LB, Seite 90–92
Newspaper article/ Shakespeare today	Kursgespräch		Leseverstehen Argumentieren	*Summing up main points Comparing arguments Writing a radio show Giving a presentation*
Why Shakespeare is for all time, 2003 (410 words)				SB, Seite 50, LB, Seite 92/93
Internet article/ Shakespeare for all time	Kursgespräch Gruppenarbeit		Leseverstehen Gespräche führen	*Discussing aspects Outlining contrasting points of view*
Shakespeare and ideology, 2006 (363 words)				SB, Seite 51, LB, Seite 93/94
Novel excerpt/The role of Shakespeare	Kursgespräch Gruppenarbeit Zusatzmaterial: Kopiervorlage 16		Leseverstehen Gespräche führen Argumentieren Recherchieren	*Summing up aspects Analysing the tone Writing a letter to the editor*
[16 ⊚] [4 🖿] Shakespeare on the silver screen				SB, Seite 52, LB, Seite 95–98
Photographs, listening texts, video clip/Film versions of "Richard III"	*Transcript* (246 words) Kursgespräch Gruppenarbeit Zusatzmaterial: Klausurvorschlag 6	*Word bank: Talking about images*	Orientierungswissen Bildbeschreibung/ -analyse Hör-/Sehverstehen Gespräche führen Argumentieren	*Talking about films Evaluating opinions Presenting a personal view Creating a video Acting out a scene Writing a film review*

5   Not for an age, but for all time   Lead-in: Not for an age, but for all time

Unterrichtsverlauf

Photos	**Lead-in: Not for an age, but for all time**	pp. 46–47

HINTERGRUNDINFO

*Shakespeare is **England's national poet**, but over the course of the centuries he has become playwright to the world. It may come as a surprise that this development has its origins in Germany. While in 18th century England he was still acclaimed primarily as a poet, it was here that such writers as Goethe and Schiller praised his style and plot structures as superior to the somewhat laboured neoclassical dramas which were popular in France, and that critics discovered his merits as a dramatist. To this day he is the most widely read and performed playwright in Germany. However, by the 20th century he had been translated into almost all major languages, and his plays were performed on every continent. The Arab league, together with UNESCO, sponsored a translation of Shakespeare's entire canon; Italians came to love him through Verdi's and Rossini's opera versions; the Japanese adapted his plays to the highly-stylised Kabuki theatre tradition; and Shakespeare festivals take place all over the world every year. All this goes to show that Shakespeare is obviously considered very relevant by an awful lot of people.*

*So what about our students? According to a poll commissioned by the **Royal Shakespeare Company**,*

28 % of the 650 young people questioned (15- to 35-year-olds) had been to see a play in the course of a year, compared with 25 % who had attended a pop concert. Only 3 % stated that they might be intimidated by a Shakespeare production. A third said he was still relevant today and 27 % said they believed his plays had an important impact on the English language. This is very encouraging news. All we have to do as teachers is get it right, and encourage students to read his plays instead of putting them off.

This topic aims at showing the students to what extent Shakespeare's plays and poems are to this day admired globally, and, hopefully, help them find a place for him in their hearts, too. For a well-structured and informative essay on the importance of Shakespeare today, see Leslie Dunton-Downer/ Alan Riding, "Essential Shakespeare Handbook". London: Dorling Kindersley, 2004, pp. 467–473. A personal and very touching acccount of the effect Shakespeare had on a young girl's life can be found here: http://www.time.com/time/ magazine/article/0,9171,1731320,00.html.

Comprehension	**1 [👥] Work with a partner to categorise the pictures on these pages.**

Lösungsvorschlag
- *Shakespeare used for advertising or selling goods: photo of Shakespeare and Company (book store), fashion show; Shakespare upon iPod*
- *Shakespeare for today's youth: Manga Shakespeare, Harry Potter Shakespeare Festival poster*
- *Shakespeare where he belongs: posters announcing theatre performances ("Twelfth Night", "Romeo and Juliet")*

Evaluation	**2 Which of the pictures in each category best fits the category's purpose?**

Lösungsvorschlag
The theatre poster advertising a production of "Romeo and Juliet" fits very well into the category. It gives all the necessary information (date, place, time), but also creates interest in the play. The two feet with the name tags on them replace the title and hint at the tragic ending of the play. The subtitle indicates that the setting the director chose for the drama might be a modern one (Shakespeare's tragedy in the suburbs).
The poster below the theatre posters showing Shakespeare with spectacles and flying above a dark, moonlit city on a giant quill is a very clever adaptation for capturing the interest of young teenagers. The fact that he has a wand in his hand suggests that his writing is just as magical as the Harry Potter stories.
The picture with a person in Elizabethan clothing listening to Shakespeare on an iPod is an eye-catcher because what is at the end of the headphones is not an iPod but a book about the Bard.

Not for an age, but for all time · Is Shakespeare still relevant today? | **5**

Evaluation — **3 Think of other ways in which Shakesepare, his name or his plays ...**

Die Aufgabe kann in Partnerarbeit gelöst oder als **Hausaufgabe** gestellt werden.

Lösungsvorschlag — *Individual solutions. Students may come up with the cinema (films about him or based on his plays), novels, books, magazines, the tourist industry.*

Erweiterung — Im Rahmen einer Internetrecherche können die S versuchen herauszufinden, welche Romane und Filme basierend auf dem Werk oder Leben William Shakespeares entstanden sind. Eine hilfreiche *Website* hierfür ist z. B. http://absoluteshakespeare.com/trivia/films/films.htm (hier findet sich eine Auflistung von Filmen, die auf seinen Stücken basieren) und http://www.nosweatshakespeare.com/resources/shakespeare-inspired-novel-titles.htm (eine Auflistung von Romanen, die von Shakespeare inspiriert sind).

Interview — **Is Shakespeare still relevant today?** — p. 48

HINTERGRUNDINFO

Jennifer Lee Carrell was born in Washington, DC, in 1962, but grew up in Arizona, where she now lives with a husband and a son. After having received a Ph.D. in English from Harvard and undergraduate degrees from Oxford and Stanford, she first started teaching literature and writing at Harvard. Her interest in literature was founded on the Arthurian legend, Norse sagas, Tolkien, and Shakespeare. The first book she wrote was a non-fictional thriller on smallpox, "The Speckled Monster", set in the US in 1721. Her second book – but first novel – published as "The Shakespeare Secret" in Great Britain and as "Interred with Their Bones" in the US has become an international bestseller. It deals with the search for a lost Shakespeare play, "The History of Cardenio", and the authorship question. In her latest book, "Haunt me Still" (US)/"The Shakespeare Curse" (UK) she picks up the legendary curse on Shakespeare's "Macbeth". For more information on Jennifer Lee Carrell, see her website: http://www.jenniferleecarrell.com/.

Lernwortschatz — scholar, to solve, drive, mischievous, affinity, lure, peril, startling, keep at bay, ulterior motive, core, elasticity, quintessential, proper, heroics, to lament

Erweiterung — The Reduced Shakespeare Company published an interview with Jennifer Lee Carrell on their website as a podcast: http://www.reducedshakespeare.com/wp/?p=436. Students can be asked to listen to parts of it (the interview is almost 20 minutes long) and summarise what she says in German as a mediation exercise.

Comprehension — **1 Point out the main features of Shakespeare's writings ...**

Lösungsvorschlag — *Shakespeare wrote about the most important experiences and emotions of life, such as love, hatred and death. Throughout his literary career, he changed the aspects of these experiences, so there are always new perspectives to discover in the plays. His plays are highly diverse, often juxtaposing elements of comedy and tragedy, written in image-filled, beautiful language and not sentimental, even if the topic (like first love, for instance) invites such sentimentality. Because his plays are so flexible, they allow for all sorts of settings and interpretations, thus enabling every reader to make sense of them for himself.*

Analysis — **2 Explain Carrell's statement that Shakespeare's plays change and grow ...**

Lösungsvorschlag — *What Carrell means by this is that readers understand Shakespeare differently at different ages. Many stories are relevant for us only at a certain time of our lives, because it is only then that we have the necessary emotional or intellectual disposition to fully appreciate them. Maybe we lay hands on the book again after some years and realise why it was that we thought it was great when we first read it, but understand at the same time that we have changed and developed, and that consequently the same story does not appeal to us any more. With Shakespeare, Carrell says, it is different. His stories reveal such a great understanding of the*

5 Not for an age, but for all time — Ourselves in Shakespeare

human soul and portray fundamental experiences in so many different ways that they permit us to find something new and relevant every time we read them, no matter how old we are. "Romeo and Juliet", for example, is a wonderful story for teenagers who have fallen in love for the first time and feel deep compassion for the tragic fate of the two young lovers, but it is a great story for adults, too, as it shows us how soon tragic events can change our lives, and how important it is to hold on to moments of bliss and happiness.

Evaluation

3 [👥] Work with a partner. Choose a Shakespeare play – maybe one …

Lösungsvorschlag Individual solutions. Students might choose a contemporary setting for "Romeo and Juliet", one in which the conflict between the feuding families is replaced by a conflict about race or social classes. The main focus of the play would then be on the conflict itself. "Macbeth" could be turned into a film in which either the supernatural plays a central role (the witches, the dagger, Banquo's ghost and how Macbeth reacts to all of them) or the relationship to his wife (how should they be portrayed as a couple?). Students may want to cast their films, too, and present to the class a film poster with photos of their stars and the entire cast.

Erweiterung *Cast your own Shakespeare movie*
- Ask students to choose a play from this book or hand out plot summaries of plays.
- Tell them to work with a partner or in groups and take notes about the main characters. What are they like? What might they look like? For more information on the characters in a play, they can browse the Internet (www.sparknotes.com).
- Distribute photos of stars in a different room, make sure to have 2–3 photocopies of one photo.
- Ask students to walk around and pick their stars.
- In the classroom, let them discuss in their own groups why they want to cast a particular actor for a role.
- Present the result to the class and explain. Would Orlando Bloom be convincing as Richard III? Can Kate Winslet play Lady Macbeth, or would Angelina Jolie – or Madonna – be a better alternative?
- Discuss.

Newspaper article **Ourselves in Shakespeare** p. 49

HINTERGRUNDINFO

The text reflects upon and at the same time offers answers to the phenomenon why Shakespeare is still so popular today even after more than 400 years. One of the most noteworthy focusses of the article is its special attention to Shakespeare's ability to raise **timeless issues of humanity** which are regaining importance in our ideological and technological age.

Lernwortschatz service, complexity, tumble, yield, to transcend, mouthpiece, wit, spark, eerie, to brood, ambition, to be destined for, cloaked, bawdy, insanity, to urge, to retrace one's steps, fate, indifferent to, raw, to despair

Brainteaser

1 To what extent do you think Shakespeare and his plays are relevant today?

Lösungsvorschlag Individual answers are possible, yet the results may probably be more widespread than expected as Shakespeare is not only a major player in today's English-speaking art world, but has left his influence in all walks of modern life, from pop and rock music, or advertising to using individual lines when looking for particularly imaginative or catchy phrases that have a high degree of familiarity. If students have already seen parts of a play or a whole production they might refer to the universality of the issues they were then confronted with.

5 Not for an age, but for all time   Ourselves in Shakespeare

Comprehension

2 Summarise the main points of the article in your own words.

Lösungsvorschlag

Every summer there are countless festivals celebrating the complex beauty of Shakespeare's words. More amazing is when the characters transcend the words and come to life to have their own identity. These fictional characters have often seemed so real that they have influenced people in politics as well as historic events. However, Shakespeare's influence is not mainly one of ideology or religion, as he does not explain higher principles or beings to the people but rather the people to themselves. His topic is humanity in all its shapes from the tragic to the most profane. In a time of necessary choices like today, Shakespeare's message is different: the most important choices are made in the human soul. His plays are not giving out simple truths, though, as everything humans experience is complex and mostly unexpected. This is why Shakespeare's characters hold up a mirror to us. In them, we see our own nature, even when it is most unpleasant and disturbing, and when they change, we see ourselves in a different light as well. So when we enter the dark theatre, we actually escape to what is most real to us.

Evaluation

3 Compare the author's arguments with the ideas you had ...

Lösungsvorschlag

The answer naturally depends on the complexity of the answers to task 1. However, it could well be possible that some students have already mentioned their expectations that Shakespeare is still relevant. It might well be expected that their answers are not as detailed as the position Michael Gerson puts forward, so that this aspect that Shakespeare does not put on a show to explain things but rather explains human behaviour might be substantially deepened.

Erweiterung

Die Argumentation Gersons kann in Form eines bestätigenden Rückblicks z. B. an der Charakterisierung Richards überprüft werden, ob, und wenn ja, welche Charaktereigenschaften Richards im menschlichen Miteinander heute nachvollzogen werden können. In dieser Art und Weise wird es relativ einfach gelingen, zu jedem bei Shakespeare im Mittelpunkt stehenden Thema inhaltliche Anknüpfungspunkte zu finden. So steht heute z. B. bei der Geistererscheinung in *Hamlet* nicht primär ein schauriger Effekt im Vordergrund, sondern die Frage von ethisch richtigem Handeln vor dem Hintergrund nicht immer eindeutiger Erfassung von Realität. *Macbeth* ist vielleicht primär ein aktionsgeladenes Drama um einen Königsmord, bei näherer Analyse wird aber eher thematisiert, wie weit krankhafter Ehrgeiz Menschen treiben kann. Eine derartige Auseinandersetzung würde es sogar rechtfertigen, die Behandlung von Dramen Shakespeares ins Zentrum eines Curriculums zu stellen und diese Möglichkeit der Elementarisierung zu nutzen, um eine verbindende Struktur von Unterrichtsthemen herauszuarbeiten.

Evaluation

4 Put together a 15-minute presentation on Shakespeare for a radio audience.

Lösungsvorschlag

Despite the historic background, there are many individual results to be expected. As preparation to the material presented, the students could be set a limited webquest exercise to find the material they would like to present additionally to the information they already have gained from the topic so far. The following linklist is meant as a means of support and is in no way comprehensive:

Life of Shakespeare
www.pbs.org/shakespeare
http://shakespeare.palomar.edu
http://shakespeare.about.com
http://kcrenfest.com
www.bbc.co.uk/history/british/tudors/shakespeare_early_01.shtml
www.elizabethan.org
http://ise.uvic.ca/index.html

The Theatre
www.globe-theatre.org.uk/elizabethan-theatre.htm
www.william-shakespeare.info/elizabethan-theaters.htm
www.elizabethan-era.org.uk/elizabethan-theatre.htm

5   Not for an age, but for all time   Why Shakespeare is for all time

Richard III
http://library.thinkquest.org/26314

Erweiterung   Aus der Vielzahl der Internetseiten zu Shakespeare sind – neben den oben genannten – die folgenden Websites für L besonders empfehlenswert:

Education
www.folger.edu/eduLesPlanArch.cfm?cid
http://shakespeare.palomar.edu/educational.htm
www.teachersfirst.com/shakespr.shtml
www.bbc.co.uk/drama/shakespeare/60secondshakespeare/
www.rsc.org.uk/learning
http://pages.unibas.ch/shine/linkseducationwf.htm

Bücher, die einen ersten allgemeinen Eindruck zu Shakespeare vermitteln können
- Shakespeare, *Court, Crowd and Courthouse (New Horizons)*, London, 1993.
- Andrew Dickson, *The Rough Guide to Shakespeare*, London, 2005.
- Janet Ware, *101 Things You Didn't Know About Shakespeare*, Avon, 2005.
- Dick Riley/Pam Mcallister, *The Bedside, Bathtub and Armchair Companion to Shakespeare*, New York, 2001.
- Laurie Rozakis, *The Complete Idiot's Guide to Shakespeare*, New York, 1999.
- John Doyle, *Shakespeare for Dummies*, London, 1999.
- Stanley Wells, *Is It True What They Say About Shakespeare?*, Oxford, 2008.
- Norrie Epstein, *The Friendly Shakespeare*, New York, 1993.
- Germaine Greer, *Shakespeare – A Very Short Introduction*, Oxford, 1986.

Internet article   ## Why Shakespeare is for all time   p. 50

HINTERGRUNDINFO

Theodore Dalrymple *is the pen name of Anthony Daniels, a British writer and retired physician. He is the son of a Communist businessman and a German-born Jewish mother, who escaped from the Nazi regime to the United Kingdom. In his extensive writing on culture, politics, education, and medicine he draws both on his experience as a doctor in Africa and as a hospital consultant and prison doctor (psychiatrist) in Birmingham. After his retirement in*

2005, writing became even more important to him. He has written for the British Medical Journal, the Times, the Observer, the Daily Telegraph, and the Spectator, among others, and published two collections of essays in 2009: "Not with a Bang But a Whimper" and "Second Opinion". For more information on Dalrymple see http://www.mondaybooks.com/theodore_dalrymple/index.html.

Lernwortschatz   *to render, notable, despot, petty, steadfastness, shrink, disparaging, unprecedented, genocide, ideological, sanction, body count*

Brainteaser   **1 [ooo] *Is drama capable of giving us help for our daily lives? Discuss.***

Lösungsvorschlag   *The question is easier to answer for students who have some experience with drama, of course. But that is what most of them have from having seen it on TV or in the cinema – even though this might not have been Shakespeare. In order to start a good debate, the teacher might start with a definition of drama, then ask what films they have seen or books they have read. From there, they may come close to having a good working definition of drama and be able to start their debate.*

Here are some definitions of "drama", which is derived from the Greek word for "action"
- *A prose or verse composition, especially one telling a serious story, that is intended for representation by actors impersonating the characters and performing the dialogue and action.*
- *A serious narrative work or programme for television, radio, or the cinema.*

	Not for an age, but for all time **Shakespeare and ideology**	**5**

- *A composition in prose or verse presenting in dialogue or pantomime a story involving conflict or contrast of character, esp. one intended to be acted on the stage; a play.*

Comprehension

2 Outline the two contrasting points of view on the relevance of ...

Die Aufgabe kann als **Hausaufgabe** gestellt werden.

Lösungsvorschlag

Dalrymple explains in the first part of his text that some Soviet poets believe that Shakespeare has become less relevant in the twentieth century. Those who committed the horrors that characterised the twentieth century did so in the name of an ideology, whether it was fascism or socialism. While Macbeth only killed a couple of innocent people, twentieth century ideologies justified the killing of thousands, making Macbeth appear like a petty criminal of little relevance today. After all, he did not kill for a higher purpose, but only to preserve his power. Dalrymple does not share that point of view. He argues that other genocides and massacres (like in Rwanda or Burundi) were not ignited by ideological ideas, and that radical evil exists without any sort of ideological justification; evil is not measured by the numbers of corpses left behind. By showing his evildoers as being free from any need for political or ideological justification, Shakespeare shows what is left of a human soul when all excuses and explanations fail to work. What is left then is simply an evil man, and these can be found today just as well as in other times.

Erweiterung

Dalrymple says in his text "I have little doubt from my medical practice that radical evil can exist on a large scale without the sanction of an official ideology. Many a man is the Macbeth of his own little world." (ll. 20 ff.)

This quotation might be used to spark off a classroom debate on the question as to what extent Dalrymple is right. In order to prepare such a debate, the students might browse the Internet, read the newspapers or watch the news in order to collect information on men and women who pursued their aims regardless of human ideals or moral values. They might come up with modern Macbeths such as Saddam Hussein, ruthless bank managers who ruined the lives of thousands of people, women who killed their children in order to keep up a certain living standard, or fathers who ignored social morals in order to maintain control of their fate. The results might be presented in class and debated afterwards: what is it that turns people into Macbeths?

Novel excerpt

Shakespeare and ideology   p. 51

Lernwortschatz

to be obsessed with sb/sth, to revolve around sth, perplexing, shallow

Comprehension

1 Sum up what importance these two texts claim Shakespeare has today.

Lösungsvorschlag

Both texts claim that Shakespeare's importance is based on his capacity to work out universal human traits and emotions in a somewhat archetypal way in which everyone finds someone else's or even his own behaviour or state of mind reflected in the dramas. As in everyday life, Shakespeare deals with characters in action and he does this in a psychologically highly convincing way. The fact that, as Gerson maintains, he ought to be placed in the self-help section of a library also indirectly criticises the traditional view of limiting the writings of Shakespeare to examples of high-art and putting the Bard onto a pedestal which distances him from us, thus also taking away some of the power of magic, which is partly created by ourselves when responding to the input we receive when studying Shakespeare or watching the plays.

Erweiterung

Ein derartiger Ansatz, die Bedeutung der Werke Shakespeares in ihrer Thematisierung allgemein menschlicher Eigenschaften zu sehen, hat in einer Vielzahl von Publikationen Nachhall gefunden, an dieser Stelle seien nur einige Beispiele erwähnt, die es Wert sind, vertieft zu werden:

- Anthony Holden, *The Drama of Love, Life and Death in Shakespeare,* London, 2000.
- Fintan O'Toole, *Shakespeare is Hard, but so is Life,* London, 2002.

93

5   Not for an age, but for all time   Shakespeare and ideology

- Harold Bloom, *Shakespeare the Invention of the Human*, New York, 1998.
- Antony Sher, *Year of the King*, London, 1985.
- John Barton, *Playing Shakespeare*, London, 1984.

Analysis

2 Analyse the tone of this text and its intended message.

Lösungsvorschlag

The overall stylistic device of this passage is that of anaphora and repetition with which Laurie Maguire points out the universality, versatility but also the familiarity that makes us respond to Shakespeare's works. She starts with the very profound yet elementary statement that the situations presented are so basically human that they are timeless. After such an almost reassuring thought she contrasts this statement with a list of everyday situations that reflect the action of our restless lives. Another row of anaphora points out the parallel emphasis on "character and situation" both on stage and off. In the third passage the text starts with an alliteration of plosives culminating in the keyword of the thought: Shakespeare is the "psychologist", which supposedly tries to get the reader off balance by going against his role expectations. This new idea of letting the playwright become part of our natural lives finally culminates in a repetition of oppositions, of "choices", with which we are faced on a daily basis. This is proof of the effectiveness of the playwright showing us our mirror of verisimilitude, as close to nature as possible.

Discussion

3 [👥] Maguire claims that Shakespeare has a universal function. Discuss.

Lösungsvorschlag

Individual responses are expected. However, as Maguire presents a lot of very convincing down-to-earth arguments taken from daily experiences which are very familiar to the reader (as she does throughout the whole book), a majority of support for the above statement is to be expected.

Erweiterung

Von der hier propagierten universellen Funktion zeugen auch die zahlreichen literarischen Adaptationen und Anlehnungen an das Werk Shakespeares. Auch hier nur einige Beispiele:

- Mike Ashley, *Shakespearean Whodunnits*, New York, 1997.
- John O'Connor, *Shakespearean Afterlives*, Cambridge, 2003.
- Humphrey Carpenter, *Shakespeare Without the Boring Bits*, London, 1994.
- Tom Stoppard, *The Fifteen Minute Hamlet*, London, 1978
- Charles Marowitz, *The Marowitz Shakespeare*, London, 1978.
- The Reduced Shakespeare Company, *The Compleat Works of Wllm Shkspr*, New York, 1994.
- Nick Page, *The Tabloid Shakespeare*, London, 1999.
- *Loves Fire (Seven new plays inspired by seven Shakespearean Sonnets)*, New York, 1993.
- James Muirden, *Shakespeare Well-Versed*, New York, 2004.
- Charles Nicholl, *The Lodger*, London, 2007.

Evaluation

4 Creative writing: Which of the points of view – Dalrymple's or ...

Zusatzmaterial

→ **Kopiervorlage 16 (Honi soit qui mal y pense – mediation)**

Lösungsvorschlag

Individual answers should critically reflect the positions the writers take, yet might come to a conclusion that besides arguing from different angles and answering the question as to a necessary ideology differently, they share a number of aspects with regard to their appreciation of Shakespeare.

Erweiterung

An dieser Stelle kann **Kopiervorlage 16** (Seite 122) eingesetzt werden. Sie bietet einen deutschen Zeitungsartikel mit einer Aufgabenstellung zur Mediation.

Not for an age, but for all time **Shakespeare on the silver screen** | **5**

| Listening texts/ Video clip | [16 ◉] **Shakespeare on the silver screen** | p. 52 |

HINTERGRUNDINFO

The fact that **Shakespeare's plays** were written as scripts for performance rather than reading material and that their main impact by what happens on the stage is a very important reason why the plays have always lent themselves to be adapted and worked over. In Shakespeare's time the flow of the play was very much like the flow of scenes in modern cinema. As the visual medium of our time is that of cinema, there is small wonder why the film industry has taken up Shakespeare's plays for a large number of productions on the silver screen. To get an impression about the sheer amount of adaptations, one may just look at the website of "The Internet Movie Database" (www.imdb.com) and look up the filmography of all films entered under the heading William Shakespeare. The appearance of the new medium film brings with it a number of very interesting new questions, like: "Can/Should the text be cut?", "What changes is the filmmaker allowed to make to adapt the material to the tastes of modern audiences?", "What new ways of expression are given to the filmmaker by modern technology and does the use of it change the original intention of the story?", etc. These are just a few questions which could be the centre of a new very worthwhile teaching unit on the differences between the artforms of theatre and film.

Lernwortschatz   *adaptation, to convey, storyteller, to knock sb dead (infml), spectacle, incredible, equivalent, to match sth, to be dependent on*

Materialien   → CD, Track 16 • Transcript (Shakespeare on the silver screen)

Empfehlenswerte Literatur zum Thema:
- Russell Jackson, *The Cambridge Companion to Shakespeare on Film*, Cambridge, 2000.
- Daniel Rosenthal, *100 Shakespeare Films, BFI Screen Guides*, London, 2007.
- Werner Kamp, Shakespeare im Film, in: Roland Petersohn/Laurenz Volkmann (Hrsg.), Shakespeare – Didaktisch (I), Tübingen, 2006, S. 119–133.

Zur Vertiefung der Arbeit an den Filmadaptationen ist neben den Zusatzmaterialien der jeweiligen DVD (Interviews mit Regisseuren oder Schauspielern, Hintergrundinformationen zu einzelnen Szenen usw.) oftmals auch das *screenplay* empfehlenswert. Hierzu einige Beispiele:
- Ian McKellan, *William Shakespeare's Richard III*, New York, 1996.
- Kenneth Branagh, *Hamlet*, London, 1996.

Für einzelne Filme wie z.B. *Looking for Richard* ist ein Filmskript aus dem Internet herunterladbar. Überaus vielfältig ist die Zahl der Medienbeispiele zu Adaptationen bei *YouTube* (siehe u.a. *Reduced Shakespeare Company*). Bei der Arbeit mit Filmen sollte berücksichtigt werden, ob es sich um eine gefilmte Theaterproduktion oder einen Kinofilm handelt. Darüber hinaus wird empfohlen, gerade auch bei der Behandlung von Adaptationen, das Medium des Animationsfilms (hier besonders: *The Animated Tales*) nicht zu übersehen.

Brainteaser   **1 *What type of movies do you like best? Explain the criteria ...***

Lösungsvorschlag   *Individual answers are expected. Although answers may vary as a result of e.g. the different ratio between male and female students and other factors of the group set-up, it is to be expected that the students will mention the most recent block busters. The elements they probably might be most interested in are action and suspense, fun or romance.*

Comprehension   **2 [16 ◉] *Outline the different aspects the two speakers refer to.***

[16 ◉]   Die Beiträge von *James Hansen (director)* und *Brent Keyes (actor and director)* werden von der CD präsentiert. Bei Bedarf kann das *Transcript* hinzugezogen werden, es befindet sich als PDF ebenfalls auf der CD.

Lösungsvorschlag   *a) The first speaker refers to Shakespeare's capacity as a fantastic storyteller as he saw this need from his daily perspective as an actor. Shakespeare primarily was the great entertainer,*

95

5 Not for an age, but for all time Shakespeare on the silver screen

who tried to stun the audiences with a vast spectrum of emotions. Shakespeare was as popular as the most popular directors of our time, like Stephen Spielberg or George Lucas.

The second speaker claims that the technology of cinematography offers new chances of presentation. If Shakespeare had to create pictures mostly with words and their sounds, today these pictures can be created on screen. Modern cameras, sound engines and computer animation have created a new genre for dramas. Shakespeare would have loved to have these sources to experiment with. The media have become a new tool for a new interpretation, while at the same time making the original text more independent of the restrictions of its historic setting.

b) *While the first speaker puts the fantastic quality of the stories and the plots in Shakespeare to the forefront and thus sees the plays within their Elizabethan context, the second stresses the new opportunities modern filmmakers get through their technological tools to put their imaginative forces into visual form. Indirectly the two speakers also stress the difference between Elizabethan and modern audiences, as Shakespeare's audience relied much more on their imaginative powers when hearing the plays while modern audiences are much more used to responding to visual impulses.*

Discussion **3 *What other film adaptations of books or plays have you seen?***

Wie relevant und vielfältig die Auswahl von Shakespeare-Vorlagen für die Bearbeitung durch die Filmindustrie ist zeigen die Produktionen, die in zeitlicher Nähe zu Luhrmans *Romeo and Juliet* entstanden (1995/96) und mittlerweile zu den Klassikern (auch für die Bearbeitung im Unterricht) zählen. Hierzu gehören neben *Richard III* besonders die Verfilmungen von *Othello* (L. Fishburn), *Hamlet* (K. Branagh) und *Twelfth Night* (H. Bonham-Carter). Alle genannten Filme sind in besonderer Weise geeignet, der Frage von Authentizität und Verfremdung im Medium Film nachzugehen. Diese Aussage gilt in ähnlicher Weise für die Vielzahl der seither entstandenen Bearbeitungen. Von den jüngeren Produktionen haben eine Reihe von Adaptationen von *A Midsummer Night's Dream* (1999), *Titus* (1999), *Love's Labour's Lost* (2000) und besonders auch *The Merchant of Venice* (2004) großes Interesse gefunden. Es bietet sich auch an, einen Vergleich zu Produktionen herzustellen, die das Originalmaterial sehr frei umgesetzt haben, z. B. *Ten things I hate about you* (1999) vs. *The Taming of the Shrew*; *O* (2002) vs. *Othello*, *King Rikki* (2002) vs. *Richard III*, *Hamlet* (2000), angesiedelt im modernen New York, oder *Makibefo* (1999), eine südafrikanische Version von *Macbeth*.

Lösungsvorschlag *Individual answers are expected. The adaptations most likely to be mentioned here could be those of the adaptation of fantasy stories like "Harry Potter", "Narnia", "The Lord of the Rings". Due to its enormous success, students may still refer to Baz Luhrman's version of "Romeo and Juliet". This could be a good starting point for further study referring to the highly successful "Shakespeare in Love". Although the latter only partly covers the plot of "Romeo and Juliet", it is a very relevant example for the question of modern adaptations.*

Erweiterung Wie bedeutsam die Wirkung elektronischer Medien umgekehrt auch für Theaterproduktionen sein kann, beweist das Beispiel der *Royal Shakespeare Company*, Stratford, aus dem Jahr 2008. Als bekannt wurde, dass David Tennant, Star der BBC Serie *Dr Who*, die Rolle des Hamlet spielen wurde, wurden für Karten im Internet astronomische Beträge geboten und das Publikum war deutlich jünger als bei anderen Produktionen (http://www.timesonline.co.uk/tol/news/uk/article4466577.ece).

Discussion **4 *Debate: This house believes that modern movie technology is needed …***

Hinweis auf die *Word bank* zu *Talking about images*.

Lösungsvorschlag *Open result of debate which should, however, be carried out under formal rules.*

Erweiterung Als Anregung für die Durchführung einer *formal debate*:
http://news.bbc.co.uk/cbbcnews/hi/newsid_4530000/newsid_4537100/4537177.stm,
http://www.educationworld.com/a_lesson/lesson/lesson304b.shtml.

Not for an age, but for all time   Shakespeare on the silver screen   5

Evaluation

5 Creative writing: Write your own shooting script for one of ...

Lösungsvorschlag *Completely open solution, which should despite a high range of creativity, however show an understanding for the rules of acting as well as the limits of what can be performed on stage.*

Comprehension

6 [4🎬] Take notes on what is said about adaptations of ...

Materialien → Film 4 (Adapting Shakespeare)

[4🎬] Die S schauen den Videoclip entweder als **Hausaufgabe** an oder er wird im Unterricht präsentiert.

Lösungsvorschlag *Ian McKellan, actor*
The principal responsibility of the actor is to make the story clear to an audience that knows nothing about the play. We tell the story as clearly as possible and that has always meant in my major Shakespeare I've always done it in modern dress. It seems to me that fancy dress gets in the way. Shakespeare isn't old fashioned to me he's bang up to date, he's modern, and one way of convincing the audience of that is to put the characters into the sort of clothes that we wear today.

Richard Lonchraine, director
- *The audience should not have to read the play beforehand.*
- *No "closed-shop" attitude.*
- *When students read the play at school because they have to study it, that's fine, but you should be able to walk in off the street and decide to go in; you shouldn't have to know the play before you get there.*
- *In a movie audiences walk out if they don't understand it, or if it's boring, but in the theatre they remain seated a little bit because it's the place to be; no one wants to appear not to understand it.*

Professor Gordon Dennis
Some critics dislike Shakespeare on film because they feel the actual text isn't being played straight. The answer to that is it never was played straight, that Shakespeare himself, who was an actor as well as a playwright, varied the words of his own plays. The second thing is some critics see themselves as members of a priesthood and it has to be said in a particular way and always their particular way.

Kenneth Brannagh, actor
It's a subjective thing, isn't it? I don't think we should proclaim him as great just because he's there, because lots of people have said he's done, but personally I feel he's a great writer. I find that he has limitless powers of observation about the human condition and many situations that human beings find themselves in with which we can still identify, laugh at, be moved by, be enraged by; and he remains wonderfully elusive about his politics, about his views on marriage and relationships and all the things that continue to obsess us. But I wouldn't impose my enthusiasm on anybody else.

Peter Greenaway, director
I do think it is extremely dangerous to put him up there as an icon in such a fashion that people genuflect in front of him – revere him – rather than like him. Every generation – certainly in France, in Russia, in Italy – they get hold of a new translator and a new adaptation is made, which can then make Shakespeare peculiarly adapt – with honourably intentions – I think to bring him up to situations of the Bosnian conflict or what is happening in Africa or making him to a colonial play. (…) We can't do that in this country; we are so stuck with this extraordinary text. Nobody is going to deny it's there, but there's a way we can't adapt it, reposition it, (…) to make it very valuable for contemporary circumstances.

English professor
It is actually a quirk, an oddity for the English-speaking world that we are the only people, we English speakers, who hear this English writer in a foreign language.

5 Not for an age, but for all time Shakespeare on the silver screen

Analysis **7 Compare how different film adaptations have created ...**

Lösungsvorschlag *The choice of scenes should be left to the students, yet some plays have had more adaptations into films than others. The most readily available film versions are probably those of "Hamlet", "Romeo and Juliet" and "Richard III".*

Evaluation **8 Write a critical evaluation of a film version of a Shakespearean ...**

Zusatzmaterial → Klausurvorschlag 6 • Revision file 5

Lösungsvorschlag Individuelle S-Beiträge.

Erweiterung
- Nach der eigenen kritischen Beurteilung durch die S kann es reizvoll sein, einen Vergleich mit den Beurteilungen professioneller Rezensenten durchzuführen. Unter IMDB lassen sich eine Vielzahl von Rezensionen zu allen Filmen finden. Besonders interessant sind in der Regel die Beurteilungen von dem amerikanischen „Filmpapst" Roger Ebert.

- Zum Abschluss des *Topics* können die S noch *Revision file* 5 (Themenheft, Seite 63) ausfüllen. Ein Lösungsvorschlag befindet sich hier im Lehrerheft auf Seite 145 (Umschlagseite 3).

Sequenzplaner | **SP**

Sequenzplaner – Differenzierungshinweise GK / LK

Topic 1   Shakespeare and his time   Seite 4–11

Titel	SB-Seite / Unterrichts- stunden	Textsorte	Thema	Kernsequenz (GK + LK)/ Vertiefung (LK)
Shakespeare and his time	SB, S. 4/5 1–2 Stunden	Combination of visuals, quotations, timeline	Elizabethan theatre	Kernsequenz 1 (GK + LK)
The Shakespeare portrait	SB, S. 6/7 2 Stunden	Factual information, visuals	Likenesses	Vertiefung 1 (LK)
Book burning	SB, S. 8/9 2 Stunden	Novel excerpt	Censorship in Elizabethan England	Kernsequenz 2 (GK + LK)
Life in the suburbs	SB, S. 10/11 1–2 Stunden	Novel excerpt, quotations	Punishment in Shakespeare's time	Vertiefung 2 (LK)

Topic 2   Shakespeare's language   Seite 12–19

Titel	SB-Seite / Unterrichts- stunden	Textsorte	Thema	Kernsequenz (GK + LK)/ Vertiefung (LK)
Elizabethan English	SB, S. 12 1 Stunde	Factual information, quotes	Elizabethan English	Kernsequenz 1 (GK + LK)
Working with Shakespeare's language	SB, S. 13 1 Stunde	Factual information, quotes	Shakespeare's language	Vertiefung 1 (LK)
Shakespeare's use of prose and verse	SB, S. 14/15 2 Stunden	Factual information	Prose and verse	Kernsequenz 2 (GK + LK)
Prose and verse in "Romeo and Juliet"	SB, S. 16 1–2 Stunden	Drama excerpt	"Romeo and Juliet", Act II, scene iv	Vertiefung 2 (LK)
Shakespeare's poetry/ Sonnet 73	SB, S. 17 2 Stunden	Factual information, poem, video clip	Love poetry, history of London	Kernsequenz 3 (GK + LK)
Sonnet 116	SB, S. 18 2 Stunden	Poem, quotation	Marriage	Vertiefung 3 (LK)
Sonnet 94	SB, S. 19 2 Stunden	Poem	Hurt feelings	Kernsequenz 4 (GK + LK)

Topic 3   Shakespeare's theatre   Seite 20–27

Titel	SB-Seite / Unterrichts- stunden	Textsorte	Thema	Kernsequenz (GK + LK)/ Vertiefung (LK)
Shakespeare's theatre	SB, S. 20/21 1–2 Stunden	Combination of visuals and quotes	The theatre in Shakespeare's days	Kernsequenz 1 (GK + LK)

99

Sequenzplaner

Touring the theatre	SB, S. 22/23 2 Stunden	Interview, map	The theatres in 16th-century London	Vertiefung 1 (LK)
What the Globe was really like	SB, S. 24/25 1–2 Stunden	Novel excerpt, interview, video clip	Life as an actor	Kernsequenz 2 (GK + LK)
Producing a play	SB, S. 26/27 2 Stunden	Factual information	Elizabethan playwright	Kernsequenz 3 (GK + LK)

Topic 4 Shakespeare the dramatist — Seite 28–45

Titel	SB-Seite/ Unterrichts- stunden	Textsorte	Thema	Kernsequenz (GK + LK)/ Vertiefung (LK)
Shakespeare the dramatist	SB, S. 28 1 Stunde	Combination of visuals	Shakespeare's plays	Kernsequenz 1 (GK + LK)
The writing process	SB, S. 29 1 Stunde	Factual information	Playwrights in Elizabethan era	Vertiefung 1 (LK)
"Richard III": What happens in the play?	SB, S. 30 1 Stunde	Factual information	"Richard III", plot summary	Kernsequenz 2 (GK + LK)
Richard's opening soliloquy – his discontent, his plot	SB, S. 31 1–2 Stunden	Drama excerpt, video clip	"Richard III", Act I, opening scene i, soliloquy	Kernsequenz 3 (GK + LK)
Richard woos Anne	SB, S. 32/33 1–2 Stunden	Drama excerpt	"Richard III", Act I, scene ii, dramatic dialogue	Vertiefung 3 (LK)
Ward je in dieser Laun' ein Weib gewonnen?	SB, S. 34 1 Stunde	German journal article, quotes	A production of "Richard III"	
Love: The balcony scene	SB, S. 35/36 1–2 Stunden	Drama excerpt, movie poster, photographs	"Romeo and Juliet", Act II, scene ii, dialogue	Kernsequenz 4 (GK + LK)
Love: Saying farewell	SB, S. 37 1 Stunde	Drama excerpt, cartoon	"Romeo and Juliet", Act III, scene v, dialogue	Vertiefung 4 (LK)
Conscience: Macbeth's guilt	SB, S. 38 1 Stunde	Drama excerpt, photograph	"Macbeth", Act I, scene vii, soliloquy	Kernsequenz 5 (GK + LK)
Order and disorder: Macbeth disrupts stability	SB, S. 39/40 1–2 Stunden	Drama excerpt, photographs	"Macbeth", Act II, scene iv, dialogue	Vertiefung 5 (LK)
The supernatural: Hamlet learns the truth	SB, S. 41 1 Stunde	Factual information, drama excerpt	"Hamlet", Act I, scene v, dialogue	Kernsequenz 6 (GK + LK)
The supernatural: Hamlet and Gertrude	SB, S. 42/43 1–2 Stunden	Drama excerpt	"Hamlet", Act III, scene iv, dialogue	Vertiefung 6 (LK)
Working with a scene	SB, S. 44 2 Stunden	Drama workshop	Acting out a scene	Kernsequenz 7 (GK + LK)
Did someone else write Shakespeare?	SB, S. 45 1–2 Stunden	Handbook excerpt	Authorship	Vertiefung 7 (LK)

Sequenzplaner | **SP**

Topic 5   Not for an age, but for all time | Seite 46–52

Titel	SB-Seite / Unterrichts- stunden	Textsorte	Thema	Kernsequenz (GK + LK)/ Vertiefung (LK)
Not for an age, but for all time	SB, S. 46/47 1 Stunde	*Combination of visuals*	*Shakespeare for all time*	Kernsequenz 1 (GK + LK)
Is Shakespeare still relevant today?	SB, S. 48 1–2 Stunden	*Interview*	*Are Shakespeare's plays timeless?*	Vertiefung 1 (LK)
Ourselves in Shakespeare	SB, S. 49 1–2 Stunden	*Newspaper article*	*Shakespeare today*	Kernsequenz 2 (GK + LK)
Why Shakespeare is for all time	SB, S. 50 2 Stunden	*Internet article*	*Shakespeare for all time*	Vertiefung 2 (LK)
Shakespeare and ideology	SB, S. 51 1–2 Stunden	*Novel excerpt*	*The role of Shakespeare*	Kernsequenz 3 (GK + LK)
Shakespeare on the silver screen	SB, S. 52 2 Stunden	*Photographs, listening texts, video clip*	*Film versions of "Richard III"*	Vertiefung 3 (LK)

KV Kopiervorlagen

KV 1a: Who stole the manuscript of *Richard II*?   p. 5, ex. 5

[👥] In 1597, London bookshops made big money with a play by Shakespeare – but he did not get a single penny for it: the money went to those who had pirated the manuscript and printed it without the author's consent, and without permission of the Acting Company that had paid for the play, Shakespeare's Lord Chamberlain's Men. On top of all that, sales were enhanced by boldly advertising that this was, indeed, one of their plays. The title of the book is "The tragedie of King Richard the second: As it hath beene publikely acted by the right Honourable the Lorde Chamberlaine his Seruants", London, printed by Valentine Simmes for Androw Wise, "and are to be sold at his shop in Paules church yard at the signe of the Angel, 1597".

You travel back in time to work as an undercover agent in the streets of London. In order to be as inconspicuous as possible, you decide to become an Elizabethan yourself. Your role card will tell you who you are. Mix with the others, talk to them, try to find out who might have stolen the manuscript – without, of course, revealing your true intentions or your own identity. That might bring you into serious trouble with the Queen's own spy master, Lord Walsingham!

Richard Burbage

You are **Richard Burbage**. Your father James built London's first theatre, "The Theatre", in Shoreditch. You and your brother Cuthbert are both actors, but you are the real star. People flock to the theatre just to watch you perform as Hamlet, or Macbeth, or Lear! Many of Shakespeare's most fantastic lead roles seem to have been written just for you. Together with your brother Cuthbert you own half of Shakespeare's acting company, The Lord Chamberlain's Men, and half of the famous Globe Theatre.

Nathan Field

You are **Nathan Field**. Your father passionately opposed London's public entertainments. Presumably you did not intend a career in the theatre at first; you were a student of Richard Mulcaster at St. Paul's School in the late 1590s. However, you were so impressed by Nathaniel Giles, one of the managers of the new troupe of boy players at Blackfriars Theatre that you joined the boy acting group Children of the Queen's Revels (also known as Children of the Chapel) and acted at Blackfriars in some of famous Ben Jonson's plays. You joined the King's Men, Shakespeare's company, in the year of his death, 1616.

Thomas Platter

You are **Thomas Platter.** You were born in Switzerland in 1574 and studied medicine, but you also travelled widely in England. You were an absolute fan of the theatre! You saw one of the first productions of *Julius Caesar* in the newly built Globe Theatre in 1599. Since you kept a detailed diary of your journey, we know that you were at the Globe on the afternoon of September 21st, 1599.

Nicholas Sandon

You are **Nicholas Sandon**, son of a farmer in Warwickshire, and were expelled from your local grammar school after only a year of education. In 1579 records show that you started writing to Sir Francis Walsingham, the Secretary of State and Spy Master, reporting in tedious detail on singularly unsuccessful attempts to discover plots against the Queen or the state. In 1584, you arrived in Stratford-upon-Avon and, with more luck than judgement, stumbled across one William Shakespeare. Suspecting him of being a Catholic, you followed the young playwright for some years, but were fascinated by his art. In fact, you are thought to be among the first, and most extreme, recorded cases of celebrity stalking. If only you could lay hands on something the star himself had touched …

KV 1b: Who stole the manuscript of *Richard II*?

p. 5, ex. 5

Anne Shakespeare

You are **Anne Shakespeare**, born Hathaway, and a frustrated mother of three. Your husband has left the family to earn a living in London shortly after the birth of your twins, Judith and Hamnet, and you rarely hear from him. For some time now rumour has it that your husband is having an affair with some mysterious dark lady. Is that what is keeping him in London all the time? You are going to find out yourself what is going on!

William Kempe

You are **William Kempe**. You were already a well known performer of jigs and jests before joining Shakespeare's troupe, the Chamberlain's Men, in 1594 and played roles in *Much Ado about Nothing* and *Romeo and Juliet*. You were one of the first shareholders in the new Globe Theatre, but the others simply refused to see the greatness of your talent, how it was really you who attracted the masses, and would not let you have more than the ordinary share of the profits. So you decided to leave the Chamberlain's Men around 1599, making sure that somehow you would get the money Shakespeare and his lot really owed you.

Marie Mountjoy

You are **Marie Mountjoy**, Shakespeare's landlady, and you really have taken a fancy to him. He has been kind enough to play a role in setting up your daughter with Stephen Belott, since you think that he is just right for her: he is an authority figure, middle-aged, successful, gentlemanly type. You are, by the way, younger than Shakespeare, and French, and rather attractive yourself. A certain Mr Wood of Swan Alley seems to have more than mere business dealings with you. And how now about that friendly lodger with the dark eyes from that rather extravagant theatre world? You wouldn't mind a little private conversation with him now and then, would you?

Elizabeth Vernon

You are **Elizabeth Vernon**, chief lady-in-waiting to Elizabeth, Queen of England. What a job! You must constantly be ready to fulfil any of the Queen's requests, and by no means ever draw the attention of a man while in the presence of the Queen: all eyes must be on her! What a disaster that you, yet unmarried, have become pregnant in 1597. Within weeks, you are married off to the Earl of Southampton and find yourself and your husband in prison in Fleet Street. If only you could see your Will again just once.

Nat

You are **Nat**, an apprentice boy in Shakespeare's acting company, The Lord Chamberlain's Men. Richard Burbage the great has taken it upon himself to teach you his art, and you love it. Your favourite role is Puck in Shakespeare's wonderful play, *A Midsummer Night's Dream* – what a show you put on, doing somersaults all across the stage! And with that fantastic body painting Master Burbage has put on you, you really do look like a creature of the forests.

Jenny

You are **Jenny**, a servant at the Mermaid Inn, London's hot spot for the theatre crowd. It is a dreary life you lead in the dirty, stinking streets of London, sharing a room and a vermin infested bed with the only other waitress, Sally. The only highlight of your days is listening in on the conversations of the big stars of the London theatre world: Edward Alleyn, star player of the Admiral's Men who perform at the Rose, or Ben Jonson, that funny and witty playwright from Blackfriars – or gentle Will Shakespeare, always willing to put an extra penny into your pocket so that you may come and see one of his plays.

KV 1c: Who stole the manuscript of *Richard II*?

p. 5, ex. 5

Richard Martin

You are **Richard Martin**, Lord Mayor of London, married to Dorcas Eccleston, translator and bookseller. Both you and your wife are staunch Protestants and feel that the Queen ought to be more strict in her policy against Catholics and should further Protestant Reformation in her realm. Your only daughter married Sir Julius Caesar, Chancellor of the Exchequer, which was probably a good thing. Maybe this helped get you out of prison, where you had found yourself after being accused of owing the Queen money. As Warden of the Royal mint and Alderman of London, you have had more than one opportunity to serve yourself from the royal funds – but being in debt meant going to prison in those days. Now if your wife was a licensed bookseller for a bestseller, that would help a lot, wouldn't it?

Andrew Wise

You are **Andrew Wise**, alias Wyse, alias Wythes – what's in a name? You are a London publisher who specialised in first editions of Shakespeare plays. You are a full member of the Stationers Company and run your own bookshop at the sign of the Angel in St. Paul's Churchyard. London is a rough place for a bookseller. If you want to make big money, you have to turn to readers other than just those learned Oxfordians who go to bed with Ovid's Metamorphoses. Why not try something new? How about that Stratford guy whose plays attract the crowds? Didn't he hit the jackpot with his lengthy poems about Venus and Adonis? In a world where noone cares about copyrights and plagiarism, you dig for gold in Shakespeare's Globe. And you hit it big time: You had *Richard II*, *Richard III* and *Henry IV, Part 1*, printed by Simmes, and struck gold three times – all of them were bestsellers.

Sally

You are **Sally**, a servant at the Mermaid Inn, London's hot spot for the theatre crowd. It is a dreary life you lead in the dirty, stinking streets of London, sharing a room and a vermin-infested bed with the only other waitress, Jenny. The only highlight of your days is listening in on the conversations of the big stars of the London theatre world: Edward Alleyn, star player of the Admiral's Men who perform at the Rose, or Ben Jonson, that funny and witty playwright from Blackfriars – or gentle Will Shakespeare, always willing to put an extra penny into your pocket so that you may come and see one of his plays.

nameless craftsmen

You are one of the **nameless craftsmen** of London. In your shop you bake bread and pies and sell them in the streets of London to passers-by. Luckily enough, the newly built theatres in your neighbourhood provide for more customers than you ever had before: theatregoers, actors, apprentices – everyone seems to be hungry before a play.

Dick

You are **Dick**, an apprentice boy in Shakespeare's acting company, The Lord Chamberlain's Men. Augustine Philips is your master, and although he never plays any of the really big roles, you have already learned quite a bit about the trade from him. With your long, dark curly hair you are just the right person to play Juliet in Will's new play. Although, to be honest, it is hard at times to crave for "Romeo, oh Romeo" – that new boy actor who plays your lover seems to have a serious dislike for soap and water.

KV 2: Shakespeare's quotes

[👥] *Cut this paper into snippets, choose a line and learn it. Then move around the classroom, address someone you meet and speak the line to him or her. The other one responds with his or her line.*

Then come and kiss me, sweet and twenty,
Youth's a stuff will not endure.
Twelfth Night

Though this be madness, yet there is method in it.
Hamlet

Bloody, bawdy, villain! Remorseless, treacherous, lecherous, kindless villain!
Oh, vengeance! Why, what an ass I am!
Hamlet

Life's but a walking shadow
That struts and frets his hours upon the stage.
It is a tale full of sound of fury,
Signifying nothing.
Macbeth

The first thing we do, let's kill all the lawyers.
King Henry VI, Part 2

Why I can smile, and murder while I smile.
King Henry VI, Part 3

Have you not a moist eye, a dry hand, a yellow cheek, a white beard, a decreasing leg, an increasing belly? Is not your voice broken, your mind short, your chin double, your wit single, and every part about you blasted with antiquity.
King Henry IV, Part 2

Wash your hands, put on your night-gown, look not so pale. I tell you yet again, Banquo's buried, he cannot come out of his grave!
Macbeth

O wonder! How many goodly creatures are there here!
How beauteous mankind is! O brave new world
That has such people in it!
The Tempest

A horse! A horse! My kingdom for a horse!
Richard III

Lord, what fools these mortals be!
A Midsummer Night's Dream

But soft! What light through yonder window breaks!
It is the east, and Juliet is the sun!
Romeo and Juliet

These tedious fools!
Hamlet

I am a Jew. Hath not a Jew eyes? Hath not a Jew hands,
Organs, dimensions, senses, affections, passions? …
If you prick us, do we not bleed? If you tickle us, do we not laugh?
If you poison us, do we not die?
The Merchant of Venice

Frailty, thy name is woman.
Hamlet

Beware the Ides of March!
Julius Caesar

"I will buy with you, sell with you, talk with you, walk with you, and so following; but I will not eat with you, drink with you, nor pray with you."
The Merchant of Venice

Double, double toil and trouble
Fire burn, and cauldron bubble.
Macbeth

He hath eaten me out of house and home, he hath put all my substance into that fat belly of his.
King Henry IV, Part 2

Oh Romeo, Romeo, wherefore art thou Romeo?
Romeo and Juliet

There are more things in heaven and earth, Horatio,
Than are dreamt of in your philosophy.
Hamlet

© Ernst Klett Verlag GmbH, Stuttgart 2010 | www.klett.de
Von dieser Druckvorlage ist die Vervielfältigung für den eigenen Unterrichtsgebrauch gestattet. Die Kopiergebühren sind abgegolten. Alle Rechte vorbehalten.

Abi Workshop Englisch
Shakespeare Lehrerheft
ISBN 978-3-12-601015-3

KV   Kopiervorlagen

KV 3: Shakespearean insult sheet

p. 25, ex. 5

Ye olde directions: Combine one word or phrase from each of the columns below and adde "thou" to the beginning. Make certain thou knowest the meaning of thy strong words, and thou shalt have the perfect insult to fling at the wretched fools on the opposite team. Let thyself go. Mix and match to find that perfect barb from the Bard!

	A	B	C
1	artless	bunch-backed	ass
2	bawdy	clay-brained	adder
3	brazen	dog-hearted	crutch
4	churlish	empty-hearted	cutpurse
5	craven	evil-eyed	drunkard
6	dull	eye-offending	egg-shell
7	fawning	fat-kidney	goblin
8	frail	heavy-hearted	hedge-pig
9	foul	horn-mad	hempseed
10	grizzled	ill-breeding	jack-a-nape
11	hideous	ill-composed	knave
12	knavish	ill-nurtured	malignancy
13	peevish	iron-witted	malt-worm
14	pernicious	lean-witted	minimus
15	pestilent	lily-livered	moldwarp
16	rank	mad-bread	mole
17	reeky	motley-minded	pantaloon
18	reckless	muddy-mettled	quintessence of dust
19	rotten	onion-eyed	rabbit-sucker
20	spongy	pale-hearted	rascal
21	swinish	paper-faced	rudesby
22	thick	pigeon-livered	ruffian
23	truant	raw-boned	scantling
24	vain	rug-headed	scullion
25	vicious	rump-fed	snipe
26	wanton	shag-eared	vice
27	weedy	shrill-gorged	waterfly
28	whoreson	sour-faced	whipster

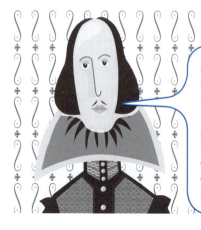

The longest insult in Shakespeare!

A knave; a rascal; an eater of broken meats; a base, proud, shallow, beggarly, three-suited, hundred-pound, filthy, worsted-stocking knave; a lily-livered, action-taking knave, a whoreson, glass-gazing, super-serviceable finical rogue; one-trunk-inheriting slave; one that wouldst be a bawd, in way of good service, and art nothing but the composition of a knave, beggar, coward, pandar, and the son and heir of a mongrel bitch.   ***King Lear*, Act II, Scene ii**

KV 4a: Drama families

p. 28, ex. 3

[👥] *Try to find the other members of your drama family. Then exchange information and agree on a way of presenting your mini-dramas to the class.*

The Richard III family

Richard
You are also called the Duke of Gloucester, and will eventually be crowned King Richard III. Deformed in body and twisted in mind, you are the central character and the villain of the play, stopping at nothing to become king. By means of your intelligence and evil nature you manage to talk the wife of one of your victims, Anne, into marrying you; have the young sons of your brother, King Edward IV, murdered; kill your own brother Clarence; and thus seize the crown of England. Ultimately, though, your enemies unite and defeat your army in the battle of Bosworth Fields, leaving you shouting for "A horse! A horse! A kingdom for a horse!" before they kill you.

Buckingham
You are the duke of Buckingham, Richard's right-hand man in his schemes to gain power, almost as amoral and ambitious as Richard himself. You campaign for him to make sure he is crowned, but he does not reward you as he had promised. This, and Richard's thirst for blood, alienate you from him.

King Edward IV
You are the elder brother of Richard and Clarence, and are King of England at the start of the play. You were deeply involved in the Yorkists' brutal overthrow of the Lancaster regime, but as king devoted yourself to achieving reconciliation among the various political factions of your reign. You are sick and close to death at the beginning of the play, and finally die when you hear of the execution of your brother Clarence, all the time unaware of Richard's scheming behind your back. If only you had known what fate awaited your wife and sons after your death!

Clarence
You are the gentle, trusting brother born between Edward and Richard in the York family. Richard murders you in order to get you out of the way. You leave two children, a son and a daughter.

Queen Elizabeth
You are also called Lady Gray, and you are the wife of King Edward IV. Together you have three children: the two young princes, heirs to the throne, and their older sister, young Elizabeth. Richard is your brother-in-law. After your husband's death, you are at Richard's mercy, who rightly views you as an enemy because you oppose his rise to power, and because you are intelligent and strong-willed. However, you can not protect your two young sons from being killed in the Tower.

Anne
You are the young widow of Prince Edward, who was the son of the former king, Henry VI. You hate Richard and blame him for the death of your husband. However, you know exactly how weak your position is at court. When Richard asks you to marry him, you know that if you want to survive you do not really have a choice. You get killed in the end anyway: Richard changes his mind, sets his eyes on young Elizabeth and needs you out of the way.

Richmond
You are a member of a branch of the royal family of Lancaster. It does not take long for the people of England to become fed up with King Richard, so when rumour spreads that you are gathering a force of rebels to challenge Richard for the throne, English noblemen defect to your side in droves. You are good, just, and fair – all the things Richard is not, but all the things Elizabethans wanted you to be (you are the founder of the Tudor dynasty). You win the battle against Richard, who is killed, and are subsequently crowned Henry VII, the first of the Tudor monarchs. By marrying young Elizabeth you secure peace between the feuding houses of York and Lancaster.

KV 4 b: Drama families

Try to find the other members of your drama family. Then exchange information and agree on a way of presenting your mini-dramas to the class.

The Hamlet family

Hamlet
You are the Prince of Denmark, the son of the late King Hamlet, and the nephew of the present king, Claudius. One night, the ghost of your father appears and reveals to you that he was murdered by Claudius and demands revenge. Melancholy and indecisive by nature, you are nearly driven mad by this request. Besides, there is the problem of Ophelia, who you would rather see in a nunnery than in a matrimonial bed with you. You stab Polonius, Ophelia's father, by accident (Why was he standing behind curtains in your mother's bedroom, for God's sake?), and are sent to England for a while so that things can settle down a bit. However, your ship is attacked by pirates, and you return just in time for Ophelia's funeral. She killed herself for grief over her father's death. Laertes, Ophelia's brother, challenges you to a sword fight to avenge his sister's death. What you do not know: Laertes' blade was poisoned by Claudius, who has wanted to get rid of you for a long time. Unfortunately, it scratches Laertes before it wounds you, but you have time enough to use it on Claudius before you yourself die.

Claudius
You are the King of Denmark, Hamlet's uncle. Your lust for power has made it necessary for you to remove the King and to think of ways of getting rid of this nerd of a prince, Hamlet. You'd much rather be in bed with his sexy mom, but he keeps moping around the castle, peeping from behind curtains – and now he seems to have a sneaking suspicion that you might be responsible for his father's death. Or what else could he have meant by staging a play in which the murder scene is the climax? You simply had to storm out of the room at the sight of it – you hope to get away with this murder.

Gertrude
Being Queen is fun, so why not remain Queen as long as possible? Isn't it only natural that you should marry Claudius after your husband's mysterious death? You really love your son deeply, and are worried about his strange behaviour. That's why you ask Rosencrantz and Guildenstern, his friends, to come to Elsinore and keep an eye on him. Unfortunately, your husband does not keep you informed of his schemes. If you had known that he had poisoned the goblet of wine he offered your son during the duel, you wouldn't have drunk from it, would you?

Horatio
You are the prince's best friend. You studied with the prince at the university in Wittenberg, you are loyal and helpful but can't do much to prevent this tragedy from taking its course. When the Norwegian Prince Fortinbras arrives at Elsinore and sees the entire royal family either slain or poisoned, but most certainly all dead, you are the only one left to tell this amazing story.

Ophelia
You are the daughter of Polonius, the Lord Chamberlain at Elsinore Castle, a beautiful young woman with whom Prince Hamlet has fallen in love. Quite the obedient girl, you agree to spy on him as your father orders you to do, but you succumb to his wish reluctantly. Besides, you don't really understand what it is the prince wants: one day he says he loves you; the next day he tells you to become a nun. All the mayhem drives you mad, and you commit suicide out of grief over the loss of your father. Hamlet's declarations of love are a bit late now.

The ghost
One night you suddenly appear and frighten the hell out of the poor guards of Elsinore castle. No one knows who or what you really are, but it is suspected that you are the spectre of Hamlet's recently deceased father. With your call for revenge you spark the whole story off.

KV 4c: Drama families

p. 28, ex. 3

[👥] *Try to find the other members of your drama family. Then exchange information and agree on a way of presenting your mini-dramas to the class.*

The Venetian family

Shylock

You are a Jewish moneylender in Venice, where Jews are not well liked. Angered by the mistreatment at the hands of Venice's Christians, particularly Antonio, you scheme to get your revenge by demanding as payment for a sum of money you lent him a pound of Antonio's flesh, which only needs to be paid if Antonio cannot pay you back within three months. But your informants tell you that Antonio's ships are having trouble reaching the Venetian shore.

Portia

You are a wealthy heiress from Belmont, beautiful and intelligent. A clause in your father's will forces you to marry whichever suitor chooses correctly among three caskets (silver, gold, lead: and the leaden one is, of course, the right one!). However, your true love Bassanio not only manages to raise the money for the journey to Belmont, but also to choose the right casket. Alas, you have to marry in haste: Bassanio's friend needs your help, and after a quick look at the other characters in the play you realize that there is no one clever enough to get him out of the grasp of the Jew – except for yourself. You dress up as a young lawyer and hurry to Venice just in time for the great showdown.

Antonio

You are a merchant who has had a bit of hard luck with his ships recently. Your beloved friend Bassanio has turned to you for money in a matter of life and death. So you agree to be Bassanio's guarantor, who intends to borrow money from the Jew (although you admit that you are somewhat prejudiced toward Jews), and you sign Shylock's contract. You consider the risk rather low; after all, you expect some vessels loaded with goods back in Venice any day now. You are sure that you will be able to pay the Jew back in time.

Bassanio

Your love for the wealthy Portia leads you to borrow money from Shylock with Antonio as his guarantor. An ineffectual businessman, you prove yourself a worthy suitor, correctly identifying the casket that contains Portia's portrait. If only you hadn't got your friend into such a mess. The Duke of Venice is a powerful man, but he, too, is bound by the law – and since Antonio signed the contract, the law is on the Jew's side.

Jessica

You hate life in your father's house, and elope with the young Christian gentleman, Lorenzo. The fate of your soul is often in doubt: Can your marriage overcome the fact that you were born a Jew? Hopefully life will be easier for you and your young husband in Belmont. But wasn't it a bit callous of you to sell a ring given to your father by your mother? Eloping must have been a terrible blow for your father, but selling such a ring might do him in.

Doctor Bellario

A wealthy Paduan lawyer and Portia's cousin, you never really appear in the play. But without your letters of introduction, Portia would never have been able to make her appearance in court and save Antonio's life. What a clever idea to let the Jew have his way – and make it impossible for him to carry out his scheme! After all, he only has the right to a pound of flesh – no more, no less – and not to a single drop of blood: So how is he going to cut that out of Antonio's breast? Wit runs in the family.

KV 4 d: Drama families

[👥] *Try to find the other members of your drama family. Then exchange information and agree on a way of presenting your mini-dramas to the class.*

The Scottish family

Macbeth
You are a Scottish nobleman and very successful warrior. After a successful battle against Scotland's enemy, you meet three witches who prophesy that you will be Thane of Cawdor and King of Scotland. Your friend Banquo, who is with you, is told that his children will be kings. At first you scoff at the words of the weird sisters, but when you return to the soldiers' camp and meet the King, you are informed that the Thane of Cawdor is a traitor and will be executed – and you inherit his title. Now that gives you something to think about!

Lady Macbeth
You are the wife of a nobleman and warrior. Although you know about his achievements on the battlefield, you realise that your husband lacks a certain recklessness to achieve the big things in life. In a letter your husband tells you about the witches, so when he returns from the battlefield, you talk him into killing the king. You see to it that the murder is blamed on the king's sons, who flee immediately. Now the way is free for your husband to be crowned King of Scotland.

Banquo
You are a Scottish warrior, loyal to the king, and good friend of Macbeth's. You are there when the three witches address Macbeth and witness their prediction that your friend will become King of Scotland. And although you do not quite believe that they are supernatural beings, you order them to tell you about your own future, too – which is that your children will become kings. Soon after Duncan's death and Macbeth's coronation you begin to fear that your former friend has killed to achieve his aims. You carefully avoid confronting him, but also make it clear that you are no blind follower. Unfortunately, such shilly-shallying does not go down very well with the new king, and you find yourself a ghost at the royal banquet.

Duncan
You are the kind king, who gratefully rewards his noblemen with titles for their fight against Scotland's enemies. Like any other king, you wish your sons to inherit your title, so you proclaim your son Malcolm Prince of Cumberland. That, however, is the cue for the Thane of Cawdor: he now knows that there is no legal way for him to become king. Sorry, but you won't survive the second act of the drama.

Macduff
Banquo was not the only one who doubted the Macbeths' version about the death of the King; you, too, felt a bit uneasy about it. Now that Macbeth is king, that uneasiness has turned into downright horror. The former honourable warrior murders anyone who is likely to oppose him. You decide to join Duncan's sons, who have gathered an army in England, when news reaches you that Macbeth has killed your wife and children. You lead the rebels' army to Scotland and confront Macbeth, whom you kill in a fight.

A witch
You are one of the three "weird sisters" who spark the story off with their predictions about the future. You just like a bit of trouble, and these humans are so easy to manipulate! It's enough to tell someone that he will climb the social ladder to stir his ambition, and if at the same time you unsettle him by telling him that this success won't last for more than one generation, a number of evil deeds are sure to ensue. Of course you expected your victim to come back and ask for more details. Only this time you give him a false sense of security by explaining that only someone not of woman born can kill him. Ever heard of a Caesarean section (*Kaiserschnitt*)? Well your Scottish Nobleman certainly never has.

KV 5: Themes of Shakespeare

p. 30, ex. 2

[👥] *In his plays Shakespeare very often took up the relevant themes of Elizabethan society as he had to cater to the public taste. Although each individual play has its own focus, the themes "conflicts of rivals in love or war", "order or disorder", "appearance vs reality" and "metamorphosis and change" can be found in every play, also in "Richard III", where the themes of "ambition vs conscience" and "contact with the supernatural" are also treated. The following passages are all from "Richard III" touching the mentioned themes.*

A conscience	B conflicts of rivals in love or war	C contact with the supernatural	D order and disorder
E appearance vs. reality	F metamorphosis and change	G ambition	H men and women

a) *Match each of the passages to one of the themes above.*

b) *Collect as much information as possible from each passage about the characters involved and their part in the plot of the play.*

			Solution
1.	For then I'll marry Warwick's younger daughter, What though I killed her husband and her father?	Richard, I.1	
2.	I do not know that Englishman alive With whom my soul is any jot at odds more than the infant that is born tonight. I thank my God for my humility.	Richard, I.1	
3.	I passed, methought, the melancholy flood, With that sour ferrymen which poets write of, Unto the kingdom of perpetual night.	Clarence, I.4	
4.	Where's thy conscience now? Oh, in the Duke of Gloucester's purse.	Murderer, I.4	
5.	Edward, my lord, thy son, our king, is dead. Why grow the branches when the root is gone?	Elizabeth, I.2	
6.	B: What shall we do if we perceive Lord Hastings will not yield to our complots? R: Chop off his head. Something we will determine.	Buckingham/ Richard, III.1	
7.	I must be marrried to my brother's daughter Or else my kingdom stand on brittle glass, Murder her brothers, and then marry her, Uncertain way of gain. But I am in So far in blood that sin will pluck on sin. Tear-falling pity dwells not in this eye.	Richard, IV.2	
8.	Let me sit heavy on thy soul tomorrow. Think how thou stab'st me in my prime of youth At Tewkesbury. Despair therefore, and die.	Ghost, V.3	

KV 6: Richard's thoughts

p. 31, ex. 3

[👥] *Speaking the hero's feelings: Alone on stage, Richard is considering his further actions and what it is that will drive him to do the things he will do. Experiment with different ways of speaking his soliloquy to bring out his various moods, or even uneasy feelings as he thinks aloud. For example, you could share the lines and whisper them, heads close together, to indicate his inner struggle. Use the following paraphrase of the soliloquy to help you with your experiments.*

ll. 1–9	Now a certain era has come to an end. Victory has fallen to our house. Yet do I like it? No! Everybody seems to be happy since the war is over, and now we seem to feel the warmth of peace. My high time is over and now is the winter of my discontent. The grim face of war has changed, has become peaceful. Yet I do not like this son/sun of York, who has brought about this change.
ll. 10–13	What kind of a soldier is this now? Rather than taking his horse and defeating the enemies of this kingdom to show our power, he jumps about following the sounds of musical instruments. Look at this weakling.
ll. 14–23	The reasons for my present mood:
ll. 14–15	But I am different. Why? Because I do not have a good-looking body and am not handsome. I don't want to play these amorous games with beautiful ladies.
ll. 16–17	I have a deformed body and lack the beauty to appear attractive to the ladies at court who are trying to impress the other wartime heroes.
ll. 18–21	I feel cheated by nature. I am angry about the unjust world that has given me this body from birth.
ll. 22–23	I am so ugly and lonely that even dogs bark at me when they see me.
ll. 24–27	These are bad times for people like me who only feel that they are of use in times of war and now feel that other people are ignoring me. All I can do is waste my time by looking at my shadow and talking about my ugliness.
ll. 28–31	Yet I am a person of action. Since I cannot play along with these new games, for which nice looks and flirting behaviour are required, I will have my own pleasure at my own game – to play the villain and let them feel what it means to be hated by me.

KV 7: Opinions about Shakespeare

p. 31, ex. 5

a) [3▶] *Read the following beginnings of statements, then watch the video clip once and finish the statements made by people in the street in no more than five words.*

	Solution
1. Shakespeare's rival, Ben Jonson called him …	
2. Although his phrases are commonly used, plays are studied at school and Shakespeare is serving many ideologies, at the heart of the fascination …	
3. Every actor …	
4. Studying Shakespeare is alright, but …	
5. Shakespeare says in a beautiful way the things that …	
6. Thelma Holt, currently producing Macbeth, has no doubt the Bard …	
7. In the London West End the public is able to see three different productions on the same night. They are …	
8. A few critical voices say that this …	

b) [3▶] *Now watch the clip a second time, concentrating on the opinion of the three experts only. Then fill in the following grid.*

	Thelma Holt	2nd expert	3rd expert
1. Personality of speaker			
2. Opinion towards the importance of Shakespeare			
3. Why do we need to keep up the work with Shakespeare's play/ fascination of Shakespeare?			
4. How should we deal with Shakespeare today?			

c) *Outline your own view on the topic.*

d) *Formulate questions that you would like to ask the three experts.*

e) *Recently the BBC has started interactive TV, asking the viewing public to respond to their broadcasts. Write an email presenting your view of the topic.*

KV 8: The meanings of *Richard III*

[👥] *Plurisignation of Shakespeare: There is no right way of thinking about or performing even an early Shakespearean play like "Richard III". Being the second most performed play of all, thousands of different productions have tried to interpret it "correctly". Thousand of pages have been written to explain its meaning on the many different levels the plot offers. However, it is possible to come to a personal interpretation of the play and find one's own way of giving it meaning. Like many Shakespeare plays, "Richard III" shows many sides of a kaleidoscope. Here are just a few examples:*

> *Richard III is ...*
> - *a play about war. It is about brutality and the killing of innocent victims.*
> - *a play that makes history exciting: What can we learn from times before our generation?*
> - *a great story: telling how human weaknesses lead to (self-)destruction.*
> - *a play about conscience or the absense of it.*
> - *a historical thriller: a murder story full of action that ends with the death of the guilty party.*
> - *a play where the weak are ruthlessly overcome by sheer power.*
> - *a psychological story giving an insight into the mind of a usurper and tyrant.*
> - *a play of political and social realism: an oppressive hierarchical society produces corrupt individuals.*
> - *a play about the battle of the sexes: how and why do men and women interact the way they do?*
> - *a play of illusions showing the effect the supernatural may have on human beings.*
> - *a play of ideas or themes: for example "private" vs "public" or "appearance" vs "reality".*
> - *a dramatic poem: showing the genius of a poet using language and imagery to great effect.*
> - *a tragedy: a great man falls due to a great flaw in his character.*

a) *Do you see other ways of seeing the play? Add your own concept:*

_____

_____

_____

b) *Choose one of the interpretations above and tell the story of Richard from that point of view, or work out a performance of an important scene seen from this particular viewpoint.*

_____

_____

_____

KV 9: Tools of language

p. 33, ex. 7

[👥] *Shakespeare was a master in using a large variety of stylistic tools to achieve his dramatic effects. Although this makes the understanding of his plays sometimes difficult for the reader, to discover the skills involved also enables us to enjoy his powerful texts even more and to enter the mind set of the plays. The following examples from "Richard III" all show one particular feature of his highly effective language.*

A rhetoric	**B** metaphor	**C** irony	**D** repetition
E insult	**F** list	**G** word-play	**H** imagery

a) *Match the stylistic tools to one of the passages below.*

b) *What hints do the quotations give you towards the plot of the play?*

			Solution
1.	Was ever woman in this humour wooed? Was ever woman in this humour won?	Richard, I.1	
2.	To fly the boar before the boar pursues Were to incense the boar to follow us And make pursuit where he did mean no chase.	Hastings, III.2	
3.	When I have most need to employ a friend, And most most assured that he is a friend, Deep, hollow, treacherous, and full of guile Be he unto me.	Buckingham, II.1	
4.	A horse, a horse, my kingdom for a horse!	Richard, V.3	
5.	Have done thy charm, thou hateful, withered hag. And leave out thee? Stay, dog, for thou shalt hear me. If heaven have any grievous plague in store Exceeding those that I can wish upon thee, Oh, let them keep it till thy sins be ripe And then hurl down their indignation On thee, the troubler of the poor world's peace.	Richard and Margaret, I.3	
6.	In God's name, what art thou? A man as you are. But not, as I am royal. Nor you, as we are loyal.	Clarence/ Murderers, I.4	
7.	I think there's never a man in Christendom Can lesser hide his love or hate, than he, For by his face straight shall you know his heart.	Hastings, III.4	
8.	Is the chair empty? Is the sword unswayed? Is the king dead? The empire unpossessed? What heir of York is there alive but we? And who is England's king but great York's heir?	Richard, IV.4	

KV 10: Richard the politician

p. 33, ex. 7

At the height of his power in this scene, Richard's allies plan to trick the Mayor of London into asking Richard to become King. Instead of appearing to want the crown, Richard pretends to have to be begged before finally accepting it.

a) *Rephrase this passage in present-day English.*

b) *Point out the arguments on the two sides of the dialogue.*

c) *This scene has been set up by Richard. Point out how specific rhetorical elements aid his deception.*

d) [👥] *Role play: Act out a similar situation. One person wants to become the head of something (a football team, etc.) but pretends not to want to.*

Catesby:	Oh, make them joyful; grant their lawful suit.
Richard:	Alas, why would you heap this care on me?
	I am unfit for state and majesty.
	I do beseech you, take it not amiss;
	I cannot, nor I will not, yield to you.
Buckingham:	If you refuse it, as in love and zeal
	Loath to depose the child, your brother's son –
	As well we know your tenderness of heart,
	And gentle, kind, effeminate remorse,
	Which we have noted in you to your kindred,
	And equally indeed to all estates –
	Yet know, whe'er you accept our suit or no,
	Your brother's son shall never reign our king,
	But we will plant some other in the throne
	To the disgrace and downfall of your House;
	And with this resolution here we leave you.
	Come, citizens, we will entreat no more.
	(Exeunt)
Catesby:	Call him again, sweet Prince; accept their suit.
	If you deny them, all the land will rue it.
Richard:	Will you enforce me to a world of cares?
	Call them again. I am not made of stones,
	But penetrable to your kind entreaties,
	Albeit against my conscience and my soul.
	(Enter the people)
	Cousin of Buckingham, and sage grave men,
	Since you will buckle fortune on my back
	To bear her burden whe'er I will or no,
	I must have patience to endure the load.
	But if black scandal or foul-faced reproach
	Attend the sequel of your imposition,
	Your mere enforcement shall acquittance me
	From all the impure blots and stains thereof:
	For God doth know, and you may partly see,
	How far I am from the desire of this.
Mayor:	God bless your grace: we see it and will say it.
Richard:	In saying so, you shall but say the truth.
Buckingham:	Then I salute you with this royal title:
	Long live Richard, England's worthy King.

Richard III, Act III, scene vii

KV 11: The cornerstone is the metre

p. 35, ex. 1

a) [👥] *Read the text "in a round", everyone reading one word only.*

b) *First on your own, then confirming with a partner, write out the verse-form of the text, including punctuation.*

c) *Put in the stress marks. Remember the rules about iambic pentameter.*

d) *Now read "in the round" again. This time everyone reads to the next comma or full-stop.*

e) *Finally, everyone reads one complete thought.*

But soft what light through yonder window breaks it is the east and Juliet is the sun arise fair sun and kill the envious moon who is already sick and pale with grief that thou her maid art far more fair than she be not her maid since she is envious her vestal livery is but sick and green and none but fool do wear it cast it off.

Romeo and Juliet, Act II, scene ii

To be or not to be that is the question whether 'tis nobler in the mind to suffer the slings and arrows of outrageous fortunes or to take arms against a sea of troubles and by opposing end them to die to sleep no more and by a sleep to say we end the heartache and the thousand natural shocks that flesh is heir to 'tis a consummation devoutly to be wished to die to sleep to sleep perchance to dream ay there's the rub.

Hamlet, Act III, scene i

Now is the winter of our discontent made glorious summer by this son of York and all the clouds that loured upon our house in the deep bosom of the ocean buried now are our brows bound with victorious wreaths our bruised arms hung up for monuments our stern alarums changed to merry meetings our dreadful marches to delightful measures, grim-visaged war hath smoothed his wrinkled front and now instead of mounting barbed steeds to fright the souls of fearful adversaries he capers nimbly in a ladies chamber to the lascivious pleasing of a lute.

Richard III, Act I, scene i

If it were done when 'tis done, then 'twere well it were done quickly if th' assassination could trammel up the consequences and catch with his surcease success that but this blow might be the be-all and the end-all – here but here upon this bank and shoal of time – we'd jump the life to come but in these cases we still have judgement here that we but teach bloody instructions which being taught return to plague th'inventor this even-handed justice commands th'ingredients of our poison'd chalice to our own lips he's here in double trust first as I am his kinsman and his subject – strong both against the deed then as his host who should against his murderers shut the door not bear the knife myself besides this Duncan hath borne his faculties so meek hat been so clear in his great office that his virtues will plead like angels trumpet-tongu'd against the deep damnation of this taking-off and pity like a naked new-born babe striding the blast or heaven's cherubim hors'd upon the sightless couriers of the air shall blow the horrid deed in every eye that tears shall drown the wind I have no spur to prick the sides of my intent, but only vaulting ambition which o'er-leaps itself and falls on th'other.

Macbeth, Act I, scene vii

KV 12: Juliet as an example of the question of gender p. 37, ex. 5

Discovery and movement of thought

a) [👥] *Start by reading the text "in a round". Then recite it by walking through the room or doing some repetitive physical activity such as bouncing a ball.*

b) *Now experiment with the text. Imagine you are speaking to an imaginative audience or another character of the play who is not present. Have fun trying out every imaginable way of speaking.*

c) *Feel Juliet's nervousness by putting two pieces of paper on the ground at a distance of about three metres from one another. These are your two stages from which you are allowed to speak. Now read the speech changing your stage at every punctuation mark.*

d) *A good way of getting closer to the meaning of the text is for one part of the group to speak the text together while the other half does not read but just listens to it and echoes every word that makes an impact on them.*

> The clock struck nine when I did send the Nurse;
> In half an hour she promised to return.
> Perchance she cannot meet him: that's not so.
> O, she is lame! Love's heralds should be thoughts,
> 5 Which ten times faster glides than the sun's beams,
> Driving back shadows over low'ring hills;
> Therefore do nimble-pinioned doves draw Love,
> And therefore hath the wind-swift Cupid wings.
> Now is the sun upon the highmost hill
> 10 Of this day's journey, and from nine till twelve
> Is three long hours, yet she is not come.
> Had she affections and warm youthful blood,
> She would be as swift in motion as a ball;
> My words would bandy her to my sweet love,
> 15 And his to me.
> But old folks, many feign as they were dead,
> Unwieldy, slow, heavy, and pale as lead.
>
> *Romeo and Juliet*, Act II, scene v

KV 13: Feel the rhythm and power p. 41, ex. 1

[👥] Many Shakespearean texts are easier to understand when you experience them physically. In the following passage from "Hamlet", young Ophelia has been sent to find out if Hamlet is really mad. She comes back to her father Polonius and in a very excited state tells him about her findings and her own emotions. Try to understand her better by working through some of the exercises below the text.

a) Stand in a circle. Everyone reads one word only as the text progresses. Try to keep up the rhythm.

b) Read it out again. Now everyone reads to the next punctuation mark.

c) Start moving through the room reading the text at your own pace, but make a sharp turn at the end of every line.

d) Repeat the last exercise, but this time you turn at every punctuation mark.

e) Turn to a partner, link arms, and repeat the last exercise. This time you turn when you feel the end of a sense unit. (Be careful!)

f) You may feel you know the passage well enough now. Recite it in whatever way you like it best. You may sing it with certain emotions, or you could whisper or shout it, changing your voice, your accent or whatever you like.

g) Finally, one of you plays Ophelia and tries to convince the group. The group, however, is just not interested.

1.	O, what a noble mind is here o'verthrown!
2.	The courtier's, soldier's, scholar's, eye, tongue, sword,
3.	Th'expectancy and rose of the fair state,
4.	The glass of fashion and the mould of form,
5.	Th'observed of all observers, quite, quite, down!
6.	And I, of ladies most deject and wretched,
7.	That sucked the honey of his music vows,
8.	Now see that noble and most sovereign reason
9.	Like sweet bells jangled, out of time and harsh,
10.	That unmatch'd form and feature of blown youth
11.	Blasted with ecstasy. O, woe is me
12.	T'have seen what I have seen, see what I see!

***Hamlet*, Act III, scene i**

KV 14: Tossing lines

p. 41, ex. 3

[👥] *How to play: Cut out the individual lines, mix and distribute them in the group. Every member of the group studies his line. After you have placed yourself sitting or standing in a circle, one by one you speak your line and throw an object (such as a ball) to another student, who then delivers his line, throws the object to someone else, who speaks his line, etc. If a word or a line has not been understood, there is a good way of finding out. Just throw the object. Try to rearrange the text. Who do you feel has the first line? Who might follow?*

Barnardo	Who's there?
Francisco	Nay, answer me. Stand and unfold yourself.
Barnardo	Long live the King!
Francisco	Barnardo?
Barnardo	He.
Francisco	You come most carefully upon your hour.
Barnardo	'Tis now struck twelve; get thee to bed, Francisco.
Francisco	For this relief much thanks. 'Tis bitter cold, And I am sick at heart.
Barnardo	Have you had quiet guard?
Francisco	Not a mouse stirring.
Barnardo	Well, good night. If you do meet Horatio and Marcellus, The rivals of my watch, bid them make haste.
Francisco	*(Enter Horatio and Marcellus)* I think I hear them. Stand, ho! Who is there?
Horatio	Friends to this ground.
Marcellus	And liegemen to the Dane.
Francisco	Give you good night.
Marcellus	Oh, farewell, honest soldier, Who hath reliev'd you?
Francisco	Barnado hath my place. Give you good night. *(Exit Francisco)*
Marcellus	Holla, Barnado!
Barnado	Say – What, is Horatio there?
Horatio	A piece of him.
Barnado	Welcome, Horatio; welcome, good Marcellus.

Hamlet, Act I, scene i

KV 15: The authorship debate – role play

p. 45, ex. 3

[👥] *Build groups of five. Choose one of the persons listed below. Your task is to defend your position at court, where the case of the authorship of Shakespeare's plays is dealt with. Make a list of the arguments you intend to put forth, and think of ways to answer the arguments of the other side.*

Henry Condell

You were one of Shakespeare's best friends and his colleague in The Lord Chamberlain's Men. You not only saw him write the plays himself, but also witnessed how he directed them as a member of the company during rehearsals. He even left you some money so that you could buy a memory ring to remember him in your will. In your opinion he was not only a great writer but also a great friend, and you simply do not want him to be forgotten. So when he died, you and others who had known him as a friend and colleague felt that his plays should be preserved for posterity, and so you started the enormous effort of collecting and editing whatever you could find: manuscripts, quarto editions, and since so many of you who had learned and performed his plays time and again were still alive, you even took the trouble to write some of them down from memory.

Ben Jonson

You were a great writer yourself, but you recognised genius when you saw it – and Shakespeare was without a doubt such a genius. And he was a good friend to boot. You will never forget the night you spent drinking with him in a pub in Stratford after his daughter's wedding. So when you heard of the project to collect all the plays he had ever written and to publish them in a complete edition, you were all for it. You even wrote a preface and an elegy for your friend, the "Sweet Swan of Avon".

Alice Bacon

Your husband was an outstanding personality. He was interested in the sciences and the arts, especially the theatre. He travelled extensively abroad and wrote essays on political and philosophical issues. As Elizabeth's counsel and James' Lord Chancellor, your husband was well acquainted with court etiquette, and due to his extensive reading and university education was a learned man. You find it unbearable that all the tribute, all the fame, all the money for the plays written by your husband should go to the heirs of an uneducated country lad, one "William Shakespeare", who probably did not even know how to write his own name.

Reporters

You have heard about the case that is being dealt with at court today and intend to write an article for your paper. Decide if you want to write for the yellow press or a quality paper and think of the type of information you might want for either of them. Remember that for a yellow press paper a scandalous story sells better, whereas a quality paper story must be filled with facts and should be kept as objective as possible.

Judge

You have to decide today whether the allegations of Alice Bacon hold true, and whether the book published by Condell, Jonson and others is a hoax. Your job is to keep order in the courtroom and to find out the truth. What do you need to know to come to a decision?

KV 16: Honi soit qui mal y pense – mediation

p. 51, ex. 3

Part of the programme of the recent school exchange was to see a production of "Richard III". The programme writes a number of different interpretations as to the meaning of the play. You find one of them particularly interesting to talk about with your friend. Explain to him the main aspects mentioned in the text.

Honi soit qui mal y pense

Oder die Kunst, sich am Allgemeineigentum zu bedienen

Richard lebt in einer Zeit, in der die Rosenkriege in England bürgerkriegsähnliche Verhältnisse geschaffen haben, in einer Zeit, die die großen Familien entzweite, in der Gesetzlosigkeit und Chaos herrscht, und die das Volk verrohen lässt. Er lebt in einer Zeit, in der das unter Heinrich V noch stabile England auseinanderzufallen droht, und die Konkursmasse des Königreiches die Barone zur skrupellosen Selbstbedienung einlädt.

Dirty Dick

Richard jedoch hat als nachgeborener Sohn des Hauses York keine Chance, über die Erbfolge an Macht und Reichtum zu kommen. Dazu noch verunstaltet, hässlich und von düsterem Charakter, voller Missgunst, Neid und sadistisch veranlagt, hat er auch keine Aussicht, in Macht und Vermögen einzuheiraten. Nur durch Mord, Betrug und Intrigen kann er an die Macht kommen. Und er nutzt diese Mittel geschickt und rigoros aus. Er beschuldigt Clarence wissentlich falsch, einen Putsch zu planen, und räumt ihn so aus seinem Weg. Er lässt die jungen Prinzen ermorden, er erteilt den Auftrag, Lord Hastings und Buckingham zu ermorden (ihr angeblicher Verrat ist wiederum seine Begründung), er manipuliert und täuscht die Bürger Londons in einer bühnenreifen Vorstellung über seine Absichten, und er versteht es auch, Lady Anne zu umgarnen, um sich so des Wohlwollens seiner Gegner zu versichern. Nach der Maxime, dass *a good fight is never clean*, schreibt er die Spielregeln um und verschafft sich so Vorteile, auf die der überraschte Gegner nicht reagieren kann. Wie ein unfairer Boxer, wie ein „Dirty Dick", *fighted* Richard, schlägt unter die Gürtellinie, setzt Ellbogen-, Kopf- und Kniestöße und kümmert sich nicht um die Spielregeln, sich sicher seiend, dass er nicht disqualifiziert werden wird, weil er ja zuvor die Ringrichter bestochen und sie von sich abhängig gemacht hat.

Doch wenn wir den Eingangsmonolog Richards genau lesen, stellen wir fest, dass Richard gar nicht am materiellen Vorteil des Machtbesitzes interessiert ist. Geld scheint ihn nur als Mittel der Bestechung zu interessieren. Ja, er erwähnt in der langen Rede, in der er dem Zuschauer seinen Charakter und seine Absichten offenbart, mit keinem Wort, dass er an der Krone interessiert sei. Sein eigentliches Ziel ist die physische und psychische Macht über andere. Er, der an die Seite geschobene Drittälteste, der missachtet am Rand stehen musste, wenn andere sich vergnügten, der verspottet wurde, mit dem niemand, nicht einmal die Hunde, spielen wollten, der sogar von seiner Mutter verachtet wird, will es den Menschen nun zeigen. Richard will die Kontrolle über das Land und die Menschen. Er, der sich als Misanthrop and als misogyn geriert, dessen jede einzelne Rede voller Zynismus ist, ist entschlossen, Macht über andere Menschen auszuüben. Er will die Menschen manipulieren können, will wie Satan die Seelen der Menschen korrumpieren und besitzen. Er will die Menschen wie Kampfhähne aufeinander hetzen, will Herr über Leben und Tod sein. Wie die Katze mit der Maus will er mit den Menschen spielen und sich an der Angst der Opfer vergnügen.

© Leonhard C. Günter, *University Players News Nr. 43*, Universität Hamburg, 2007/2008.

Lösungen zu den Kopiervorlagen

Kopiervorlage 5
1. – B, 2. – E, 3. – F, 4. – A, 5. – D, 6. – G, 7. – D + B + A + H, 8. – C

Kopiervorlage 7
a) 1. … a man for all times. 2. … the play is the thing. 3. … wants to play Shakespeare. 4. … it's quite difficult to understand. 5. … seem ugly in everyday life. 6. … deserves the superior status. 7. … *Macbeth, Richard III, The Tempest*. 8. … obsession has gone too far.

b) **Thelma Holt:** 1. producer, 2. cannot be regarded highly enough, 3. Shakespeare is a genius, 4. the obligation to produce "good" Shakespeare only
2nd expert: 1. professor of literature, 2. critical; too much "bardophilia" at the expense of other important playwrights, 3. no answer, yet indirectly afraid of overemphasis on Shakespeare, 4. regard the other writers as well
3rd expert: 1. historian, 2. positive towards "bardophilia", yet looking from a historical perspective; highlight in 19th century, today more seen in a more complex light, 3. wonderful language; terrific characterisation; super plots; great moral sense; wonderful parts, 4. historically: person to love and adore; nowadays seen in a more complex light

Kopiervorlage 9
1. – D, 2. – H, 3. – F, 4. – B, 5. – E, 6. – G, 7. – C, 8. – A

Kopiervorlage 16
Honi soit qui mal y pense (the motto of the Royal Knights of the Garter)
Or the art of living of the common good
Richard lives at a time when the War of the Roses has created conditions similar to a civil war, ripping great families apart, a lawless and chaotic time and the people are losing any sense of justice. The country which during the reign of Henry V was stable is in danger of falling and the barons are invited to pick up the remains.
As Richard is very low in the hereditary line of the House of York, there is no chance for him to reach power and wealth by inheritance. Additionally being physically handicapped, ugly and of sombre mind full of envy, vain and sadistic traits, he does not stand a chance of marrying into power. The only way left for him seems to be that of treason, plotting and murder and he takes advantage of this option without any scruples.
He accuses Clarence, despite knowing better, of preparing a plot against the king and thus gets him out of his way. He has the young princes murdered and gives the order to murder Hastings and Buckingham (again accusing them of treason). He manipulates the citizens of London in a show worthy of being presented on stage about his intentions and he also manages beautifully to woo Lady Anne, in order to obtain the support of his opposition.
He acts according to the motto "a good fight is never clean", changes the rules of the game and gains advantages which cannot be matched by his surprised opponents. Like an unfair boxer, a "dirty dick", he fights, hits below the belt, uses his elbows, head- and knee-butts, absolutely sure he won't be disqualified, as he has bribed the referees beforehand.
Yet when reading the first soliloquy more closely, we find out that Richard is not at all interested in the material gain of his position. To him money is only a means for bribery. In his long speech in which he reveals his character and his intentions to the audience, there is no mention of his interest in the crown.
His main objective is the physical and psychological power against others. The person who did not inherit anything, who was set aside when others were enjoying themselves, who was laughed at and shunned by everyone – even by the dogs – who is despised even by his mother, will show it to the world. Richard wants to gain control over the country and its people. The misanthrope, whose every speech is full of cynicism, is determined to use his power over others. He wants to be able to manipulate everyone, and corrupt and own people's souls as Satan does. He wants to set them against each other like fighting cocks, he wants to be master over life and death. Like a cat playing with a mouse, he wants to play with his victims and indulge in their fears.

KL | Klausurvorschläge

Klausurvorschlag Topic 1: A Sense of History

by Michael Wood

All families have tales about their past. Today, they might be about the Second World War or the Depression, centred on an old box of photos, service
5 medals and cuttings. One particular tale suggests that the Shakespeares were like that too. In 1596, when William was thirty-two and famous, he and his father went to London to try to obtain a coat of arms for John, to gain him the status of a gentleman. In the files of the
10 Royal College of Arms their submission survives, including a rough draft with the herald's notes. That day Shakespeare claimed that long ago an ancestor had won reputation and "lands and tenements" when he had done King Henry VII "valiant and faithful service".
15 That meant deeds in war, and implies that William's ancestor had fought with Henry Tudor against Richard III at Bosworth in 1485. Of course, it may have been pure fantasy, a family myth that had lost nothing in the retelling. But maybe the tale was true: handed down
20 from the grandparents, or gleaned from a crumbling old title deed bearing the king's name in the family box under the bed. […]
   The real point here, though, is not whether the tale is true or not, but that it was a family tradition. Because
25 it comes from words spoken and jotted down that day in 1596, it enables us to say confidently that history – national history, indeed – was part of the Shakespeare's family story.
   As an adult Shakespeare would be fascinated by
30 English and British history: the national narrative of the past two centuries with its good kings and bad kings; the sacredness of monarchy; the struggle between justice and might, power and conscience; the relation of poor people to the mighty; and what constitutes
35 patriotism. All this was of particular fascination because the national narrative was up for grabs in Elizabeth's day as history was being rewritten root and branch. His early fame would rest not on comedy or tragedy, but on history. There are many ways in which history
40 is important. It shapes our identity; it gives reality and authenticity to our family and communal life; it creates for us a sense of a shared past; and, not least, it fashions our sense of justice. The Shakespeare family motto – composed, it would seem, by William for that
45 meeting with the herald, and intended to sum up the family and their ancestry – makes precisely that point: "Not without right".

(414 words)

Annotations

line 8:   **coat of arms** – a design on a shield used by a family as their own special symbol
line 10:   **submission** – a formally presented document asking for consideration
line 11:   **draft** – a first sketch of a design, text or picture
line 11:   **herald** – someone who designs coats of arms
line 13:   **tenement** – a large building
line 20:   **to glean** – to conclude
line 21:   **title deed** – a document that shows the legal right to possess sth, e.g. land
line 30:   **narrative** – story
line 36:   **to be up for grabs** – to be available for anyone to take
line 37:   **root and branch** – entirely, from the very beginning to the present day
line 43:   **to fashion** – to form or shape
line 46:   **ancestry** – those members of your family that lived before you

Tasks

1 Contents/Comprehension

Outline the author's view on history.

2 Form/Analysis

The author says that in Shakespeare's time, history was being "rewritten root and branch".
Explain why that was so and what effect it might have had on society.

3 Comment/Text production

The Shakespeare family motto as proposed to the herald in 1596 says "Not without right".
Interpret this choice: why might Shakespeare and his father have chosen such a motto? In order to answer that question, draw on the information you have already gathered about Shakespeare and his family.

KL — Klausurvorschläge

Klausurvorschlag Topic 2: Sonnet 130

My mistress' eyes are nothing like the sun;
Coral is far more red, than her lips red:
If snow be white, why then her breasts are dun;
If hairs be wires, black wires grow on her head.
5 I have seen roses damask'd, red and white,
But no such roses see I in her cheeks;
And in some perfumes is there more delight
Than in the breath that from my mistress reeks.
I love to hear her speak, yet well I know
10 That music hath a far more pleasing sound:
I grant I never saw a goddess go,
My mistress, when she walks, treads on the ground:
And yet by heaven, I think my love as rare,
As any she belied with false compare.

(123 words)

Annotations

line 3: **dun** – grey
line 5: **damasked** – of more than one colour
line 8: **to reek** – to smell unpleasantly
line 4: **wires** – fine gold thread used in jewellery
line 14: **belied** – lied about

Tasks

1 Contents/Comprehension

Summarise the contents of the sonnet.

2 Form/Analysis

Analyse the structure of the sonnet. How does Shakespeare develop his argument? What is his point?

3 Composition/Text production

a) In the Elizabethan sonnet tradition, poets praised the beauty of their lovers in elaborate metaphors. Explain why Shakespeare might have decided to diverge from this standard.

b) Discuss how important looks are in a relationship.

Klausurvorschlag Topic 3: Teachers "leave children bored by the Bard"

by Martin Bentham

Globe director condemns poor funding of Shakespeare training

A director of the Globe Theatre has given a warning that pupils are being "turned off" by "dull" Shakespeare lessons because the Government is failing to invest in the teaching of England's greatest playwright.

Patrick Spottiswoode, the Globe's director of education, said that despite the success of films such as *Romeo and Juliet*, starring Leonardo DiCaprio, and Kenneth Branagh's *Much Ado About Nothing*, which had made Shakespeare "cool and sexy", some schools were failing to capitalise on the Bard's popularity.

He said that the reason was that their teachers did not teach the plays in a lively and imaginative way. Courses to help them do so have been provided by the Globe Theatre for three years, but, because of a lack of Government funding, attendance by British teachers has been "disappointing".

Instead, places have been filled by Americans, whose government has given staff incentives to sign up. While pupils in the United States are benefiting from "exciting" teaching, some of their counterparts in Britain are being subjected to uninspiring lessons.

Mr Spottiswoode's comments will embarrass the Government, which has emphasised the value of Shakespeare as a central and compulsory element of school English lessons.

Teaching unions said that there was a danger that pupils would be discouraged from studying literature if Shakespeare, which was complex and difficult, was not taught well. This required better training. Mr Spottiswoode said that the overall quality of teaching of Shakespeare had improved in recent years.

There was now a greater focus on studying his plays as scripts for performance, rather than as dry texts to be pored over. There was still a minority of teachers, however, who were "nervous" of the subject. He said: "There are some teachers who are scared to teach Shakespeare and the problem is that there is no encouragement from the Government for them to learn how to do it better. Schools have to pay an extortionate amount for cover to take a teacher out of school, the teachers don't get paid more for taking courses and there is no tax incentive. For American teachers it's a completely different picture. We are inundated with them. They get credit for going on the course, can write the cost off against tax, and get points to improve their salary. We don't have that in this country."

Mr Spottiswoode said that more than half the places on summer courses at the Globe, which last between one and three weeks, were filled by teachers from overseas, particularly the United States. […]

Peter Smith, the general secretary of the Association of Teachers and Lecturers, said that the requirements of GCSE and A-level exams meant that pupils had to concentrate on the text of Shakespeare, rather than the stage play.

He agreed with Mr Spottiswoode, however, that lessons needed to be made more lively, particularly for younger pupils. He said:
"Shakespeare is a very difficult playwright and there are plenty of examples of children being turned off his plays, and theatre in general, because they have to study him too soon." […]

Under the National Curriculum, pupils must study at least two Shakespeare plays between the ages of eleven and 16. There is also a compulsory Shakespeare test for 14-year-olds. The Department for Education said: "We believe that pupils are well taught and that sufficient money is spent on ensuring that teachers have the skills to do that."

(562 words)

Annotations

line 37:	**to pore over sth** –	to look over sth carefully
line 43:	**extortionate** –	being extremely expensive
line 47:	**inundated** –	to give too much of sth so that it cannot be handled

KL | Klausurvorschläge

Tasks

1 Contents/Comprehension

Outline the positions, as given in the text, regarding the role of Shakespeare in the English National Curriculum.

2 Form/Analysis

a) Examine how the structure of the text is determined by the type of text.

b) Analyse how the use of language corresponds with the type of text.

3 Comment/Text production

Comment on the claim that teaching Shakespeare in schools is important.
Write a letter to the editor stating your personal opinion. *Or:*
Write an article about at a scene of your choice how you would like it to be taught in school.

Klausurvorschläge KL

Klausurvorschlag Topic 4 (Text 1): Romeo and Juliet (The Prologue)

Enter Chorus

Chorus
Two households, both alike in dignity,
In fair Verona (where we lay our scene);
5 From ancient grudge break to new mutiny,
Where civil blood makes civil hands unclean.
From forth the fatal loins of these two foes
A pair of star-crossed lovers take their life;
Whose misadventured piteous overthrows
10 Doth with their death bury their parents' strife.
The fearful passage of their death-marked love,
And the continuance of their parent's rage,
Which but their children's end nought could remove,
Is now the two hours' traffic of our stage;
15 The which if you with patient ears attend,
What here shall miss, our toil shall strive to mend.

Exit

(104 words)

Annotations

line 5:	**grudge** – a strong feeling of anger
line 7:	**loins** – part of the body above the legs and below the waist
line 9:	**piteous** – causing to feel sadness and sympathy
line 9:	**overthrows** – circumstances
line 10:	**strife** – violent disagreement
line 13:	**nought** – nothing

Tasks

1 Contents/Comprehension

Describe in your own words what the prologue is about.

2 Form/Analysis

a) Analyse the atmosphere the text attempts to create.

b) Analyse the function this scene has for the whole play.

3 Evaluation

Examine the extent to which the form of the prologue corresponds with the contents of the play.

4 Text production

Imagine you are a theatre director. Describe how you would transfer the setting of the Elizabethan play from the stage to a modern environment for your new film.

Klausurvorschläge

Klausurvorschlag Topic 4 (Text 2): Macbeth

In scene ii, Act 1 of "Macbeth" Duncan, the Scottish king, has just received news that his captains Banquo and Macbeth have won the decisive battle against the traitor Macdonwald, who was supported by Norwegian troops and the Scottish Thane of Cawdor, a traitor. In the third scene of the play Macbeth meets three witches who tell him that not only will he become Thane of Cawdor, but also King of Scotland. Shortly afterwards, the King's messengers arrive to tell Macbeth that Duncan has rewarded him with the title Thane of Cawdor. The following is an extract of scene iv.

```
       DUNCAN:      Is execution done on Cawdor? Are not
                    Those in commission yet return'd?
       MALCOLM:     My liege,
                    They are not yet come back. But I have spoke
  5                 With one that saw him die: who did report
                    That very frankly he confess'd his treasons,
                    Implored your highness' pardon and set forth
                    A deep repentance: nothing in his life
                    Became him like the leaving it; he died
 10                 As one that had been studied in his death
                    To throw away the dearest thing he owed,
                    As 'twere a careless trifle.
       DUNCAN:      There's no art
                    To find the mind's construction in the face:
 15                 He was a gentleman on whom I built
                    An absolute trust.
                    Enter MACBETH, BANQUO, ROSS, and ANGUS
                    O worthiest cousin!
                    The sin of my ingratitude even now
 20                 Was heavy on me: thou art so far before
                    That swiftest wing of recompense is slow
                    To overtake thee. […]
       MACBETH:     The service and the loyalty I owe,
                    In doing it, pays itself. Your highness' part
 25                 Is to receive our duties; and our duties
                    Are to your throne and state children and servants,
                    Which do but what they should, by doing every thing
                    Safe toward your love and honour.
       DUNCAN:      Welcome hither:
 30                 I have begun to plant thee, and will labour
                    To make thee full of growing.
                    […] Sons, kinsmen, thanes,
                    And you whose places are the nearest, know
                    We will establish our estate upon
 35                 Our eldest, Malcolm, whom we name hereafter
                    The Prince of Cumberland; which honour must
                    Not unaccompanied invest him only,
                    But signs of nobleness, like stars, shall shine
                    On all deservers. From hence to Inverness,
 40                 And bind us further to you.
       MACBETH:     The rest is labour, which is not used for you:
                    I'll be myself the harbinger and make joyful
                    The hearing of my wife with your approach;
                    So humbly take my leave.
 45    DUNCAN:      My worthy Cawdor!
```

MACBETH: [Aside] The Prince of Cumberland! that is a step
On which I must fall down, or else o'erleap,
For in my way it lies. Stars, hide your fires;
Let not light see my black and deep desires:
50 The eye wink at the hand; yet let that be,
Which the eye fears, when it is done, to see.
Exit
DUNCAN: True, worthy Banquo; he is full so valiant,
And in his commendations I am fed;
55 It is a banquet to me. Let's after him,
Whose care is gone before to bid us welcome:
It is a peerless kinsman.

(504 words)

Annotations

line 8: **set forth a deep repentance** – showed that he regretted his deeds
line 12: **trifle** – a small thing of little importance
line 21: **swiftest wing of recompense is slow to overtake thee** – Macbeth continues to do so much for Duncan that he will always be in his debt, no matter how fast he tries to make up for it
line 36: **Prince of Cumberland** – the Prince of Cumberland in Scotland was the same rank as the Prince of Wales in England, and thus Malcolm is now next in line to the throne
line 50: **wink** – quickly close and open an eye
line 53: **valiant** – courageous
line 54: **in his commendations I am fed** – I am full of praise for him

Tasks

1 Contents/Comprehension

Briefly summarise the scene.

2 Form/Analysis

a) Explain what exactly goes on in Macbeth's mind at this crucial moment of the play. What does he mean when he says "The Prince of Cumberland, that is a step …"?

b) One of Shakespeare's common themes is appearance and reality. Analyse the way in which this theme is represented in this scene.

3 Comment

Discuss the extent to which a topic such as appearance and reality is relevant today.

Klausurvorschlag Topic 5: Othello in Earnest

by Perry Pontac

LADY BRABANTIO and OTHELLO, just after tea. They speak in the distinctive accents of, respectively, Lady Bracknell and John Worthing.

	LADY BRABANTIO:	Excellent cucumber sandwiches, Mr Othello.
5	OTHELLO:	I'm so pleased you enjoyed them, Lady Brabantio.
	LADY BRABANTIO:	And now, to our business. You wish to marry my daughter, Desdemona, I believe.
	OTHELLO:	Yes, Lady Brabantio, very much so.
	LADY BRABANTIO:	I see. In that case I have a few questions to put to you. (*She takes out her notebook and pencil.*) What is the source of your income?
10	OTHELLO:	I am a soldier, Lady Brabantio – from an old military family.
	LADY BRABANTIO:	(*taking notes*) Ah.
	OTHELLO:	I am, I'm afraid, often out of Venice, slaughtering the infidel, sacking and burning towns, beheading prisoners.
15	LADY BRABANTIO:	I am pleased to hear it. A man who remains at home can do incalculable harm. My husband Lord Brabantio is a case in point. The more domestic he becomes, the more savage his behaviour seems to be. And now, your property.
	OTHELLO:	Two main residences, Lady Brabantio. A bachelor flat near the Bridge of Sighs and a large Gothic mansion on the Rialto.
20	LADY BRABANTIO:	That is most satisfactory. And were you born in one of the great houses on the Canal, or did you rise from the rural simplicity of a country seat?
	OTHELLO:	(*reluctantly*) I'm afraid I was born … elsewhere, Lady Brabantio.
	LADY BRABANTIO:	(*surprised*) Elsewhere, Mr Othello?
	OTHELLO:	Yes. (*Evasively*) Rather far away, in fact.
	LADY BRABANTIO:	(*disapprovingly*) Far away? And where, precisely, 'far away' were you born?
25	OTHELLO:	In … in Africa, Lady Brabantio.
	LADY BRABANTIO:	(*Lady Bracknell-like*) Africa?
	OTHELLO:	Yes, in a tiny village in Africa. Kajabufu. I was born in a small military fortification as it happens, a simple hut made of mud and dung; my nappy a banana-leaf, my rattle a quiver of poisoned arrows, my cradle a sandbag.
30	LADY BRABANTIO:	(*even more Lady Bracknell-like*) A sandbag?
	OTHELLO:	Yes, Lady Brabantio. There in a clearing in the great jungle where the she-elephant suckles her young.
35	LADY BRABANTIO:	(on a rising note of disapproval) And how, if I may ask, did you come to be raised on a sandbag in a hut in a clearing where the she-elephant suckles her young? It seems most improbable.
	OTHELLO:	My parents were Africans, Lady Brabantio – as am I.
	LADY BRABANTIO:	(*appalled*) Indeed? Not Blackamoors?
	OTHELLO:	Quite. Father was a warrior-chief, Mother his favourite wife. (*Shakespeareanly*) Haply, for I am black …
40	LADY BRABANTIO:	Not happily at all, Mr Othello. I had assumed, from your appearance, that you had recently been basking in the sun at one of our well-known seaside resorts. Indeed, this puts, if I may say so, an entirely new complexion on the matter. Yet, let us continue. I have almost completed my questions and I always finish what I begin, especially if there is no reason to do so. That is the meaning of thoroughness.
45		(*She takes up her pencil.*) Now, your education. Which of our great universities did you attend?
	OTHELLO:	None, I'm afraid. No formal education at all. My childhood was spent climbing the banyan tree, sporting naked in the sunshine, foraging for nuts and grubs with 'Maputu' the wart-hog.
50	LADY BRABANTIO:	(*not impressed*) I see. And as an adult?
	OTHELLO:	As a soldier I have had many remarkable adventures which Desdemona, dear girl, has often begged me to recount. I have known disasters as well, Lady Brabantio: sold into slavery, shipwrecked on the Isle of Wight for several weeks, and I have

		been scalped – on two different occasions – by the dreaded Norijwanee tribe of Sumatra.
LADY BRABANTIO:		To be scalped once, Mr Othello, may be regarded as a misfortune; to be scalped twice looks like hairlessness.
OTHELLO:		(*continuing his story, trying to impress her*) In Kashina I was nearly eaten by a lion who sprang upon me in the most unexpected manner. (*Lady Brabantio remains unmoved.*)
		It was a fierce Nemean Lion, Lady Brabantio.
LADY BRABANTIO:		The lion is immaterial. Mr Othello, I confess your history has filled me with disquiet. A life such as yours, with a person such as yourself, is hardly the destiny I have in mind for Desdemona.
OTHELLO:		But what is it you advise me to do? I adore the divine Desdemona.
LADY BRABANTIO:		I advise you to quit your suit and to avoid my daughter forever. Desdemona has a noble nature and will be certain to forget you almost instantly.
OTHELLO:		I see. Ah, the pity of it, if I may say so, Lady Brabantio, the pity of it.
LADY BRABANTIO:		Mr Othello, you seem, if I'm not mistaken, to be displaying signs of considerable self-esteem.
OTHELLO:		(*sadly*) On the contrary, Lady Brabantio. I've now realised for the first time in my life the vital importance of being burnished.

They freeze in tableau. Black-out.   *(810 words)*

© Perry Pontac 1995 (see credits page for full details and performing rights)

Annotations

- **line 2:** **respectively** – belonging to each of the characters just mentioned
- **line 3:** **Lady Bracknell and John Worthing** – protagonists of Oscar Wilde's play "The Importance of Being Earnest"
- **line 12:** **infidel** – having no belief; *synonyms:* heathens, pagans
- **line 12:** **sacking** – another word for plundering and pillaging
- **line 17:** **Bridge of Sighs** – famous bridge in Venice (*Seufzerbrücke*)
- **line 18:** **Rialto** – famous main street in Venice
- **line 37:** **Blackamoors** – archaic and racist term for a black person
- **line 38:** **Shakespeareanly** – *here:* to speak in an old fashioned, over exaggerated way
- **line 39:** **haply** – perhaps
- **line 72:** **burnished** – shiny, glossy

Tasks

1 Contents/Comprehension

Outline the themes picked up by this scene that are also relevant in Shakespeare.

2 Form/Analysis

a) Describe the setting of this scene.

b) Analyse the tone of the scene with special regard to the language of the two protagonists.

c) Analyse the tools the author uses to create this scene.

3 Comment/Text production

This scene is taken from a highly successful revue using Shakespearean plots as background material to be put into new contexts. Discuss the extent to which it is legitimate to play around with classic elements like this by transplanting them into contexts like that of another famous play.

Erwartungshorizont zu den Klausurvorschlägen

Topic 1: Textinformation

Autor: Michael Wood
Titel: A Sense of History
Quelle: *In Search of Shakespeare*. London: BBC Books, 2005, pp. 18–20.
http://www.pbs.org/shakespeare/theshow/mike.html (geprüft: 20.4.2010)
Textformat/Textlänge: Dokumentation, 414 Wörter

Erwartungshorizont

1 Contents/Comprehension

In the extract form *In Search of Shakespeare*, published in London in 2005, the author Michael Wood claims that history is an important part of human life. It is not only world history, or the great political events in the past that shaped a nation, but begins with the stories and tales that each family cherishes as their own personal history. Such tales and stories are often preserved in photos and other memorabilia. Thus, history has a double function for people. It creates an identity for a person or a community by giving them a past, and the traditions and stories of the past shape the way in which that community functions.

2 Form/Analysis

Shakespeare's parents had seen three changes of religion in ten years: from Catholicism to Protestantism, back to Catholicism, and back to Protestantism again. Elizabeth's reign was marked by a cultural revolution. After the definite separation from the Church of Rome, many of the traditions held dear by the English for centuries were forbidden, like the pilgrimages to holy places or certain Catholic holidays, and whereas it was good and right to go to church and celebrate mass there on Sundays, you were now fined for it. Monasteries, which had been places of learning, refuge and caring for the sick for hundreds of years, were closed; shrines, ornaments, images and stained glass windows had to go. With all that, an essential part of the nation's history was subdued. Within thirty years, Henry and his successors Edward and Elizabeth had changed England forever, and by imposing Protestantism on England and Ireland laid the seed for civil unrest and hysteric fear of conspiracy that marked the reign of Elizabeth I. Henry had refused to accept the authority of the Pope, and he had bishops imprisoned and executed, but in doing so left a void. The people were shaken and confused, and it is not hard to imagine that some took up arms and tried to revolt against the new religion. But in such situations of trouble and change there also lies a chance for those who search for power. Some people who because of their social standing would not have had a chance to climb the social ladder in any other period of English history could now make an impressive career, like Thomas Cromwell, a layman who became Vicar General under Henry VIII.

3 Comment/Text production

William Shakespeare was the son of a respected Stratford citizen. His father John was a well-known and respected man who held various important public offices such as alderman and high bailiff. His mother came from a prestigious Warwickshire family, the Ardens. "Not without right" is a wary motto for dangerous times. Shakespeare's family had seen how monasteries and nunneries all over the country were closed and the possessions handed over to noblemen. William himself played in a theatre in London that was situated on the grounds of a former monastery, Blackfriars. The motto might suggest that the Shakespeares did not want to accept anything that was not rightfully theirs. It also implies that the Shakespeares thought they were certainly worthy of the status of gentlemen. In the submission William claimed that his ancestors had fought for Henry VII, Elizabeth's grandfather, and that consequently he and his family had a right to a coat of arms. He was only a playwright and actor, so to be granted the status of gentleman was unusual at the time, and the motto defies any criticism aimed that way.

Erwartungshorizont

Topic 2: Textinformation

Autor: William Shakespeare
Titel: Sonnet 130
Quelle: http://www.shakespeares-sonnets.com/sonn02.htm#anchor073 (geprüft: 20.4.2010)
Textformat/Textlänge: Sonett, 123 Wörter

Erwartungshorizont

1 Contents/Comprehension

In this sonnet Shakespeare describes his mistress as someone who is not very beautiful. She neither has beautiful eyes, nor nice hair; her breath smells unpleasant and she does not have a nice voice. In spite of this, he thinks that his love for this woman is unique.

2 Form/Analysis

The sonnet is written in the typical structure of Elizabethan sonnets. It consists of three quatrains that rhyme abab cdcd efef and a couplet, which rhymes gg. In the first two quatrains, he picks up metaphors which are used to describe the beauty of a woman (eyes like the sun, lips which are red as coral, white breasts, rosy cheeks), but states that his mistress does not correspond to these ideals. In the last line of the second quatrain he even deliberately uses an unpoetic word ("reeks") when he talks about the unpleasant breath of his mistress. After having made it quite clear that his mistress cannot be compared to the beauty standards of the time, Shakespeare in the third quatrain refuses to compare his mistress' voice to music or her way of walking to the heavenly gait of goddesses, but simply says that music sounds nicer and that she walks like any other human being. The last two lines then come as a surprise. The poet does not conclude by saying that there is some other inner quality that makes him love his mistress and singles her out among all other women, as one might have expected, but simply says that his love is very precious to him, just as precious as all those women who are glorified with wonderful metaphors in other sonnets.

3 Composition/Text production

a) In this sonnet, Shakespeare does not mock the looks of his girlfriend but the Elizabethan sonnet tradition. He rejects the exaggerated comparisons they use: no women's eyes are like the sun, which is always a lot more radiant than any other thing on earth; their breasts are never as white as snow; and as women are not heavenly creatures, they simply walk like human beings, not like goddesses. Shakespeare seems to consider such comparisons as were the fashion at the time as lies ("belied with false compare"). To him they probably just serve as a sugar coating that hides true feelings. The last two lines simply say that he loves his girlfriend, and that it is enough to say that she is exquisite and precious to him without glorifying her with unrealistic and hollow comparisons.

b) Individual solutions. The students might mention the following aspects:
- appearances are important because they attract you to someone else
- it is difficult to look at someone daily whose face you do not really like
- trying to make the best of your outward appearance is also a mark of respect for your partner: after all, it is he/she that has to look at you most of the time
- a good-looking partner is something many people are proud of
- on the other hand, looks are not of utmost importance because they cannot stabilize a relationship (especially since appearances change with age, whims, and time)
- it is more important to find a partner who shares common interests
- if there are problems, good looks alone cannot solve them; other qualities are needed
- when people grow older, looks fade, but love can grow
- inner qualities such as wisdom, compassion, forgiveness, trustworthiness, honesty, kindness, courage, patience, tolerance, and understanding contribute a lot more to a stable relationship than just good looks
- a good-looking woman or man attracts others, too, and jealousy might then become a problem

EH | Erwartungshorizont

Topic 3: Textinformation

Autor: Martin Bentham
Titel: Teachers "leave children bored by the Bard"
Quelle: Published on Sunday, August 6, 2000 by The Sunday Telegraph.
Textformat/Textlänge: Sachtext, 562 Wörter

Erwartungshorizont

1 Contents/Comprehension

Some aspects Patrick Spottiswoode claims include
- students are not motivated by dull methods of teaching Shakespeare
- some schools are not able to use the overwhelming global interest in Shakespeare to their advantage
- the government does not give enough funding to British teachers for special projects
- Shakespeare is considered to be important, yet difficult to teach
- there is a new focus on teaching Shakespeare as a script rather than a text
- some teachers are still too nervous to use this concept
- there are too few incentives for those who are willing to be trained

Peter Smith, representative of the teachers' association maintains
- the test formats still requires the students to read texts in an analytical way
- there is agreement that lessons ought to be more lively
- the teaching of Shakespeare starts at too early an age
- there is even a compulsory test on Shakespeare for 14-year-olds

The Government believes that nothing is wrong with the present status and that enough money is being spent and teachers are already competent enough.

2 Form/Analysis

a) This journalistic (non-fictional) article from a British quality newspaper tries in a mainly expository and descriptive way, in which it also presents the key arguments, to analyse the situation regarding the teaching of Shakespeare in schools.
The structure of the text clearly meets the requirements of a quality paper. The author tries to remain neutral, yet the number and order of arguments show that he is in favour of the criticism uttered by Mr Spottiswoode, although this is not directly argued. The text clarifies a number of positions by providing relevant quotations supporting the different points of view.
The text presents the criticism, mainly directed at the government, at great length. The first argumentation against this harsh criticism is trying to find a middle way, agreeing partly, yet referring to the official requirements of the curriculum.
It is the quoted official view of the government that finally makes quite clear where the position of the author has to be seen. The reader may come to the conclusion that the early criticism is not without justification and really more could be done to improve the situation.

b) The author starts the article with a direct reference to the tone: an authority on the subject gives a "warning"; this is given some urgency by the following superlative "England's greatest playwright". The author increases his authenticity and presence to the reader by using words as direct quotes of the person he has interviewed on the subject.
He organises his introductory presentation of the problem by using opposing word pairs and phrases to stress the contrast between what the text sees as the criticised and the desired situation: turned off / dull vs. lively/ imaginative; lack of funding vs. incentives; disappointing attendance vs. filled places; students are benefiting from vs. are being subjected to; uninspiring lessons vs. exciting teaching.
The author uses repetitions of phrases as well as a number of very lively adjectives to stress his urgency: failing to invest; failing to capitalise; lack of funding. The register and the choice of words in the exposition as well as those by Mr Spottiswoode are used to give the position more authority.

Erwartungshorizont | EH

Rather than describing the opposing viewpoints himself, the author has chosen and structured direct quotations or passages of reported speech to present others' positions in detail. In the author's selection of quotes and reported phrases the differences between the quite fervent and critical language of Mr Spottiswoode – showing his enthusiasm as well as his frustration openly – the rather understanding position of Peter Smith – trying to take a middle ground in order to have as many supporters to his position as possible – and the lifeless, formalistic language of the government – quite anticlimatic in tone – give the article a very wide range of expression. It is this mix of seemingly neutral reporting yet cleverly arranged material that shows the article to be a good example of a "quality press" text.

3 Comment/Text production

a) The outer form of the text should qualify for the text type required in the task. The personal opinion should be worked out clearly using argumentative material from the text. The solution itself is left to the personal opinion of the student

b) This creative form enables the students to show a personal understanding of contemporary forms of working on Shakespeare's text and give them the opportunity to develop their own creative ideas.

Topic 4 (Text 1): Textinformation

Autor:	William Shakespeare
Titel:	Romeo and Juliet: The Prologue
Quelle:	http://www.clicknotes.com/romeo/P1.html (geprüft: 20.4.2010)
Textformat/Textlänge:	Drama, 98 Wörter

Erwartungshorizont

1 Contents/Comprehension

The prologue presents two noble families in Verona who have been fighting against each other for a long time and have killed members of the opposing families in a long-standing feud. When a member of one family falls in love with a member of the opposing family and they eventually kill themselves, the ancient fight between the two families finds a tragic ending. In the prologue the speaker announces to the audience what will happen during the two hours of the play. The development of the relationship and the death of the two lovers becomes a foregone conclusion and is in the centre of the play. The lovers' struggle against their families and their parents' rage, which nothing but the death of the lovers could end, is the central theme of the play. The speaker of the prologue asks the audience to follow the play kindly and apologises for any mistakes the actors might make during the play.

2 Form/Analysis

a) The atmosphere is that of an official announcement ("where we lay our scene") but tries to create interest among the audience members by mentioning the themes (war, love and death) and the information that the duration of the play is limited ("two hours' traffic"). The choice of words creates immediate suspense (civil blood/ hands unclean/fatal loins/star-crossed/misadventured/death/strife/fearful/death-marked love/rage). Apart from trying to appeal to the groundlings with these words, the speaker also tries to address the nobility when he uses words like "alike in dignity", "fair" and "ancient". At the beginning the speaker also points out the fact that the tragedy is only one on stage, and that the end of the performance will be kind: "our toil shall strive to mend".

b) The prologue has the function of informing the audience about the necessity of understanding the play, the "quiddities" answering the questions as to the who?, where?, when?, what? and why? of the story. The aim is to attract the audience's attention at the beginning of the play and quieten the rowdy crowd of the groundlings to be able to allow the performance to begin. One of its purposes is to prepare them to decide on sympathies with chosen characters. The speaker gives away the plot so that the audience can concentrate on the question of how the story is acted out rather than what is being presented.

© Ernst Klett Verlag GmbH, Stuttgart 2010 | www.klett.de
Von dieser Druckvorlage ist die Vervielfältigung für den eigenen Unterrichtsgebrauch gestattet. Die Kopiergebühren sind abgegolten. Alle Rechte vorbehalten.

Abi Workshop Englisch
Shakespeare Lehrerheft
ISBN 978-3-12-601015-3

Erwartungshorizont

3 Evaluation

The form of the prologue technically is that of a sonnet, here transformed into a monologue. The first verse ("ABAB") is the presentation of the background, the second ("CDCD") is a short presentation of the plot, the third ("EFEF") is a variation of the question about the reasons for the tragedy, the final two lines ("GG") appeal to the audience to follow the production with a kind ear. The first verse thus shows the initial situation between the two parties, the second the love between the protagonists and the third muses on the tragic ending.

4 Text production

The answer is open to individual answers, yet should refer to the specific tools of film as they are used by Baz Luhrmann in his interpretation of *Romeo and Juliet*, particularly at the introduction to the film, where after a rapid sequence of visual impulses the prologue is presented in the form of a newsflash.

Topic 4 (Text 2): Textinformation

Autor:	William Shakespeare
Titel:	Macbeth
Quelle:	http://shakespeare.mit.edu/macbeth/index.html (geprüft: 20.4.2010)
Textformat/Textlänge:	Drama, 504 Wörter

Erwartungshorizont

1 Contents/Comprehension

In this extract from *Macbeth*, the Scottish king Duncan is talking to Malcolm, who reports on the execution of the traitor Cawdor. Duncan explains that he had trusted Cawdor, then turns to greet Macbeth and thank him wholeheartedly for having fought so bravely against Scotland's enemies. Macbeth states that he did his duty and was glad to do so. Duncan turns to the other persons present, Ross, Malcolm, Banquo and Angus, and tells them that he has decided to make his son Prince of Cumberland, which means that after Duncan's death he will become king of Scotland, and that he plans to stay at Macbeth's castle that night. Macbeth turns to go and inform his wife about the king's visit and in an aside gives away his dark and ambitious thoughts.

2 Form/Analysis

a) Duncan has made Macbeth Thane of Cawdor, so one of the witches' prophecies has come true. Until the moment when Duncan named his son Prince of Cumberland, there was still a small chance for Macbeth to lawfully succeed Duncan to the throne. That has now become more difficult: The Prince of Cumberland is the designated successor, and if Macbeth wants to become king himself he has to move him out of the way. "The Prince of Cumberland, that is a step / On which I must fall down, or else o'erleap / For in my way it lies." Macbeth does not explicitly say so, but murder is on his mind. He does not want anyone to penetrate his thoughts; he does not even want his own eyes to see what he is about to do. "Stars, hide your fires / Let not light see my black and deep desires / The eye wink at the hand, yet let that be / Which the eye fears, when it is done, to see." At this moment Macbeth's conscience and better knowledge succumb to his ambitious desires.

b) The difference between appearance and reality plays an important part in this scene. At the beginning, Duncan explicitly says that he was wrong when he trusted Cawdor. The thane who seemed to be a valiant fighter for Scotland proved to be a traitor in reality, and Duncan regrets that there is no possibility for a man to read the truth in someone else's face: "There's no art / to find the mind's construction in the face. He was a gentleman / On whom I built an absolute trust." Ironically, Macbeth steps onto the stage at that precise moment. He is another gentleman whom Duncan trusts, but who, as we shall soon see, deserves this confidence even less than the Thane of Cawdor. The last lines of the excerpt reveal that Macbeth is already thinking of how to become king himself by unlawful, even sinful means. When he talks of loyalty, love, honour and duty towards the king, he puts on a show, but again Duncan fails to read the mind of the person he is talking to. He thinks that he is going to be the guest of a faithful servant and worthy gentleman that night, but in reality he marches straight into the arms of his murderer; along with the title of the traitor (Thane of Cawdor) he has passed on access to treason to Macbeth.

3 Comment

The topic has lost none of its relevance to this day. At all times in history people have pretended to be someone or something they were not, lied their ways into the confidence of others and abused it. A good present-day example is probably the global financial crises the world has witnessed in the past years. Countless people trusted bank managers with their money and were confident that it was safe with them because that is what they were told. They believed in the promises of financial profits and security, but found out that bank managers cannot be trusted, and that in reality the global financial market cannot guarantee keeping such promises.

Another example for the difference between appearance and reality are politicians who make promises before an election that they do not even intend to keep afterwards. Public political deceit has become such an integral part of election campaigns that many voters are disgusted to the point of refusing to vote at all. But appearance and reality often play a role on a much smaller scale. People apply for a job pretending to have the right qualifications although they do not; partners cheat on each other; friends who you trusted divulge your secrets. But the fault does not always lie with the others. We are frequently disappointed because our conception of reality proves to be incorrect, but then maybe our conception was wrong in the first place. Some of the people who trusted the bank managers refused to read the information about the risks they were actually taking because they were fascinated by the prospect of fast profits. Similarly, some people glorify their partners and fail to see that they are only humans, too. All this is part of human nature today as much as in Shakespeare's times, and that is why the topic of "appearance and reality" is timeless.

Topic 5: Textinformation

Autor: Perry Pontac
Titel: Othello in Earnest
Quelle: Christopher Luscombe/Macolm McKee: *The Shakespeare Revue*. London, 1995, pp. 40-43.
Textformat/Textlänge: Drama, 810 Wörter

Erwartungshorizont

1 Contents/Comprehension

Some examples for themes are
- status, "from an old military family" / "born in one of the great houses?" / "a sandbag?" / "most improbable" / "what do you advise me to do?"
- pride, e.g. "father was a warrior chief" / "to be displaying signs of considerable self esteem"
- race, e.g. "not Blackamoors?"
- love vs. (arranged) marriage , e.g. "to our business. You wish to marry my daughter"
- gender, e.g. Lady Brabantio appears superior to Othello and her husband
- education, e.g. "which of our great universities did you attend?" / "no formal education"
- reality and appearance, e.g. "I had assumed from your appearance" / "you seem to be displaying signs of considerable self-esteem"

2 Form/Analysis

a) The setting is an absurd mix taken from the two sources of *Othello* and *The Importance of Being Ernest* with the addition of Othello's invented African background. The story is made timeless due to the references to the classic setting (Venice, Bridge of Sighs, Rialto) as well as modern times (e.g. cucumber sandwiches; bachelor flat; Gothic mansion; universities, military fortification, seaside resorts).

Despite the references to the original plot of *Othello*, the overall impression is that *Othello* has been transferred into Victorian times, hence the title. The playful question of this scene is, what would happen if the powerful hero of Shakespeare's tragedy was reduced to a suitor being rejected by Lady Bracknell / Lady Brabantio (her name of course is changed, too, to increase the humour)?

b) The overall tone is dominated by the upper-class accent and language of Lady Brabantio, which is (unlike in the original) matched by that of Othello. Despite Lady Brabantio's open display of greed and display of superiority, increased by her superficiality and pretended understatement and class distinction, the overall tone is humourous. This is mainly a result of the reversal of gender roles which lets Othello appear in the inferior situation. The language of the two is full of phrases of decorum, which receive a very absurd note when put into the context of Othello's fairly ordinary biography.

Othello tries to adapt himself even to the negative attitudes of Lady Brabantio (e.g. "mother, his favourite wife") and when bragging about his rather special education.

The language of the text is marked by the large number of contrasts and elements of irony sometimes stressed into absurdity. Throughout the passage Lady Bracknell is shown as pretending to be educated, yet only utters common stereotypes and is openly shown to be quite stupid and of low moral standards (e.g. "not Blackamoors?"), while the supposedly uneducated Othello proves to be intelligent by changing his tone all the time. Appearing quite naïve in the way he presents himself throughout the scene, Othello changes the overall tone of the scene with his final sentence, setting things right by using yet another play on words ("burnished" rhymes with "Earnest", which is the last word in this scene in the original play by Wilde).

c) Some of the tools that could be mentioned include
- very contrastive characterisations (Lady Brabantio: pretended wisdom: "A man who remains at home …" / "your history has filled me with disquiet" vs. Othello: naïve presentation: "I'm afraid … out of Venice, slaughtering the infidel" / "foraging for nuts and grubs with 'Maputu' the wart-hog")
- contrasts (e.g. "one of the great houses on the Canal"; "a sandbag")
- understatement ("rise from the rural simplicity of a country seat")
- (self-)irony (e.g. "I always finish what I begin, especially if there is no reason to do so" / "you seem to be displaying signs of considerable self esteem")
- puns and ambiguity (e.g. "a new complexion on the matter")
- quotations (e.g. "Happily for I am black", "Ah, the pity of it")
- anticlimax (e.g. "shipwreck on the Isle of Wight")
- punch line ("a sandbag" – rhymes with "a handbag" from the original; "the vital importance of being burnished")

3 Comment/Text production

The answer is open to the opinion of the students. There could be good reasons to feel that this use of the material from *Othello* is stretching things too far. On the other hand, it could be seen as a good example of viewing Shakespeare as the great entertainer, who himself constantly adapted his material to suit the needs and tastes of his audiences.

Erwartungshorizont zu den *Revision files*

Revision file 1: Shakespeare and his time (Topic 1)

Add words and phrases next to each picture that belong to the specific topics.
Arrange them in coherent categories or in logical order.

William Shakespeare

- Born in Stratford, probably on 23rd of April (baptized 26th).
- Married in 1582, wife is eight years older.
- Daughter Susanna is born six months later, twins Judith and Hamnet in 1585 (Hamnet dies in 1596).
- 1586–1591: No documents, maybe toured the country with the Queen's Men, maybe studied on the continent or at least travelled there, maybe was a tutor in Lancashire.
- 1592: First mentioned as a playwright in London.
- Returns to Stratford in 1612.
- Wrote 39 plays, plus sonnets and long poems, is considered England's greatest writer.
- Died in Stratford in 1616.

Historical context

- A time of learning (Renaissance)
- Renewed interest in classical literature, access to books, more schools, discovery of new countries, more people moved to the big cities.
- Church of England separated from Rome (Henry VIII).
- Three changes of religion within two decades: from Catholicism to Protestantism (Henry VIII), back to Catholicism (Queen Mary), back again to Protestantism as only religion tolerated in the state (Elizabeth).

Political situation

- Trouble at home: constant fear of conspiracies and rebellion.
- Trouble abroad: war with Spain, the Netherlands, Ireland.
- Successful defeat of the Armada under Elizabeth I.
- Continuous fear of Catholic plots → lead to execution of Mary Stuart, Queen of Scots.
- Death of Elizabeth in 1603, succeeded by Mary's son James.

Everyday life

- Increased mobility, growth of cities.
- Bad hygienic situation – many diseases and deaths (Bubonic plague).
- Cruel forms of entertainment: bear baiting, public executions.
- Police state: fear of spies and denunciation.
- Harsh punishments for minor offences, e.g. death penalty for repeated begging.

RF | Revision files

Revision file 2: Shakespeare's language (Topic 2)

List the main aspects of Shakespeare's language in the left-hand boxes and add relevant information to the right.

Elizabethan English

grammar vocabulary syntax	• flexion of some verbs (thou hast, thou seest, he hath, thou knoweth) • different pronouns: thou, thee, ye • flexible rules for syntax • constant influx of new words due to contacts with other languages (wars, trade, exploration, diplomacy), e.g. tobacco, mandolin • many new words and expressions coined by Shakespeare (assassination, gossip, luggage, too much of a good thing, wear my heart on my sleeve)

Forms of verse and prose

metre iambic pentameter sonnets	• iambic metre: unstressed syllable is followed by stressed syllable (mis-take, re-venge, de-cide) • pentametre: five such iambs in a line • resembles human heartbeat, can have a soothing or intensifying effect • verse for high-status characters, prose for low-status characters (but no hard and fast rule for Shakespeare) • sonnets: iambic pentameter, usually three quatrains with rhyme scheme abab, followed by couplet (aa).

Shakespeare's style

soliloquies creativity	• use of meters: intensify soliloquies or change their tone • highly inventive; new expressions • imagery, metaphors, similes

Shakespeare the poet

narrative poems	• Venus and Adonis, The Rape of Lucrece • dedicated to Henry Wriothesley • published by Shakespeare himself
sonnets	• 154 sonnets, probably not meant for publication • written in iambic pentameter, 14 lines • three quatrains with rhyme scheme abab, followed by couplet (aa)

---

142   **Klett**

© Ernst Klett Verlag GmbH, Stuttgart 2010 | www.klett.de
Von dieser Druckvorlage ist die Vervielfältigung für den eigenen Unterrichtsgebrauch
gestattet. Die Kopiergebühren sind abgegolten. Alle Rechte vorbehalten.

Abi Workshop Englisch
Shakespeare Lehrerheft
ISBN 978-3-12-601015-3

Revision file 3: The theatre (Topic 3)

Collect words and phrases from the texts which relate to the subtitles below.

Development of the Elizabethan theatre

<u>touring companies • inn-yards • apron stage</u>
Early forms of theatre: Amateur actors in morality plays and pageants on temporary stages or in guild halls; later travelling players with low reputation; serious actors joined companies with a prominent patron; inn-yards the first theatres for Elizabethan plays; audience viewing from inside the inn; this arrangement resulted in the shape of the first purpose-built theatres in London with their apron stage reaching out to the middle of the yard surrounded on three sides by the groundlings.

Shakespeare's playhouse – The Globe

<u>open air theatre • yard and 3 tiers • tiring houses and galleries • props • trap door and heavens • machinery</u>
Globe Theatre was a 24-sided polygon around an open yard of 30 m in diameter, up to 2,500 people. Extreme closeness between actors and audience; apron stage with no backdrop but three doors for the actors; tiring houses to get changed; a recess to serve as tomb or extra room; a small gallery above as room for the musicians; in front of the stage two massive columns holding the roof and serving as props; very few extra props on stage; in the middle a trapdoor to the underworld, above the "heavens" and the special machinery, e.g. for flying and sound effects.

People in the production process

<u>the company • shareholders • no female actors • apprentices • clown vs. fool • bookholder</u>
To secure their reputation, actors formed companies, preferably playing at fixed playhouses; the most important members were part owners (shareholders) of the company which also owned the rights to the plays. Elizabethan customs did not allow women on stage; their parts were taken by boys before their voices broke, often living with senior actors as apprentices; actors entertaining as clown or fool were particularly important. The clown simply had to entertain while the fool was allowed to speak the truth even if not very pleasant. The bookholder also held a higher position than the hired men (minor actors and musicians) as he was responsible for keeping the official text and not allowing it to be taken by rivalling companies or to be produced to the Master of the Revels.

Theatre versus public life

<u>ban on the theatres • censorship • competition with the entertainment industry</u>
The authorities were afraid of public unrest and diseases and often closed the theatres (e.g. 1592); actors answered by moving outside the city limits; companies were under the control of the Master of the Revels; every play had to be licensed and was subject to censorship. The theatre companies had to compete with the other forms of mass entertainment, e.g. "bear-baiting".

Producing a play

<u>hard life of actors • costumes • props • special effects</u>
Actors had to learn and rehearse new plays alongside productions for up to six plays a week; they learned stagecraft as well as fencing; highly elaborate costumes and make up; props on stage rather sparse; sound effects and music to heighten the atmosphere; no breaks or intervals during the plays; "brevity is the soul of wit".

RF | Revision files

Revision file 4: Shakespeare's plays (Topic 4)

Collect information from the texts about these four plays. You may have to do a bit of extra research to complete some blocks.

Play	Main themes	Main characters	Plot
Richard III	plotting and power, appearance and reality, the supernatural	Richard III, Lady Anne, Richmond, Edward IV, Clarence, Lord Buckingham, Lord Hastings	Edward IV lies dying, his brother Richard wants to become King although he is not next in line. He has his adversaries and competitors either killed or imprisoned and is crowned Richard III. In the Battle of Bosworth, Richard is defeated and killed by Richmond, who has gathered an army against him. Richmond becomes King.
Romeo and Juliet	love, revenge, appearance and reality	Romeo, Juliet, Mercutio, Tybalt, the Nurse, Friar Lawrence	Romeo and Juliet are from two feuding Veronese families. They meet at a ball and fall in love. In a quarrel, Mercutio, Romeo's friend, is killed by Tybalt, so then Romeo kills Tybalt, a Capulet. He is banished to Mantua for the deed. Before leaving, he gets Friar Lawrence to marry him to Juliet. Friar Lawrence plans to fake Juliet's death so that she can escape with Romeo, but Romeo only hears that she is dead and kills himself when he sees her in the tomb. She awakes from her deep sleep, sees Romeo dead beside her, and kills herself.
Macbeth	ambition, power, conscience, order and disorder, the supernatural	Macbeth, Lady Macbeth, Banquo, Duncan, Macduff, the witches	Macbeth is a Scottish nobleman and cousin of Duncan. He is told by three witches that he will be Thane of Cawdor and the next King. In order to make the prophecy come true, he kills Duncan, egged on by his ambitious wife, and blames the murder on the king's chamberlains. He is crowned King, but in order to feel safe he starts to kill all those who threaten his position. Macduff and Duncan's son Malcolm gather an army in England and march against the tyrant. Macbeth is killed by Macduff.
Hamlet	power, revenge, the supernatural	Hamlet, Prince of Denmark, his mother Gertrude, his uncle King Claudius, a ghost	Hamlet's father is dead. His mother has married his uncle, who is now King of Denmark. From his father's ghost Hamlet learns that he was poisoned by Claudius. Hamlet feigns madness, which worries his mother and uncle alike. He accidentally kills Polonius, the father of the girl he is in love with (Ophelia) and gets sent to England for that. But he returns just in time for Ophelia's funeral (she has killed herself out of grief). Laertes, Ophelia's brother, is now quite mad at Hamlet and challenges him to a sword fight. The tip of the sword is just as poisoned as the goblet of wine for him (Claudius' work: he wants to get rid of the troublesome prince). Hamlet is wounded, but kills Laertes first, Gertrude accidentally drinks the wine, and when Fortinbras from Norway arrives at Elsinore the entire royal family is dead.

144 | Klett

© Ernst Klett Verlag GmbH, Stuttgart 2010 | www.klett.de
Von dieser Druckvorlage ist die Vervielfältigung für den eigenen Unterrichtsgebrauch gestattet. Die Kopiergebühren sind abgegolten. Alle Rechte vorbehalten.

Abi Workshop Englisch
Shakespeare Lehrerheft
ISBN 978-3-12-601015-3